CHRISTOPHER STIFFLER

TRAIL
HEADSPACE

FINDING MY BEST SELF ON
THE COLORADO TRAIL

Praise for Trail Headspace

"A stunning blend of honesty and insight, this book takes you on a journey not only through the wilderness but into oneself. With every step, you'll feel the weight of the trail, the resilience of the human spirit, and the transformation that only nature — and self-discovery — can bring. A must-read for anyone seeking meaning and inspiration."

- *Stephanie Wilson, Author of "Big Waves & Wooden Benches"*

"I have zero interest or knowledge regarding hiking, but I still found Trail Headspace to be a captivating page turner. This hike-in-a-book is a fantastic peek into the physicality and mindset of a subculture that I knew existed but had no clear idea about. Stiffler changes that with his insider account of his journey that (emotionally, physically and literally) had its huge ups and downs. Made me want to go hiking for days on end to see if I change, too."

- *Mike Lukas, Comedian and Author of "Finding Your Funny Muscle"*

"Stiffler's book reflects his approach to life in every capacity. He shares his personal journey along the CT with humility and honesty. And, he weaves in research to add depth and appreciation on a variety of topics related to thru-hiking. It's the first book about the CT of its kind. A truly fun and enjoyable read."

- *Jan M. Rastall, Author of "Living, Fully, The Colorado Trail"*

"Trail Headspace is relatable to so many who also desire to set their out-of-office reply as "If you need me in person, I can be found on the Colorado Trail!" He energizes the reader with his humor and wit, sharing his raw thoughts and experiences that captivate any lover of the outdoors. Certainly, the value of human relationships, especially with fellow thru-hikers, may be the best and most captivating part of this book as his desire for simultaneous wilderness isolation and companionship weaves its way through his 486-mile journey."

- *David R. Witte, Author of "World War II at Camp Hale: Blazing a New Trail in the Rockies"*

Contents

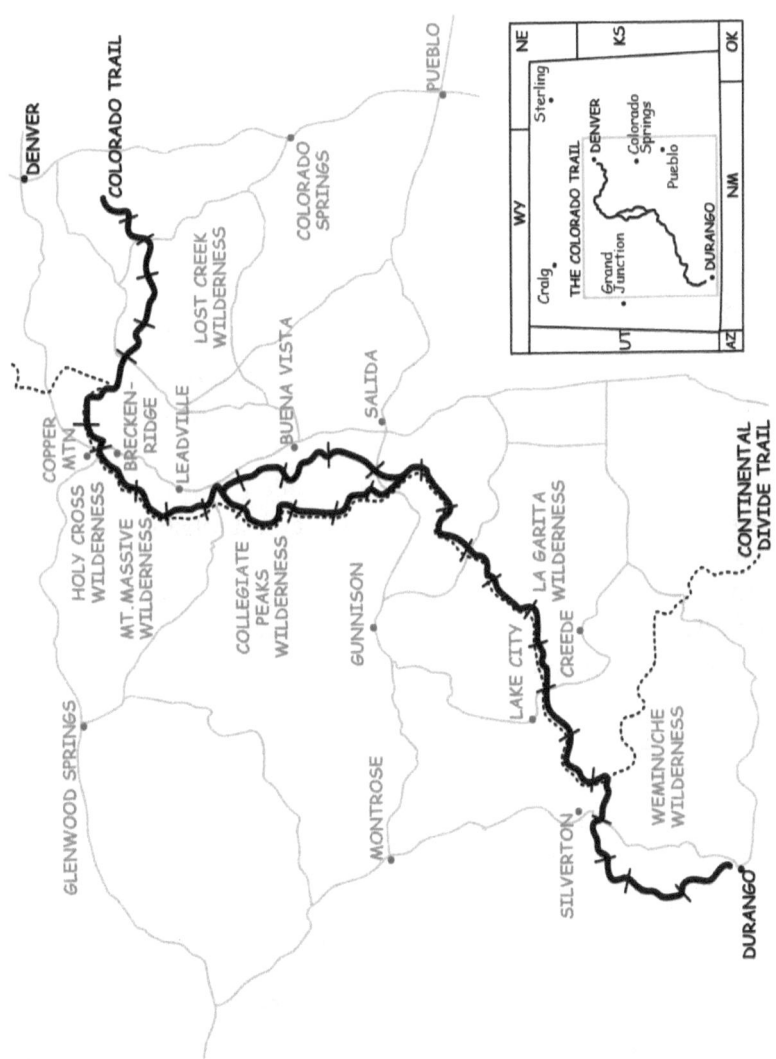

Preface: My Best Self

The aim of this book is to share with you my day-to-day hike experience on the 486-mile Colorado Trail (CT) and the knowledge I gained tapping into the thru-hiker community as someone new, though not new to backpacking. There's a distinction.

"Thru-hiking" (yes, it's really spelled that way) according to Wikipedia is "the act of hiking an established long-distance trail end-to-end continuously." So, not segments of a trail over a few summers. You're taking on the whole enchilada all at once, hiking as many miles as you can every day and then getting up and doing it all over the next day.

Sprinkled along the way are a bunch of nuggets on things like the history of the Colorado Trail, wilderness areas, wildflowers, hiker lingo, hiker hacks, naming origins, a famous cannibal, trail name stories and tips to bring back from trail life. The book also contains the anecdotes and advice of the quirky people I met along the trail and the transformational experience I had on the (mile-for-mile) most beautiful trail in America.

I hope the narrative will jumpstart, freshen and transport previous Colorado Trail hikers back to their own experience. I also intend to paint a picture for new hikers of what daily trail life looks like hiking all day and eating your meals seated in the dirt. I see this book as much as a trail journal for those looking to plan a big thru-hike as well as a wellness guide that highlights how trail life might just be the antidote to the burnout, brain frazzling, social media-addicted and argumentative world we find ourselves trapped in.

As an economist, accustomed to backing up my assertions with academic studies, I dove into the academic literature of psychology, neuroscience, philosophy, sleep science and biology to help figure out how what I was doing during a 35-day thru-hike that made me feel so damn good. These insights are scattered inside the narrative.

I quickly discovered some good news from the research: many of the things that helped me find my best self on the trail are easy to adopt back in the modern world, like getting sun in your eyes in the morning, limiting artificial light before bedtime to improve your sleep, setting appropriate goals and seeing every situation, even annoying instances, as opportunities for stories.

Maybe one of my biggest hopes is that this book will tip those contemplating a big thru-hike into the "yes, let's do it" column.

Happy Trails
Christopher Stiffler

Prologue: Mountain Passes in Between

As I boiled a packet of ramen noodles, I was being laughed at. "Do you really think there's room with a parasite stirring up a storm in here?" my gut taunted. "Plus, I'd prefer more than ramen noodles," added the parasite. I was currently a month into a thru-hike of the Colorado Trail. I was zapped of energy, and there were 25 miles and several mountain passes between me and the nearest road. And I had giardia.

Giardia is an intestinal infection caused by a parasite commonly found in streams in remote areas. Its symptoms are far from positive traits like optimism, strong legs, stamina or powerful lungs. Instead, they manifest as the complete opposite.

You don't really want nausea, stomach cramps and fatigue when backpacking the most remote stretch of the 486-mile hiking path across the Rocky Mountains. There's no cell service and no easy way out — other than hiking.

But that's where I found myself.

A month earlier, a setback like this would have sent me down a rumination spiral. I would have cursed the situation. I would have been cranky with everyone, thrown blame around and looked for pity. Or I would have called up my

mom and dumped my misfortune on her as I'd been unfortunately trained to do since childhood.

But I didn't do any of those. Instead, I smiled. "Let's
dance," I told the parasite.

The trail was changing me.

How did I get here?

Let's start at the beginning.

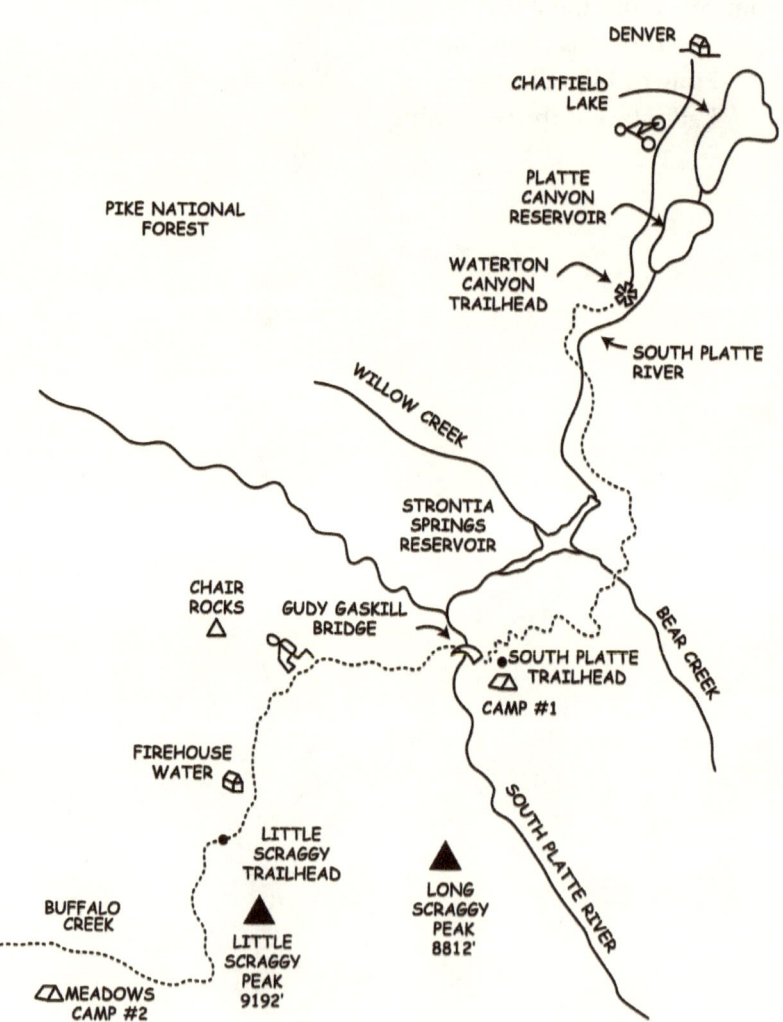

DENVER

CHATFIELD LAKE

PIKE NATIONAL FOREST

PLATTE CANYON RESERVOIR

WATERTON CANYON TRAILHEAD

SOUTH PLATTE RIVER

WILLOW CREEK

STRONTIA SPRINGS RESERVOIR

BEAR CREEK

CHAIR ROCKS

GUDY GASKILL BRIDGE

SOUTH PLATTE TRAILHEAD

CAMP #1

FIREHOUSE WATER

LITTLE SCRAGGY TRAILHEAD

LONG SCRAGGY PEAK 8812'

BUFFALO CREEK

LITTLE SCRAGGY PEAK 9192'

MEADOWS CAMP #2

SOUTH PLATTE RIVER

CHAPTER ONE:

Out-of-Office Reply

The Colorado Trail begins at Waterton Canyon on a gravel road next to the South Platte River, which is 25 miles southwest of downtown Denver. Most hikers catch a ride to the start of the trail, but I wanted to start my self-powered adventure from the front door of my Denver home. So, I decided to bike to the trail's starting point instead.

It was a sunny Denver day in June, two days before the longest day of the year. The last thing I did before I slipped my trail runners into the baskets of my road bike pedals and headed for the South Platte Path that connects to the start of the trail was send an email to myself.

Then I read the final sentence of the automatic reply:
If you need me in person, I can be found on the Colorado Trail!
"That's right," I thought, "I'm not answering your email because I'm walking across the state of Colorado."

For the next five weeks, anyone contacting my work email would get an automatic reply with the details of my sabbatical, the contact info for my coworkers along with my line about where to find me.

A typical Monday would find me in my office with my second cup of coffee, sitting in front of my computer parsing Colorado tax data. You know, an economist's version of fun. Instead, I was rolling south next to a river, with the wind condensing and evaporating the beads of sweat accumulating under my bike helmet as I set off toward Durango. I had no email, no responsibilities, no obligations, no one to answer to. All I had to do was motor myself each day in a southwesterly direction for as many miles as I felt like. That was an intensely freeing feeling.

I had fully intended to broadcast my plans for the sabbatical. I was proud of my adventure, even though I hadn't taken a single step yet. It was a bit zany, a bit outside the norm, but it was a bold step in the spirit of "Go do it." I didn't want to be the kind of person who talks about the adventures they hope to have. I wanted to take the leap. As a single, 35-year-old guy, I couldn't use family, relationships or ancient ligaments as excuses to skip this adventure.

I can't quite remember a comparable time when I had the same feelings. The closest experience was probably when I was moving into my freshman dorm at the University of Richmond. It was a time of uncertainty, a completely new environment and a new challenge.

The Colorado Trail stretches 486 miles and is divided into 28 segments. To contextualize this, if you drove from Pittsburgh to Chicago, you'd still need to drive around Wrigley Field a few times to put 486 miles on your tires. But even more daunting is the elevation gain, requiring 89,000 vertical feet of hiking. That's three times the height of Mt. Everest from sea level. Oddly enough, it wasn't those intimidating figures that made me nervous.

It was the mental side of thru-hiking that scared me. Can I camp in the wilderness alone? Would I have to hitchhike alone? Would I get spooked in my tent at night? Do I have the mental game for this? Can I eat that many Pop-Tarts?

Mentioning the Colorado Trail in my out-of-office message was a psychological strategy; it was for my own personal motivation.

It's called a pre-commitment device. It's a strategy you put in place to help you get to your goal. To fight off your impulsive short-term self, you can have your planning/long-term self set up a mechanism to prevent your short-term self from succumbing to temptation. In the case of a thru-hike, that urge would be quitting.

I took a page from the playbook of the character whose name literally became synonymous with "a long, eventful journey." The classic example comes from Homer's epic, where Odysseus wanted to hear the sirens' song but didn't want to be lured toward them and wreck his ship. So, his planning-self instructed his sailors to plug their ears and tie him firmly to the ship's mast. The ropes saved him from making a bad decision when in a state of temptation.

I've used commitment strategies in the past. My weight-lifting partner from my undergrad days at the University of Richmond operated the same way. Most days we'd plan to work out together at 8 a.m. I had extra motivation to get out of bed and get across campus to the gym, otherwise I would have let my partner down.

Publicly stating my mission of hiking the trail was a commitment strategy. It was insurance against the I'm-lonely-and-sick-of-rain-and-sleeping-on-the-ground self. I didn't want my impulsive self, caught in a temporary low point, to be able to override an adventure that was nearly a decade in the making. It was a good ol' case of external accountability.

The seed of hiking the Colorado Trail was planted in 2014. While I was doing the final inspection to buy my first home in Denver, the owner mentioned the house's proximity to the South Platte Bike path and how it connects to the start of the Colorado Trail.

"I had always planned one day to leave this front door and connect the South Platte Trail to the Colorado Trail and walk to Durango," the homeowner told me. "Yeah, I regret never pulling the trigger on that adventure."

There was a somber tone to his speech. He averted his eyes. I could tell he was disappointed that he never got to realize his idea, to take the leap and to fulfill that longing. He had an idea, an adventure, a dream, and he never fulfilled it.

That desire stuck in the back of my mind for many years — the idea of leaving my front door and self-powering myself to Durango. Eight years later, I'd make that idea a reality.

If the seed of the Colorado Trail idea was planted by the previous homeowner, the urge to push my comfort zone on some madcap expedition would have been the fertilizer. I had previously been scratching that itch with Colorado Fourteeners, a journey that took me nine years to summit all the peaks above 14,000 feet. Now, I needed a new challenge, and thru-hiking was it.

My feelings were a moving target on day one of my Colorado Trail expedition. One moment it was giddiness, the next it was uncertainty. When I turned the lock on the front door of my Denver home on June 20, 2022, I wasn't certain if I was feeling excitement, pride, or fear. But I was sure of one thing: a big adventure was on my horizon. I wasn't standing still anymore. I wasn't going to leave an adventure on the shelf. I was headed to Durango.

My bike ride to the start of the trail was not without a mistake. In Chatfield State Park, which is built around a large reservoir, I mistakenly followed the paved road farther around the southern part of the water. I learned the hard way that the most direct route to the mouth of Waterton Canyon from the state park was on a dirt road that ran parallel to Wadsworth Boulevard. This turned my roughly 17-mile ride into about 20 miles total.

When I initially realized I was off-track, I turned my bicycle around and began pedaling as fast as I could. I didn't like the feeling of being off track. It was like I had a nervous ball of energy in my stomach, and I wanted to rid myself of that feeling as quickly as possible. Once I was back on the correct path, that nervous feeling began to fade.

But this feeling was silly. I had no deadlines, and I had the freedom to hike as far as I wanted and camp where I chose. There was no need to feel anxious.

I need to ditch that mindset.

I rolled into the Waterton Canyon parking lot around noon to meet Ed, my 75-year-old best friend in Denver, who sat waiting with my heavy pack. A big smile stretched across his grey-goateed face. Ed was the star player in my support team and road crew.

He made me put some calories in my body in the form of peanut butter crackers as I loaded my bike into his car. Then he helped me swap out my small backpack I had brought with me on my bike ride for my pack which weighed 32 pounds at the time and would become an extension of my body for the next 35 days. Though I had a fully loaded backpack on my shoulders, I felt a silly sense of lightness.

A liter of water weighs 2.2 pounds. While leaving the trailhead, I had two liters of water in my pair of plastic Smartwater bottles. These are emblematic of the thru-hiker, not the Nalgene bottles you see on the packs of weekend hikers. An empty Nalgene weighs 6 ounces, but an empty plastic Smartwater bottle holding the same volume weighs only 1.2 ounces. So, two plastic bottles instead of two Nalgene containers will save you almost 10 ounces. This seems trivial for a weekend hike, but it's a lot to an ultra-lite thru-hiker, who is meticulous about pack weight.

I also had four individual gallon Ziplock bags filled with a day's calories. Each bag, now weighing a little over 2 pounds, contained a combination of foods intentionally selected for their calorie-to-weight-ratio, from Swedish Fish and Pop-Tarts to oatmeal packets and beef sticks, to ramen and dehydrated meals.

This system allowed me to know how many calories I had allocated for each day. It also kept my food organized for resupply points. A few weeks before my trail runners hit the trailhead at Waterton, I packed 40 Ziplock bags of daily food. I stocked them for the points where I'd meet up with my Ed-led resupply team.

Without water and food, the base weight of my pack was about 20 pounds. "Base weight" is a backpacker's term for "how heavy is my carry-on luggage?" It's your pack's total weight with gear, shelter and sleeping pad. It doesn't include consumables like water, food and stove fuel. Let alone the waffle iron or the hibachi grill. When big mile days are your chief goal, the lighter the pack the better. Thru-hikers shoot for a 15- to 20-pound base weight. The crazy ultralight backpackers aim for targets even lighter. In the tradeoff between creature comforts and weight, weekend backpackers tend to favor the comforts.

After applying some sunscreen, Ed and I left the parking lot and walked over to the Waterton Canyon Colorado Trail sign where Ed took several photos of me with a huge smile. I am wearing my black T-shirt with the name of my hometown, "Bedford," written in cursive across the front (which carried sentimental value to me because it had the same design as the baseball jersey my dad crafted when I was 10 years old), my fresh white trail runners, white running shorts (both of which would end up looking closer to my black shirt by the end of the trip), my green backpack and trekking poles. I had customized a pair of Oakley sunglasses. The M-frames were blue, the ear socks were red, and the wings were white with a yellow Oakley circle to mimic the yellow sun cradled by the red "C" of the state flag.

After photos at the trailhead sign, Ed, even though his knee was bothering him, shared my first steps on the trail

"I'll tell you what. I'll walk you to that tree up there," he said.

When we got to that geographical feature, Ed paused, rubbed his throbbing knee and said, "I'll take you up a little farther . . . to that next tree."

As much as I wanted to relieve his knee of any further pain by saying no thanks, I smiled and said, "OK."

I had met Ed four years earlier in a coffee shop. I was injecting caffeine before teaching my 10 a.m. lecture, and he was there solving the world's problems with some other coffee shop friends. (Before their second cup of coffee got cold, they had already found solutions to global warming, the Bronco's running game, and the sudden popularity of Pickleball.) He saw I needed a place to sit and invited me over. I've been sitting at his table ever since.

I ask him things like: "Ed, I'm going to take country two-step dance lessons during the pandemic, do you and Julie want to join?"

"Sure," says Ed without hesitating. He then asks, "What's two-step dancing?"

He plays a grandfather and mentor role, and I keep him young.

We are making our way up the start of the trail. "I wish I was able to hike this whole thing with you, Chris," Ed said. "Though I won't be hiking, I'll be as much a part of this as I can."

Ed's plan to walk the first 100 yards turned into the first 200 then into the first 300. I was a 35-year-old aiming to hike across the Centennial State, but it felt like I was starting my first day of kindergarten — and Ed didn't want to say goodbye.

After his last time saying, "I'll walk you up a little farther," Ed gave me a big bear hug and said, "I'll see you at Kenosha Pass in five days. Love you, kid."

He then turned and limped back to the trail's start. I watched him walk for a bit back toward his car. Then I turned toward Durango and made my way up the Denver Water Board service road, alone.

The start of the Colorado Trail is gentle. It begins at an elevation of 5,500 feet and climbs a mere 40 feet per mile for the first six miles. To a Coloradan, that's essentially flat. There would be times farther west when the trail climbed 1,000 feet per mile. It starts rather shallow, but the canyon grows higher and more rugged as it gets farther from the trailhead.

While these first few miles were physically easy, they were emotionally difficult. I didn't know what to expect on the trail. I didn't know for sure if I would be able to handle the solitude. Muscle- and endurance-wise, I knew I was well prepared, but the emotional and spiritual side of the long distance thru-hiking still spooked me.

Walking up the dirt road, I passed several day-hikers, people fishing, and some mountain bikers. And each time, I yearned for someone to chat with me, to notice my hardy hiker backpack and rugged figure, and ask questions like, "How far are you hiking?" or "Hey, you look like someone who doesn't want to be on his death bed regretting the adventures he didn't have the guts to take, just like the previous owner of the house you bought who never took his shot at hiking the Colorado Trail. Elaborate." Or something to that effect.

But nobody did. Until I passed mile marker four.

"That's a hefty pack," said a stranger leaning on his mountain bike. "You must be planning a few days out here, huh?"

"I'm hiking the Colorado Trail," I blurted out before I could catch myself.

"Ha! I hope you keep that enthusiasm the whole trip," he said.

His name was Kyle and lived in Denver. He was spending his day off doing a little wildlife watching, and it wasn't long before he directed my attention to the neighboring cliffs.

"Do you see the four mountain goats up there? I don't want you to miss 'em," Kyle said, pointing upward.

Thinking I was new to Colorado, he took pleasure in sharing the joy of nature with someone who hadn't seen mountain goats before.

"I like your enthusiasm to share Colorado," I told Kyle.

I pondered Kyle's modus operandi of making sure people don't miss out on the excitement of Colorado as I walked up the trail toward the reservoir.

I came up with a goofy ritual to mark my daily progress and create an occasional mental checkpoint victory. When I passed the five-mile marker, I turned around facing the start of the trail and took 48 normal-size backward steps and one half-step. This was my best approximation for 48.6 backward steps to signify the 486 miles of the Colorado Trail. Backward walking had been a big part of my pre-trail training routine to strengthen my legs and knees.

Once past the reservoir, the Colorado Trail moves from the service road to a single-track path and begins hiking uphill into the trees. The trail starts at 5,500 feet, but Segment One's high point reaches an elevation of 7,500 feet. The 40-feet-per-mile road is replaced with the 380-feet-gain per mile path.

This meant my easy introduction was over and that it was time to really start testing the quads I had been training — partially by that backward walking on the treadmill and mostly by pounding the stair climber with my 30-pound pack — all winter. I felt strong.

At mile 8.7 at Bear Creek, I turned a corner in the forest. and there, I met my first fellow hikers. They were Ian, Kelly and Mountain Goat. No, not the animals Kyle was eager to point out belonging to the genus *Capra*. Mountain Goat was the hiker's "trail name" and who I would later learn has a home in Salida, Colorado.

"Where are you headed?" I asked.

"Durango," Ian said.

"Oh, good. Me, too," I said, as I instantly swelled with pride at that declaration.

It was a cool feeling knowing that I'd met fellow hikers headed to the same destination, even if that destination was 477 miles away and that we'd only completed 1.7% of the trail thus far. I knew I wasn't the only one who had the idea of hiking this trail, but to be in the presence of others felt welcoming in a weird sort of way that I didn't quite fully understand — like we were kindred hikers.

Bear Creek, a stream tucked among the trees and small enough to jump across, is the first water source hikers cross on the Colorado Trail, and it's likely the first time hikers on the trail can test their water filtration system in the field. I pulled out my Sawyer Squeeze and began running the creek's water through my filter and into my water bottle.

Bear Creek also offers the earliest real camping spots along the Colorado Trail. For those looking for an easy day one introduction to the trail, Bear Creek is a good spot to spend the night. I, however, had another eight miles and a fair bit of gain to tackle before I would get to my Camp No. 1 spot. I wanted to finish Segment One on my first day.

As the trail wound upward to the high point of Segment One, it revealed a vantage point where I could see the skyline of Denver. But it didn't take long before that view was blocked by geography, and foothills came between me and the Mile High City.

Last view of the city, time to lose myself in the country.

At the 10-mile marker, I turned around and did another 48.6 backward paces, but quickly realized that this was much harder on single track, rocky terrain than the flat smooth path of the Waterton Canyon service road. It's funny how the plan you see in your head changes once you're out there.

It wasn't far from this point that I diverted off the trail for two mountain bikers speeding down the well-banked trail of Segment One. The first biker stopped.

"Hey, I know you. You're Ed's buddy," he said, looking through his single-lens biking glasses.

Turned out the mountain biker was a neighbor of Ed's. What a welcome and well-timed run-in, because at that point I was feeling a bit low. I wasn't sure if I needed company or calories. But after chasing a snack, my demeanor came back to positive. I recorded the following message in my phone:

"It's amazing how quickly your attitude can change when you stop and take a break, drink some Gatorade, protein, sugar, snacks in your belly, and have a little chat with some people. It can really boost your spirit. Really like that. I got a little pep in my step again!"

That enthusiasm would wane just a bit as I ran out of water a little past the high points on Segment One. The lesson about checking for water availability was reaffirmed as I, with my dry mouth, headed down the switchbacks toward the South Platte that seemed to never get any closer. The trail drops you 1,400 feet from the 7,500-foot-high point to the South Platte River Trailhead and the beginning of Segment Two.

At this point in the journey, I wasn't attuned to long dry stretches on the trail. Had I known that the next reliable water source was eight miles away, I'd have filled up both of my water bottles at Bear Creek instead of just one.

I began to daydream about cold beer.

And it sent me reminiscing about a weekend back in Richmond, Virginia, when my friend Wilk and I ran the James River 10K on a Saturday afternoon. At the end of the 10k, we each received two beverage tickets, which we quickly exchanged for ice-cold Blue Moon beer in a plastic Solo cup complete with orange garnish. Sitting on the grass recovering from a hard six-mile run and sipping a cold beer with a great friend was one of the best drinks I ever had.

Am I craving a cold beer? Or am I craving my good friends? What makes a top beer experience?

Ever so slowly, the South Platte River got closer and closer as I descended the trail's switchbacks.

I made it to the end of Segment One of the Colorado Trail at 7:30 p.m. Before crossing the Gudy Gaskill Bridge to find a flat spot to lay my tent next to the Platte for the night, I filtered two liters of water. I had completed 37 human-powered miles on Day One of my trek: 20 miles by bike and 17 miles on foot. My Whoop app told me that I had burned 4,700 calories that day, more than double my normal daily caloric burn. My stomach felt empty, my shoulders were sore, my feet felt raw, and I was worried that my cranky calve muscles would be screaming the next morning.

I found a sandy spot a few paces from the river to pitch my Zpacks Altaplex, a single-person tent that sets up using one trekking pole. When set up, it looks like a small white triangle. Then, I used my MRS PocketRocket stove to boil water for my dehydrated chicken teriyaki and rice dinner. As I ate, I saw Ian and Kelly setting up their tent 50 yards away. Having fellow hikers nearby felt reassuring.

As the water was heating up, I checked messages on my Garmin Inreach Explorer+. I had received several messages from friends and family wishing me good luck on my trek and noting that they were following my dot along the map of the Garmin device. I was shocked by how much those messages meant to me. I had spent most of my 10 hours hiking and biking on day one in solitude. With limited cell service, I decided to upgrade to the unlimited Garmin text plan for the next two months, hoping that my friends and family would continue to reach out.

I made a mental note to myself that I wanted to find the next night's camping spot by 7:30 p.m. Because once I set the tent up, changed clothing, made dinner and journaled, I was out of daylight.

That wouldn't be much of a problem as my body adapted to the rhythm of the Colorado sun and my start times got earlier. But that was still a few days away.

I smirked listening to the sound of the South Platte River flowing by my tent as the thought about how many people today received my automatic email reply breezed through my mind:

If you need me in person, I can be found on the Colorado Trail!

CHAPTER TWO:

Burn Scar

woke up on Day two, a Tuesday, nervous that my sore shoulders and cranky calves that I went to bed with would be worse in the morning. I was wrong. I was delighted to find out that my body had somehow hit the refresh button overnight. "Let's even hike backwards," it said.

Day two on the trail started around my normal wake up time in the off-trail world at 7:45 a.m., which I would quickly learn is a late start for a thru-hiker. As I was breaking down my tent and allowing my oatmeal water to reach a boil, I spotted a conga line of hikers headed up the steep side of the trail where Segment Two of the CT climbs from the South Platte River on several switchbacks (zigzag sections). The leader of the group wore a white, blue and peach flannel shirt and gave me a wave. I waved back from my campsite.

After breakfast and coffee (a powdered coffee that also has 15 grams of protein in it called Strong Coffee), I made my way to the latrine at the trail head on the other side of the river. So, I re-crossed the bridge which honors Gudy Gaskill, the "Mother of the Colorado Trail."

Without Gudy's effort, the Colorado Trail wouldn't be here today. While the genesis of the Colorado Trail began in 1973 as a federal bicentennial project, the subsequent years saw a stalled campaign to build a footpath across Colorado. That's when Gudy (pronounced *GOO-dee*) took the reins.

She drew routes through Forest Service districts connecting a patchwork of existing trails, mining and logging roads, and railroad grades. She spent the early 1980s recruiting volunteers and leading trail-building parties that would eventually connect a continuous trail from Waterton to Durango.

An avid mountaineer who climbed all of Colorado's Fourteeners, Gudy was the Colorado Mountain Club's first female president. She was inducted into the Colorado Women's Hall of Fame in 2002. The bridge crossing the South Platte River built in 1999 in her memory is the start of the second segment of the CT. Only a few wooded spots dot an otherwise barren and treeless stretch of 12 miles of trail on this segment. I loaded up my bottle from the river, knowing water wouldn't come until the fire station faucet at the end of Segment Two. (Hey, I'm learning.)

A few miles south of the trail, Long Scraggy Peak (8,812') looks like several giant tan shark fins popping out of a sea of evergreen trees. Further down the trail is Little Scraggy Peak (9,198') whose name is used at the trailhead at the start of Segment Three.

The dominant feature of Segment Two of the Colorado Trail is the 12,000 acres of former forest burned in 1996, known as the Buffalo Creek Fire. Approximately 8,000 of those acres were burned by high-intensity crown fires, which consume the entire length of the tree. They burn so hot they devastate the soil and its ability to retain moisture, which explains why this part of the trail is so barren and hasn't grown back over 25 years.

Prior to 2002, no fire in Colorado history ever exceeded the 100,000 acres mark or even came close until the Hayman Fire. It struck a few miles south of Segment Two of the

Colorado Trail in that same Buffalo Creek area. Hikers on the CT won't see evidence of the Hayman Fire, but bicyclists on the CT detour will.

For 18 years, the Hayman Fire was the largest in the state's history at 138,114 acres burned.

Then 2020 came. The devastating fire season ignited with a lightning strike 18 miles north of Grand Junction sparking the Pine Gulch Fire. The Hayman Fire was quickly eclipsed in acreage by the Pine Gulch Fire. Unlike The Hayman Fire's 18-year reign, it only maintained its No. 1 spot for seven weeks until the Cameron Peak Fire in Larimer County displaced it as the largest fire in Colorado history.

Since 2000, there have been 60 forest fires in Colorado that torched more than 10,000 acres. The top 20 largest forest fires in Colorado's history all occurred since 2000. To put those 12,000 scorched acres of the Buffalo Creek Fire into perspective, the Cameron Peak Fire in 2020 burned about 207,000 acres.

Eight weeks after the Buffalo Creek Fire, a massive rainstorm hit the area sending a torrent of water across the denuded area into Buffalo Creek then onto the South Platte River. That deluge carried away the 20-foot bridge used by CT hikers to cross the Platte River.

The new bridge's construction is a testament to the commitment, effort, overcoming of red tape and toil of trail building. It took two years to get another bridge built after bidding, contracting, permitting, arrangements with the Forest Service, fights with Denver Water, acquiring permits from the United States Corps of Engineers and Douglas and Jefferson County governments, applications for a matching grant from the Colorado Lottery and State Trails, several construction delays and finding the only crane in the entire region large enough to pick up a 26-ton bridge, swing it out over a river, and place it on the foundations.

Between the Colorado Trail Foundation volunteer hours, the Colorado Lottery cash grant, and other donations, the total cost of just the bridge and trail improvements was $250,000.

Excited to get a photo of myself and the bridge in the morning sun, I vowed to get an early morning start on this section: 8:30 a.m., which I learned after a couple days on the trail was not even remotely close to an "alpine start."

I quickly worked up a sweat heading uphill from the Platte River. I stopped to drink some water and shed the one piece of hiking gear I was most proud of: my trail sweatshirt, handmade special for this trip by my mother from micro-grid Polartec fabric. It was basically a customized, homemade version of the popular Melanzana hoodies sold by the company of the same name in Leadville, Colorado.

I dolloped some sunscreen on my face and continued up the steady switchbacks. Segment Two begins with a steady five-mile ascent gaining 1,760 feet — for about 380 feet of elevation per mile. My general rule for the trail was that anything under 400 feet a mile wasn't too bad. I could maintain a steady pace with hardly any rest at that grade. Anything steeper required some breaks.

I was surprised to realize that I craved some human interaction. The trail feels desolate, dusty and a bit like the setting for a post-apocalyptic movie. The benefit of the burn scar is that there are no trees to block your view of the trail several hundred yards ahead. This allowed me to locate up the trail the conga line of hikers I saw as I broke down my tent earlier. I pushed a little harder uphill to catch up to the group.

Before I met the conga line and less than two miles into my day, I caught up to the "Sweep." (No, this wasn't someone's trail name.) The term is used in the outdoor expedition community to refer to the last hiker that takes up the rear to ensure that every hiker in the group makes it safely to the destination. Bringing up the rear means the sweep is stuck with the slowest hikers in the group all day. That hiker turned out to be a friendly female hiker with dark hair from Ohio.

"You're hiking the whole trail! Good for you. I'm rooting for you. I wish I was able to do the whole thing, but being from Ohio doesn't allow me to acclimatize very well to Colorado. I'm afraid I'm a bit slow," she told me.

The Sweep's eyes said, "Yeah, that's an understatement."

What she lacked in hiking speed, she more than made up for with her caring, enthusiastic personality.

"Thanks for the motivation," I said. "It's easy to take things like this for granted when you live here."

They had fallen several hundred yards behind the group, and it was still early in the day. Having observed the pace I was making uphill, the guide hinted to me that if I was looking for someone to chat and hike with, I'd do better to leap-frog them and catch up to the main party.

So, I did.

I quickly caught up to a line of hikers who all wore day packs: no 58-liter overnight packs, no tents, no pads no quilts nor hibachi grills. They were led by Colorado Mountain Expeditions — a Colorado-based guiding service owned by Chris and Jeanne Szczech. I realized that it was Chris who wore the flannel shirt and waved at me that morning beside the river. Chris's company hikes the Colorado Trail over seven separate weeks during the summer. Each new week is a fresh set of clients seeking to conquer another 70 or so miles of trail.

This week's expedition would cover the mileage between Waterton Canyon to Kenosha Pass. Several of the group members had signed up for two weeks and were set to rejoin Chris and the guides later in July for another portion of the CT. Several other hikers from out of state had been doing a week each summer with the group to slowly hike the trail in segments. Each day, the guides would shuttle the group to the start of the day's hike, pick them up at the end of the day and shuttle them back to the base of operations — complete with mess hall and dining tent. Their base of operations for three nights was the Meadows Group Campground.

"Are you hiking the whole trail?" the first hiker asked.

"Yes, I hope to," I responded.

"That's so cool! Are you alone?" the second hiker asked.

"I'm hiking alone, but I met you today," I said.

I felt like a low-key celebrity.

I began to thrive off their energy. They were all Colorado Trail enthusiasts set on completing the trail in segments over several years. What better place to find a bunch of like-minded Colorado Trail hikers than on the Colorado Trail. And to think, I had been looking for them at bars in Denver.

They didn't have five weeks to do the whole thing in one push. Nor did many of them want to set out solo. A guiding service like Chris's was a perfect option for them. And they appreciated someone who had the time and daring to set out solo on the 486-mile hike.

It was at that moment that I hit it off with a curious woman from Denver who had an intoxicating, cheerful way of speaking with people that instantly made them feel valued. I introduced myself as Chris. She introduced herself as "Rosy Maple." I later learned that she shared Alma Maters with my parents, Temple University.

Rosy Maple got her trail name hiking in Tennessee while wearing brightly colored hiking socks with the Rosy Maple Moth on them. The Rosy Maple Moth is an insect with pink and yellow wings and body. Like Pepto-Bismol pink. As she was hiking, the actual moths kept landing on her shins to check out their knitted 2D cousins.

In my pre-trail research, I read a book on Colorado's naming origins. I guess I figured that pointing out things like

"Weminuche means *canyon people"* would be a sure-fire way to make trail friends.

"That reminds me about how the 'Mosquito Range' got its designation," I said. "Rosy Maple isn't the only thing in Colorado that's named after an insect."

The legend goes like this: there was a meeting in 1861 for the purpose of establishing a mining district and town after gold was discovered in the area. The meeting's participants couldn't agree on a town name. I imagine that argument went like this:

Prospector 1: I say Minersville.

Prospector 2: I say Minersburgh.

Prospector 3: I say Charlestown.

Prospector 4: Shut up, Charles.

Unable to agree, they left a blank spot for the name in their meeting's notebook. When they reconvened the committee, they discovered — when opening the minutes journal from the prior meeting — directly on the page where the blank spot had been left for the town's name was a squashed mosquito. The group that couldn't agree earlier quickly approved the use of "Mosquito" for the district and town's name. The use of the moniker for other neighboring national features quickly followed. There's Mosquito Peak, Mosquito Pass, Mosquito Creek and the Mosquito Range. But oddly no *Swat Lake* or *Itchy Bump Bend.*

The conga line group was mostly composed of women at or beyond retirement age. There was one gentleman from New Jersey. There was also one recent high school graduate set to start his freshman year at college in two months. The guides would take turns on who was the sweep, who led the main group, who drove the shuttle van and who cooked dinner. The main group on this day was led by Chris, the owner.

You know those people who talk about themselves for five minutes without really saying anything of weight — the kind of people who quickly drain the introvert's social battery? Chris wasn't that way at all. He was intentional when he spoke.

"In preparation for my trip, I read some studies on the benefits of being in nature," I told Rosy. "That led me to some more studies about how terrible social media and screens are for us. The trail is a nature antidote to all that stuff."

"Sounds like a good book idea," Rosy said. "People need more trips in nature — seeking areas without cell service."

That's when Chris interjected from the front of the conga line, "How would they advertise such a book? On Instagram? Seems a bit of a Catch-22 since the people with the most need to read a book like that and get off social media are the ones not reading."

"Fair point," I admitted. "Someone needs to change that."

The hikers then began lamenting Gen Z's obsession with phones, screen time and social media. They directed a lot of their derision of Gen Z at the recent high school graduate in the group. But after six miles of hiking that day, when we stopped for a snack, it wasn't the 18-year-old who pulled out his phone and buried his nose in the dopamine dispensing device, it was the Sexagenarians.

I guess two days in nature isn't enough time to break our phone addictions.

I couldn't have hoped for better weather through this section. It wasn't an overcast day; it was beautifully sunny with just enough sporadic cloud cover to give consistent and staccato-like breaks from the direct Colorado sun. I would have sweated a lot more and exhausted my limited water a lot faster had it not been for the partial cloud cover.

The group's hiking day ended in the early afternoon after 11.5 miles at the end of Segment Two. As we approached the North Fork Volunteer Fire Department, which generously allows hikers to use its water faucet, we met a frazzled woman waiting for her hiking partner she had split away from and sped ahead of. I didn't stay around to get the full story because I was out of water and needed to walk over (about 200 yards northwest of the CT) to the fire department building and find their outdoor faucet at the back of the building.

When I returned to the trail after filling up my water and checking in with my parents (I learned that there's decent cell phone reception at the fire station), the group was gone.

Dang!

I didn't get to say goodbye to Rosy Maple and the other hikers with whom I had bonded over the last four hours. The boost I got from talking with my parents was replaced with a deflated feeling of losing the group of hikers with whom I spent the morning.

They left me. I still needed to be around people right now, and I needed them. Wasn't there some tiny etiquette to wait for someone on the trail?

I put my head down and continued to the Little Scraggy Trailhead and the start of Segment Three. Glancing at a white van parked by the Little Scraggy day-use sites, I felt a rush of excitement. As I approached the van from a distance, I thought I could make out a guide's logo on the side panel. That's when Chris popped out of the vehicle and handed me an ice cold can of Sprite.

"A cold soda after a hot morning for you," he said.

The cold, sugary, carbonated liquid was a heavenly experience after a half day of hiking through the Buffalo Creek burn area. The group hadn't forgotten about me. They had delayed their shuttle back to their base camp long enough to deliver me a soda. I felt honored. (Or they might have been waiting for the Ohioan and the Sweep. I chose to believe they waited for me.) So, with newfound energy, I was also eager to log another eight miles of hiking.

Just like yesterday, I rebounded from a low moment.

After a snack and a Sprite, I started Segment Three in the middle of the afternoon. The pine and fir forest sprinkled with large boulders was a nice change of pace to the treeless landscape of Segment Two. The trail here is relatively flat. But it's also the first time the trail crosses the 8,000-foot elevation mark.

I didn't have a set destination to spend night two on the trail, so I figured I'd hike until I was tired. After not seeing another person for an hour, I got a little anxious. The previous night at my camp site, I had been within a stone's throw of other hikers. Would I get lucky again? I'd never camped alone in the Colorado backcountry like this before. That thought snowballed into an emotional low point.

After hiking half the day in great conversation, the loneliness of hiking without the group really got to me in the late afternoon. I began to have doubts about my ability to do this for another month. Physically I was doing great. It was the mental side letting me down. Gripped by a tightening of the stomach and an anxious worry, I continued slowly down the trail. A depressing thought began to occur to me: this wasn't much fun.

Two hours after leaving the group, emotionally in a pit, I checked my FarOut app to see where I was on the trail. That's when I noticed a feature on the map that was only three miles away. It was called "Meadows Campground."

Wait, that's where Rosy Maple and the Colorado Mountain Expeditions group are camped.

I had a definitive goal for the day, now. Not an undecided camping spot alone, but a spot with my new team. I decided to power myself to the Meadows Campground and surprise the group. With a tangible goal, I began to inch my way out of my emotional pit. It was 5:30 p.m. — an absolutely gorgeous time to hike through Ponderosa Pines as the sun's rays began to cast longer shadows from each tree trunk. Be it from a new-found purpose to make it to Meadows or great lighting, I was able to knock out those three miles in less than an hour.

The Meadows Campgrounds requires a slight diversion off the Colorado Trail up a dirt road. Arriving at the wide-open group camping area, I didn't see the white van. No Chris, no Rosy Maple, no 18-year-old hiking with senior citizens, no Ohioan, no sweep.

Maybe they aren't here?

My emotional high of anticipating surprising the group turned into a low. What a roller coaster — low to high back to low again. The group camp area was reserved by a mountain biking group. I must have misheard them when they told me the location of their base camp.

With my head hanging low again, I slowly ambled back toward the trail and resigned myself to a night eating dinner and camping alone. Almost missing it entirely, I happened upon a small sign that said "Site 1" on it.

If this is Site 1, then that means there must be a Site 2, right?

I turned around and headed back up the road that meandered through some trees before revealing a second group camping site in the hopes of finding my new friends.

As I strolled into the campsite uncertain if I was imposing on strangers, a woman cried out, "Hey! It's our backpacker! It's Chris, he made it." It was the Ohio woman whom I met with the sweep that morning. I'd found my friends.

I had hiked an extra eight miles to meet back up with them. I mostly wanted to reconnect, to chat, and dig my way out of my emotional low.

I got that, and I also got tacos.

But only because Rosy Maple, sensing I was too shy to ask for food, asked the guides if I could join them for dinner.

"If there's not enough, Chris can have some of my portion," added the Ohio woman.

I felt like I was back with my team again. What a relief. And I wouldn't have to camp alone.

If that chilly Sprite was pure bliss, then the fresh tacos and homemade guacamole were orgasmic! I was spoiled. Only two days into my adventure and I had been treated to fresh quesadillas, tacos and homemade guacamole. Not really roughing it. In exchange for dinner, I offered to help with dishes, which also gave me the opportunity to chat with the guides. They offered me a cold beer, but I turned it down, telling them that I'd save my first trail beer for Breckenridge. The company and the conversation about Colorado's outdoors was enough for me.

Day Two on the trail had me cover 19.6 miles on the CT. If you included the extra half mile I walked up to Meadows Campground, I had put more than 20 miles of wear and tear on my trail runners on my second day on the trail. After two days of thru-hiking, I had knocked out 37 miles of the Colorado Trail and had a belly full of fresh guacamole.

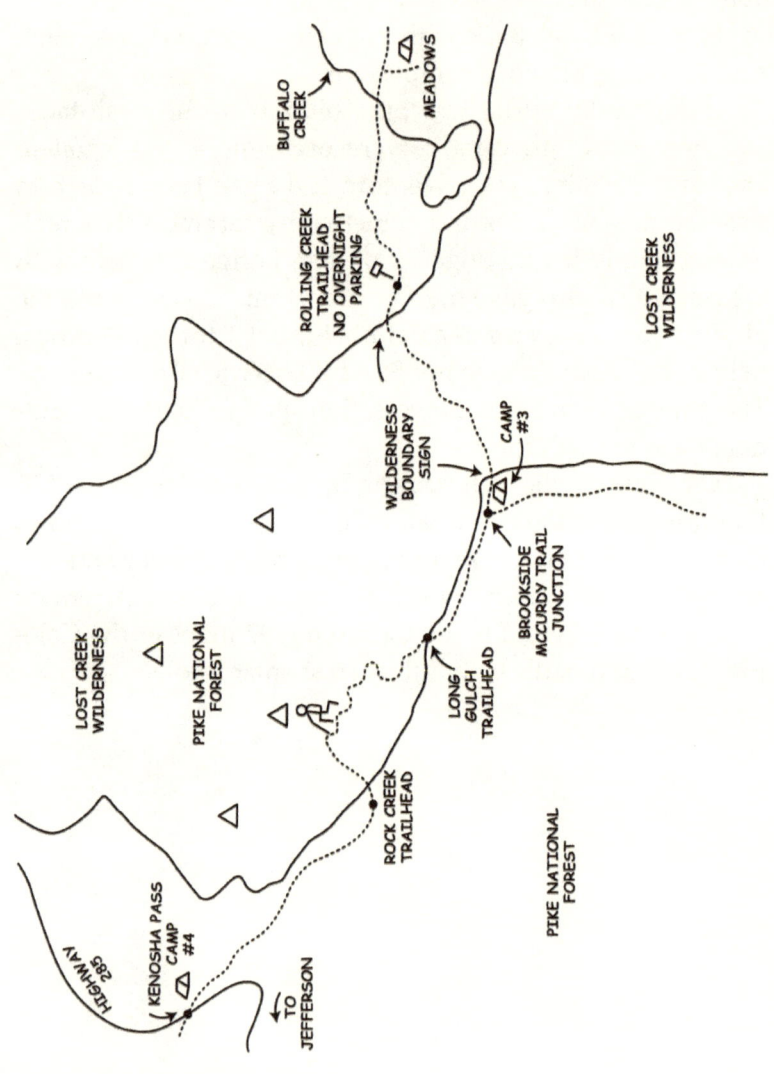

BUFFALO CREEK

MEADOWS

ROLLING CREEK TRAILHEAD NO OVERNIGHT PARKING

LOST CREEK WILDERNESS

WILDERNESS BOUNDARY SIGN

CAMP #3

BROOKSIDE McCURDY TRAIL JUNCTION

LOST CREEK WILDERNESS

PIKE NATIONAL FOREST

LONG GULCH TRAILHEAD

ROCK CREEK TRAILHEAD

PIKE NATIONAL FOREST

HIGHWAY 285

KENOSHA PASS CAMP #4

TO JEFFERSON

CHAPTER THREE:

Adopted

I n preparing for the trail, I came across a recurring piece of advice on the thru-hiking blogs that on my third day finally started to make sense. To block out the sunshine peering through my tent, I pulled my down quilt over my eyes and caught a sweet pungent whiff of myself. I smelled like a half fermented, half rotten peach.

"Embrace the stink!" the blogs said.

Like a stench was the secret ingredient to unlocking some kind of outdoor enlightenment.

I nailed the stink part, but when it came to embracing it, I was still uncertain. It seemed ironic to take advice from someone who showers once a week about embracing odors, like a mosquito advocating for the joy of itchy bug bites.

Just after I had broken down my tent and organized my backpack, one of the guides, Cory, delivered a freshly made breakfast burrito to me before jumping into the vans to shuttle the group back to where they left off the day before.

I was getting faster on breaking down my gear. Only 70 minutes elapsed from when I awoke to the time I started hiking. I made my way from the Meadows group campsite area back to the trail to finish the several remaining miles of Segment Three.

Once back on the trail hiking, I filled my water bottles at Buffalo Creek, which offers some great camping spots for those not lucky enough to mooch their way into free tacos and a sleeping spot at the pre-paid Meadows group camping sites.

To remember my adventure, I dictated video messages into my iPhone as I hiked. Between the crunch of trail gravel under my shoes, I said, "I was more efficient this morning than yesterday in breaking down my tent. Beautiful day, just a few clouds in the sky, calves are a little sore, but I got a pep in my step. I wonder what adventure the trail will deliver today. I did 20 miles yesterday. It's going to be a good day."

One little habit I picked up months before my hike, aimed at boosting my mental fortitude, is called positive self-talk. This involves recalling past challenges I've conquered. When faced with a similar difficulty, I replay those victorious moments in my mind. That's why, after completing a 20-mile day, I revisited that memory.

Self-talk doesn't have to be positive, however; it can go the other way too if you're not careful. "I can't do that." "This is miserable." "I want to quit because I smell like rotten cabbage." Those words harm you, shrink your options and capabilities. But sayings like: "I got this." "I've done this before." "I'll lick this steep section." "I can embrace the stink." Those are positive ways of self-talking.

For me, I found that controlling the narrative in my head made the difference between quitting and accomplishing big things.

I began to stroll down the trail with a general excitement in my stomach. I had hiked about a mile when I reiterated to myself, "I wonder what adventure the trail has in store for me today?"

It wasn't a few minutes later as I weaved my way through pine trees that I spotted a group of hikers ahead. That's when I met Laura, Lilly and Charlie: The LLC (Or that's at least what I called them in my journal). They had camped by the river sites beside Buffalo Creek and had gotten out of camp a few minutes before I came through.

Laura and Lilly were a mother and eighth-grade daughter pair of thru-hikers from the Evergreen, Colorado area. They planned to hike the whole trail. Charlie was the female friend of Lilly who had agreed to join for a few days.

"You're welcome to join us or leapfrog us if you want to go faster." Laura said.

I decided to join them.

Is that sort of strange for an introvert like me?

I made their threesome a foursome as I filed to the back of their line. We knocked out the last few miles of Segment Three together. The segment ends at the Rolling Creed Trailhead where this crew had shuttled and parked a camper, apparently directly in front of a sign that read "no overnight parking." The group half expected to arrive to either a ticket or a tow that would have left them without their re-supplies.

The grade over this section was about 330 feet of vertical gain per mile over smooth pine-needle-padded tread as it crossed the 8,000-foot mark, an elevation the trail wouldn't drop below until Gudy's Rest four miles from the very end of the whole trail. And while the trail wasn't so steep that heavy breathing replaces all conversations, I was still amazed by the speed at which these eighth-grade girls chatted. And they also hiked briskly too. After I overheard the scoop on the rival games between Evergreen and Conifer high schools and learned about their friend's mullet haircut, Lilly directed a question at me.

"Why do cows have hooves and not feet?" she asked.

Before I could decide if this was a joke or serious inquiry, she said chuckling, "Because they lactose . . . *lack toes*, get it?"

I chuckled more audibly than normal to make sure that Lilly felt appreciated, and deep down, I found the silly joke endearing.

When we got to the end of Segment Three, the crew breathed a sigh of relief. Their truck was there along with their fresh fruit, which they shared with me. I thanked them for the snacks, the morning company, and the cow jokes. Then, I turned and started Segment Four as the trail headed toward the Lost Creek Wilderness.

Segment Four starts with two miles on Jeep roads before the trail enters the Lost Creek Wilderness.

Bicycles are not permitted in wilderness areas, hence, detours are established for those biking to Durango. The CT triangle signs which mark the trail, which I welcomed and had gotten accustomed to seeing, are absent in the Lost Creek Wilderness because confidence markers aren't allowed in these areas.

A mile into the wilderness area, the trail crosses 9,000 feet in elevation right around a water source called Cold Stream. As I approached, I saw a guy and gal standing up from their rest.

"Don't take it personally, but we were just about to leave," the woman said as I dropped my backpack and reached for my water filter. I was glad they announced their departure. If they would have just gotten up and left without saying a word, I'd have wondered if it was my hiker stench. I guess it was bad timing; they had just finished a nice long break and were preparing to start hiking again when I showed up.

Rats.

It had been an hour since I left the LLC, and to my surprise, I was craving more camaraderie. I was hoping to meet some more fellow thru-hikers. I refilled my bottles, downed a snack, then set out down the trail determined to catch up to the pair.

It didn't take me more than 10 minutes of fast hiking before I was within earshot of some heavy breathing. I heard Ross before I saw him. He was in his 60s. Coming from the lower elevation of California, it was quickly obvious he was still acclimatizing to oxygen levels above 9,000 feet.

I slowed my pace so that I could join him.

"We are in the first of six designated wilderness areas that the CT wanders through," I told Ross. "The other five are the Holy Cross, Mount Massive, Collegiate Peaks, La Garita and Weminuche."

"How many wilderness areas are there in Colorado?" he asked.

"Forty-Two," I told him, like I was thru-hiking Rain Man.

We hiked about two miles in a good conversation flow until we caught up with Ross's fellow hiker named Ann. She was snacking, filtering water and preparing for the 1,300-foot climb over the next two miles. The grade was 550 feet per mile, the kind of grade where you want to take an occasional breather. This climb would put us above 10,000 feet of elevation for the first time.

I filtered some water, ate some trail mix and a beef stick while I got to learn about Ann, Ross and Ian, who was ahead of them on the trail and would see them in camp. They were a three-hiker *tramily*, who started from Waterton together the day before I did. A *tramily* (a combination of *trail* + *family)* is a unit that makes daily decisions to ensure they remain together. "Close-knit group" is a good definition. Or "thru-hikers who travel in a loose group."

I learned their group formed a year prior on the Pacific Crest Trail (PCT). They each started the thru-hike at the

Mexico border alone, but met each other along the way and stuck together for another 1,400 miles.

In 2021, forest fires drove them off a portion of the PCT in Oregon. Their original plan for 2022 was to hike the remaining mileage of the PCT they were forced to skip because of those fires. But when June 2022 rolled around, the snowpack in Oregon was well above average. So, they called a sudden audible and decided to hike all 486 miles of the Colorado Trail.

Now here they were, in the Lost Creek Wilderness cursing the elevation. Ian, the third member of their trio, was a faster hiker. He had made plans to meet back up with the group in camp at mile marker 52 next to the Brookside-Mc-Curdy Trail junction.

There was another seven miles between us and that spot. This was the first time I really started to notice the benefit of the FarOut app. The app is free to download, but each trail/map costs extra. The Colorado Trail download was $19.99 when I got it. It made planning and coordinating evening rendezvous points very simple. Each evening Ian, Ann, and Ross would decide how many miles they'd tackle the next day and where they'd camp together that night. This also afforded Ian the ability to leave camp earlier and hike faster than the group, but still be able to reconnect each evening.

I finished my snack with some sugar from an Airhead candy bar to give me a boost up the hill. Ann and Ross told me to push on ahead and find Ian; they were going tackle the incline at a slower pace. An hour later, I hit the high point for the day of 10,656 feet. From that point, the trail descends. As you exit the Lost Creek Wilderness area at 8.2 miles into Segment Four, the trail then emerges into Long Gulch, an open meadow that runs about seven miles.

Walking a half mile into that meadow, I caught movement in the willows out of the corner of my eye. About 75 yards away was a lanky, dark brown shape in the brush that looked like an elk at first glance. Then it raised its head out of the branches, and I saw the broad, flat shape of the antlers. It was a bull moose.

Nowhere to run to in the wide-open meadow if it charged me, so I quickly and vigilantly hustled down the trail.

The grade in the high alpine meadow is a gentle 150 feet of gain per mile. This makes for extremely enjoyable hiking at the end of the day. Actually, it's extremely enjoyable hiking anytime. I just happened to be crossing in the late afternoon.

A few miles into Long Gulch, I noticed a reddish-orange tent set up right beside the trail with a man lounging inside.

"Are you Ian?" I asked.

"Uh-oh, you must have met Ann and Ross," he said.

I laid my pack down as a backrest and lounged beside Ian's tent.

Once I learned Ian was from Oregon, I was eager to share some Colorado factoids.

"Where we are at, the Lost Creek Wilderness is named because the river here disappears underground and reappears down the valley. About 100,000 acres of the Lost Creek Wilderness were created in 1980," I explained. "Another roughly 15,000 acres were added later."

We hit it off immediately. We chatted about a wide range of subjects from inflation to psychology, to the Pacific Crest Trail as we waited beside the trail so the other two wouldn't miss us and walk past.

Usually, it takes a while before I let someone behind my introversion armor. That day, it took all of five minutes.

What's going on? Was there something magical about the trail?

Once Ann and Ross arrived, we set up camp in a great spot about 40 yards off the trail just inside the trees. Seated on top of my foam butt pad, I was boiling water for my evening dehydrated beef stroganoff when Ross said he was trying to airdrop to my iPhone a few photos of me from earlier in the day.

The first image was a picturesque little dell with great afternoon light shining among the tree trunks. I was a small figure in the picture facing away from the camera.

"Wait, is that photo of me peeing?" I asked.

"Yeah, I didn't know if you were peeing or just holding a tiny crayon," Ross said.

Wait, did he just make a small dick joke? Boy I'm going to fit right in with this group!

I sent the same message to my mom and to Ed through my Garmin: "I think I've found a tramily."

I camped on day three at mile marker 52 by the Brookside McCurdy Trail Junction. I was averaging 17.3 miles a day on the Colorado Trail through three days.

I walked into it a solo hiker, and I would exit the Lost Creek Wilderness adopted.

CHAPTER FOUR:

RAT

D ay Four on the trail found me at Mile 57 saying, "Dust . . . Cereal . . . Fish."

Ian responded, "Rust . . . Cereal . . . Fish?"

"No, no, *dust* with a *D*," I repeated.

We hiked another 50 yards and Ian said, "Hmm . . . dust . . . cereal . . .fish . . . let me think . . . dust-*buster* would work, but there's no *buster*-fish or fish-*buster* is there?"

No, our brains weren't in a hypoxia-induced hysteria (we hadn't even gone over Georgia Pass yet. We were still in the Lost Creek Wilderness under 11,000 feet in elevation). We were distracting our sore knees with a sort of cognitive brain teaser known as a Remote Association Test (RAT). It's used by researchers to measure creative thinking and insight problem-solving. A RAT poses a series of three seemingly unconnected words that are linked by a common word. For example, cottage/cake/Swiss would all three be linked by "cheese." (Cottage Cheese, Cheesecake, Swiss Cheese.)

We hiked along the single-track trail another quarter mile.

"It's bowl!" Ian finally says, "Dust bowl, cereal bowl and fishbowl." He got it.

I first introduced Ian to the Remote Association Tests the previous evening at camp. I set an eight-minute timer and had him try one of the RAT quizzes.

"I have to say, I was thinking about RAT clues as I was drifting off to sleep last night and while I was packing up my gear this morning," Ian said.

That morning was the first time on the trail I really noticed the crisp, cold dawn mountain air when I woke up at 6:40 a.m. I had coffee and oatmeal, packed my gear and hit the trail at 7:30 a.m. Ian was the first one up and out of camp in the morning followed by Ann and Ross. I caught up to Ross about a mile down the trail, then I leapfrogged Ann and finally caught Ian about five miles into the day. And it wasn't long after that I was quizzing Ian with RAT clues.

This same Remote Association Test was used in a 2012 study that confirmed that time spent in nature improves our creativity[1]. Participants who got four out of ten correct pre-hike, got on average six out of ten after four days backpacking.

The curiosity about the connection between the human mind and nature started in the 1970s with a husband and wife at the University of Michigan — Stephen and Rachel Kaplan. Both psychologists had the idea that time in nature could recharge the brain. They called it the *Attention Restoration Theory*[2].

According to Kaplan[3], the theory proposed that for attention to be repaired, the environment must be complex, and away from distractions. In other words, your brain battery won't recharge if you're pulled away by Facebook notifications, text messages and fantasy football score updates.

In a 2007 study, participants who walked among trees did much better on the math test than people who walked in the city. Direct attention is required to walk in a city, so you don't get hit by a car. This is not restorative. But walking along the Colorado Trail where the chance of a Subaru-driving texter is considerably lower, is restorative.

But here's the big kicker: It seems those breaks in nature only help if we put down our phones — even if you're in the fairest and most fascinating forest in Colorado.[4] In one study, people remembered numbers better after they took a break in nature compared to the same break in a brick-lined alley.

That shouldn't be a surprise. You don't need multivariate analysis to know that bricks are boring.

But what was more interesting about this study was the subjects who took their break in a verdant park but were allowed to enjoy that 15-minute break with their laptop performed just as poorly as those staring at a brick wall. To enhance your attention power, it's not enough to go to green space; you also need to also holster your notification box.

There have since been many studies that document nature's health and wellness benefit.

Schools with greener views from classroom windows had significantly higher graduation rates and better test scores[5]. Even having plants in your office can increase productivity; workers whose offices had greenery got 15% more work completed[6]. People who walked for 90 minutes in nature compared to those who walked in a city showed less activity in the parts of the brain linked to depression[7]. Gallbladder surgery patients whose hospital rooms faced a cluster of trees recovered faster and took fewer painkillers[8]. Taking a 20-minute walk in nature lowers stress hormone levels[9].

In a paper titled, "Of Cricket Chirps and Car Horns," researchers found that listening to natural sounds like crickets or rainfall improved people's attention capacity[10]. Nature scenes with water are especially restorative compared to other nature views[11]. People who pass more green space commuting to work tend to have better mental health[12].

So being among the trees is an anti-aging tonic, an immune-booster, therapist, meditation-instructor, creativity booster and an attention-recharger. If you put all that in pill form, it would be more popular than REI garage sale Saturdays in Denver.

"Put simply: time in nature is good for us," I told Ian as we strolled along the trail in Segment Four.

"I'm starting to notice what they call the three-day effect," I continued.

Three days in nature will find you more present and more at peace. On day one, there's a small improvement in stress and health markers, but you're still adjusting to the discomfort of hiking. We're thinking about our sore knees, our uncomfortable sleeping pads, and the dirt we will sit in to cook. We are also missing our phones and the warm showers. Work life is still on our mind. Day two finds our minds a little more settled and your sense of presence sharpening. We are spending less time worrying about the business we left behind and focusing more on the sounds, sights and smells of the trail. Day three washes over us like a warm wave. The discomfort of the backcountry ain't so bad. A wave of calm and inclusiveness comes over us. Our minds are still and passively and effortlessly soaking in nature. We just feel . . . good. (Even though that's about when we start to smell . . . bad.)

Prior to my time on the trail, I had been reading studies on the benefits of nature. As an economist, I wanted to use myself as a test subject. So, I recruited my Aunt Nancy and my cousin Amanda to help me create 12 days' worth of RAT quizzes for me to test the benefits of nature. I included extra copies in case I had other participants.

I wanted to see if I objectively got more creative the more time I spent on the trail. Each quiz consisted of 10, three-word clues on note cards. I had done quiz No. 1 at the end of my first day on the trail beside the South Platte River. I gave Ian the same clues. I won the first matchup of RAT quizzes. He got three out of 10 correct. I got four out of 10.

After chatting about the benefits of nature, I told Ian, "We can due RAT No. 2 later today."

I shared the trail for the next eight miles with Ian.

Two miles from Rock Creek, we ran into Beth, a guide from the Colorado Mountain Expeditions, strolling toward us. She was acting as the "Front Sweep" today. She drove the shuttle to the point where the group would end their day and began hiking backward as the group headed her way.

After we chatted with Beth, Ian asked me, "What do you call a snowboarder who breaks up with his girlfriend?"

"What?"

"Homeless," Ian said.

Ian was 66 years old with short white hair and had raised a family in Park City, Utah. He has an undistracted manner about him when you talk that lets you know he's really listening.

We got to Rock Creek, which is about eight miles into Segment Five, at 2 p.m. We hiked 13 miles. This is where Ian would stop for the day and wait for Ann and Ross. I wanted to get a few more miles because the Colorado Mountain Expeditions group moved their base camp to the camping area at Kenosha Pass for the last two days of their guided adventure. With the taste of fresh guacamole still fresh in my mind, I had some good motivation. Plus, I wanted to reconnect with my new friends.

While I was waiting for the boiling water to cook my lunch, we did another RAT test. We set the eight-minute timer and began Quiz No. 2. Ian got six out of 10 while I only got three out of 10. Our second matchup went to Ian.

"Okay, so we will plan to meet you at Kenosha Pass at 9:10 a.m. tomorrow," Ian said.

"Yep, sounds good, and you'll get to meet Ed and Julie." I responded.

Up until this point, I was a solo hiker who didn't have to make rendezvous points, I needed to adjust now.

As I left Ian and hiked up hill away from Rock Creek, I pondered a few of the clues I missed and smiled at the fact I had found someone to share the RAT experiment with.

A mile later around 5 p.m., despite the Gatorade and energy beans I ate, I really bonked (hiker term for a sudden loss of energy) three miles from Kenosha Pass. Like the previous three days, negative thoughts invaded my mind.

This is only day four. Can you do this day in and day out?

I don't know why, but I just felt depressed.

I rebounded slightly when the trail topped out in a large Aspen tree grove, and it gave me an expansive view of the valley of South Park (made famous by the cartoon of the same name). I could also see the town of Jefferson and the first view of where the trail was headed: Georgia Pass — the first foray above timberline. I caught a glimpse of snow fields on the big peaks ahead of me with the Continental Divide looking fearsome to the west.

Still feeling glum, I made it to Kenosha Pass just after 6 p.m. to find the Colorado Mountain Expeditions basecamp a third of a mile off the trail. I was a bit tentative strolling into their camp.

Would I be welcomed? Or would it feel like I've invaded their campsite and am mooching?

"Hey, look who it is!" the guide named Cory yelled out as I made my way into their camp next to their cooking tent. My fears were quickly allayed. They made me feel like part of their crew.

Chris then invited me to dinner if I agreed to help with the dishes. That was an easy choice. I was treated to a feast: spinach sausage tortellini pasta, fresh garlic bread and peach cobbler. Oh boy, was that rejuvenating. In the first 71 miles on the Colorado Trail, I'd been treated with two banquets. Over dinner, I was able to catch up with my new trail friends.

I stayed up until sunset chatting with the guides and hearing their stories before I crawled into my tent to write in my journal by headlamp light.

Before hitting the trail, I'd been reading about the benefits of journaling and how it belongs in the toolbelt of self-care along with things like exercise and meditation. Journaling boosts memory and communication skills. Journaling is associated with better sleep, more self-confidence and higher I.Q[13]. It helps us label our emotions and organize our thoughts. As we process things while we write them down, our brains free up space for better memory and sleep. Done right, journaling can help unload anxiety and unclutter the mind.

But before I penned my day's adventures and thoughts into my Rite in the Rain trail journal, I read over the three notecards in my journal. The first three-by-five index card had the following:

I am hiking the Colorado Trail because....
- I need a difficult adventure
- I want time to evaluate the next phase of my life

- I want to find FLOW
- Looking to find stillness
- Want to upgrade my physical and mental resiliency
- Wish to push my comfort bubble
- Want to write a book about wellness
- Want to test the benefits of nature
- Learn to suffer so everything else is sweeter
- Want to re-wire
- Want to break technology addiction

Two days before I began the trail, I sat on the front porch of my house in Denver and thought for about 10 minutes about the purpose of my trek. It really helped calm my nerves as I put my thoughts to paper. I came across this method in the book "Appalachian Trials: The Psychological and Emotional Guide to Successfully Thru-Hiking The Appalachian Trail" by Zach Davis. The book has wonderful advice on the pre-trail mental preparation. The other two cards had the following written on them in my handwriting.

If I give up on the Colorado Trail, I will:

- Not enjoy the rest of my sabbatical
- Not like who I see in the mirror
- Have less confidence in making the next decision about the next phrase of my life
- Not be able to teach about wellness
- Have less confident posture

When I successfully thru-hike the Colorado Trail, I will:

- Have a story for a lifetime
- Find presence
- Be a better listener
- Write a book within 12 months
- Have unshakable confidence
- Be a better Christian
- Have clarity in what I want in life

Zach describes how 70% of the people hiking the Appalachian Trail won't make it to the end. Those who do are able to find their *why*. Those who are successful are those who have a purpose. The notecards are a way of reminding myself, while I hiked the Colorado Trail, of my purpose.

Clues to RAT Quiz #1:
law, birthday, case
stop, ground, ache
off, beer, way
wash, food, off
good, salad, head
hat, poll, last
work, back, line
wreck, town, shape
silver, hard, house
back, camp, enemy

Clues to RAT Quiz #2:
without, Indian, dinner
new, through, loose
school, ball, chair
paper, castle, bag
coffee, dance, down
bottom, hard, music
rest, chair, side
sheet, bed, out
see, horse, dust
moon, shoe, sun

(Answers in the appendix)

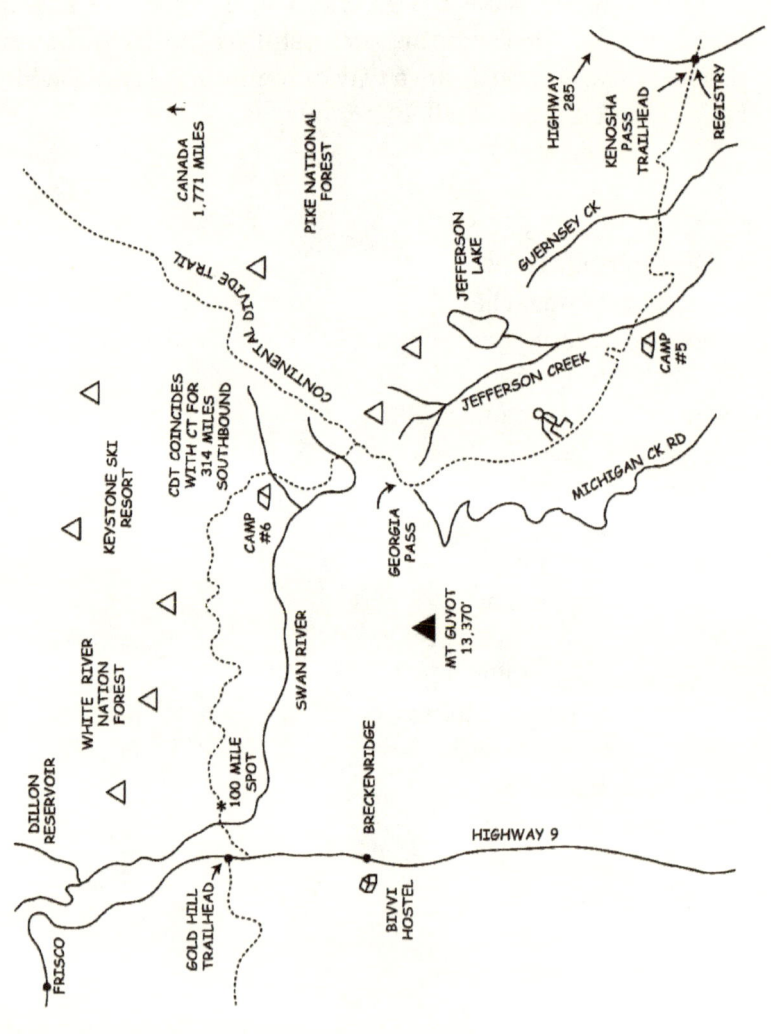

CANADA 1,771 MILES

PIKE NATIONAL FOREST

CONTINENTAL DIVIDE TRAIL

HIGHWAY 285

KENOSHA PASS TRAILHEAD

REGISTRY

JEFFERSON LAKE

GUERNSEY CK

JEFFERSON CREEK

CAMP #5

MICHIGAN CK RD

KEYSTONE SKI RESORT

CDT COINCIDES WITH CT FOR 314 MILES SOUTHBOUND

CAMP #6

GEORGIA PASS

WHITE RIVER NATION FOREST

SWAN RIVER

MT GUYOT 13,370'

DILLON RESERVOIR

100 MILE SPOT

BRECKENRIDGE

HIGHWAY 9

FRISCO

GOLD HILL TRAILHEAD

BIVVI HOSTEL

CHAPTER FIVE:

Trail Registry

My anxiety was still lingering in the morning of Day Five on the trail when I woke up at 7:30 a.m. This was the first day on the trail that I woke up feeling low — not physically low, but mentally anxious.

I took my time packing up because I still had two hours before Ed and his partner Julie would meet me. Beth from Colorado Mountain Expeditions saved me some French toast and ham from their breakfast. I gobbled it up like I was being timed.

After packing up my gear, I crossed Highway 285 at 9 a.m., found the trail registry and penned:

"6/24 Chris Stiffler - left Denver Monday am headed toward Durango"

I closed the register lid, then I found some shade by Kenosha Pass.

Kenosha Pass derives its name from a stagecoach driver named Clark Herbert who named the pass after his hometown in Wisconsin. Highway 285 at Kenosha Pass follows an important toll road that linked Denver to California Gulch (the future Leadville). The spot is a popular destination for Aspen-peeping in September. That's when people from Denver make the one-hour drive to see the changing colors of the leaves on the Aspen grove I'd hiked through the previous day.

I decided to read my novel while I waited for my resupply team to arrive. I didn't get through more than five pages before two friendly couples in their 70s strolled up to me and noticed my backpack.

"Are you hiking the Colorado Trail?"

"Yep!"

"All the way to Durango?"

"Yep, I hope to. I'm 71 miles in so far. The next segment is 32 miles until the town of Breckenridge."

"That's such an adventure. Do you know how difficult this trail is? We planned to hike about two miles then turn around."

This segment is the longest of the Colorado Trail. It runs from where the trail crosses US Highway 285 at Kenosha Pass until Breckenridge. The high point on the segment reaches about 11,874 feet.

"Well, it gets above timberline, but that's not for another 12 miles, though. The next two miles should be doable," I said, happy to fill them in on the details I'd been studying.

Then one of the husbands was eager to give me some advice. He said, "I've been to 471 breweries in my life, and Broken Compass Brewery in Breckenridge makes my top 10 list. If you're looking for a beer after all that hiking, that's what I'd suggest."

Did he really have an accurate tally of the several hundred breweries he'd been to or was that a joke? Either way, I am so going.

Ed and Julie arrived in their automobile about five minutes before Ian showed up on foot. Ten minutes later, Ross and Ann trickled in around 10 a.m. They had already hiked seven miles that morning. Ed and Julie brought the works for us: chips and guacamole, bananas, apples, sandwiches and diet Cherry Coke. I resupplied my pack with three Ziplock gallon bags that contained each day's rations.

Then, Ian and I packed into the car with Ed and Julie and drove to Jefferson to retrieve the re-supply box from the post office.

From an outsider perspective, Ian thought that Jefferson was a regular-sized town, but it's tiny. The post office isn't a stand-alone office. It's incorporated into the Jefferson Market. Their hours aren't 9 to 5.

We got there right at 11 a.m., right when the post office opened — or so we thought. Turns out they didn't open until noon. Ian was not-so-politely told that it was a federal offense to even look to see if his package was there until noon. So, we sat in the Jefferson Market and ate some fudge. I also used the time to charge my Anker portable charger.

Ian was visibly stressed that he was forcing Ed and Julie to wait an additional hour. But they didn't mind at all. Ed is a big extrovert who soaked up the opportunity to sit in the Jefferson Market, sip coffee, nibble on fudge and chat. Ian didn't know that, however.

When noon finally rolled around, Ian discovered that his package wasn't there. It had been delivered to Jefferson but was returned to the sender. And it got worse.

"That package had food for Ann and Ross, too." he barked.

"Oh no. What can we do to help?" asked Julie.

"I think I can make do with what's here," Ian said noticeably flustered.

Ian was able to buy some snacks and some overpriced dehydrated meals in Jefferson. Then we got back into Ed's car and headed back to the pass.

"'If you can, avoid re-supplying in Jefferson. My advice instead is to find yourself an Ed and Julie and have them re-supply you at Kenosha' will be some advice I add to my trail blog about this incident," Ian told us, still looking stunned.

Looking back, I had extra Ziplock bags of food stashed in Ed's car I should have shared with Ian. At that point, however, I was still in my solo-hiking selfish mindset and didn't know if I would have enough food bags prepared for later in my journey.

The kerfuffle at the post office added to the anxious and low feeling I had that morning. The weather didn't help brighten my mood as dark clouds rolled in, spitting rain as we began Segment Six in the early afternoon.

About half a mile west of Kenosha, I ran into the two couples I'd met earlier that morning. They were on the back portion of their out-and-back hike.

The husband who had been to 471 breweries told me, "After we left you this morning, my wife was worried about the difficulty of this hike. She said by the look of that guy, this is a pretty tough trail, that guy looks like he's from Seal Team Six!"

OK, that pumped me up. It's amazing how a single positive interaction like that can change your mood.

I gave him a big smile and bumped fists with him. It took a stranger's positive talk to remind me to focus on a positive mindset.

From Highway 285, the trail climbs about 400 feet over the first mile then a nice downhill for the next 2.5 miles. The trail through the Aspens offers great views of the Continental Divide. There were still snowfields visible. After three miles into Segment Six, we hiked into a clearing and noticed about 20 women swinging pickaxes into the tundra dirt and grass. The all-woman crew was rerouting a short portion of the trail to avoid a low area prone to flooding and erosion. This was the second day of the "Women's Only Guernsey Creek" four-day crew. The 21 volunteers built a 0.18 mile reroute to replace an eroded section of the trail.

This crew was one of 19 trail crews that the Colorado Trail Foundation organized in 2022. The trail crew volunteer opportunities varied from three to seven-day commitments. From 5,633 volunteer hours working on the CT in 2022, trail crews constructed or repaired three bridges, cleared avalanche debris, built rock walls and constructed/realigned a mile of trail.

For those interested in joining a trail crew, the Colorado Trail Foundation publishes the crew schedule in February for the summer's projects. This is the earliest you can register for a project.

I got an insight on the power of volunteer labor reading early editions of "Tread Lines" the Colorado Trail newsletter from 1986. Trail construction that cost the Colorado Mountain Club $2,500 would have cost the Forest Service, who would have to hire a crew, $260,000. "Not a bad return for a $2,500 investment!" the newsletter stated.

We got to Jefferson Creek at mile 78 at 3 p.m. This put us 5.5 miles and 2,000 feet of elevation gain from Georgia Pass, which we'd save for first thing the next morning. This was an easy day for me; I hiked seven miles with 1,000 feet of elevation gain. Setting up camp at 3 p.m. felt too early. I got anxious again. I even journaled about it that evening writing, "I need to work on calming my brain and enjoy my present company. Why am I dreading down time in the afternoon?" I had no deadlines. I had worries. I had all my necessities.

Why couldn't I just be still? How do I drop the city-life, ramped-up, anxious-living mentality and sink into trail life?

As I was soaking my feet and washing up in Jefferson Creek ("Oh no, save me" cried my stank), my trail family was doing some conspiring. I strolled back into camp drying my hair from the cold water at 10,000 feet of elevation to find the three sitting together with almost mischievous grins — like they were plotting a prank on me.

But to my delight, they weren't pranking me, they were about to give me something I had been craving and pondering ever since my Colorado Trail hike began to materialize.

"We've decided to dub you 'Nugget,'" said Ross.

They decided it was time I got a trail name. And they sensed this was a special moment for me.

"Wait . . . why Nugget?" I asked.

"Because of all the factoids about Colorado's mountains, and the 14ers, and things that you add to the conversation like telling us that Kenosha pass was named because of a stagecoach driver, we dub you 'Nugget' for the nuggets of information you add to the conversation," declared Ross.

"We went back and forth on whether it should be 'Nugget' or 'Nuggets,'" interjected Ann.

"But 'Nuggets' sounds too much like you have big balls or something," said Ross.

"And 'Nugget' is a lot better than 'Crayon,'" he croaked harking back to our first day together.

"I like it!" I blurted out. "What now, is there like a knighting ceremony where you confer my trail name by tapping my shoulders with your trekking poles like the flat side of a knighting sword?"

Ian smiled and said, "Nope, you just have to accept."

It's usually understood that someone else must give your trail name. Trail names allow you to separate yourself from normal life. There's usually a story behind those names, which makes for great conversation as you walk the trail. "Nugget" wasn't merely a nickname; it was another identity freshly opened to me.

I then got to learn the trail names of those three. No longer were they Ann, Ross and Ian. From that point on, I knew them and addressed them by their trail names.

At that moment Ian became *Bad Foot*. He earned his trail name on the Pacific Crest Trail in 2021 after suffering for 400 miles through a massive blister on the sole of his foot.

Ross's trail name was *Hairy Potter*. Surprisingly, his moniker doesn't come from the J.K. Rowling epic. It was because the guy was both hirsute and hand-crafted his own ceramics. He literally is a Hairy Potter.

You know the scene in Forest Gump when the Tom Hanks character starts running across America and grows out his hair and beard? Well, Hairy Potter only needed to buy the iconic Bubba Gump Shrimp Co. red hat to complete his Forest Gump Halloween custom last year. He already had the thigh-length running shorts (which he wore on the CT), the beard and the hair.

Then there was *Tall Tale*. The 47-year-old brunette whom to this point I knew as "Ann" got her trail name during a 2021 Pacific Crest Trail thru-hike.

Along the trail, Ann came across some fishermen at a remote alpine lake. Wanting to help out the thru-hiker with some food, the fishermen gave her one of the fish they had caught. But to a thru-hiker whose only cooking equipment is one small boil mug, a fully scaled fish is more of a burden than benefit. Ann didn't have a knife to fillet the fish nor aluminum foil to wrap it in before tossing it into the coals of a fire to cook. She wasn't making fires anyway. She was basically saddled with a smelly fish that she didn't want to reject out of politeness.

Naturally, when she reconnected with some fellow hikers on the trail, they asked her why she was lugging around a fish. She informed them about the fisherman and her inability to reject a gift.

Like a childhood game of telephone, the story morphed as it got retold.

"Did you hear about the gal who is spearing her protein with a trekking pole?" "Have you met Ann? She kills fish with her hiking poles!" Ann's legend began spreading up and down the trail. Then, a few days later, Ann met some other female hikers. After they learned her name, they of course burst out, "Are you the Ann who is spearfishing with her poles?" And so, Ann became *Tall Tale*.

With a newfound sense of joy to my day, I decided to pay them back with a little poetry recital as we ate dinner together. I had been memorizing Robert Service poetry for months leading up to the hike for occasions just like this.

"Robert Service was known as the 'Bard of the Yukon,'" I explained.

Though critics called his poetry "doggerel," Service never wanted to be the poet recited in the ivory towers, he wanted to be heard in pubs. Service said, "Verse, not poetry, is what I was after . . . something the man in the street would take notice of and the sweet old lady would paste in her album; something the schoolboy would spout and the fellow in the pub would quote."

I sat cross-legged in the dirt and recited from memory two of my favorite poems: "The Cremation of Sam McGee" and "The Spell of the Yukon."

"The Spell of the Yukon" is about a successful prospector who, after striking it rich, got sick of the rich life and preferred to go back into nature. The poem finishes with these two stanzas:

> They're making my money diminish;
> I'm sick of the taste of champagne.
> Thank God! when I'm skinned to a finish
> I'll pike to the Yukon again.
> I'll fight—and you bet it's no sham-fight;
> It's hell!—but I've been there before;
> And it's better than this by a damsite—
> So me for the Yukon once more.

> There's gold, and it's haunting and haunting;
> It's luring me on as of old;
> Yet it isn't the gold that I'm wanting
> So much as just finding the gold.
> It's the great, big, broad land 'way up yonder,
> It's the forests where silence has lease;
> It's the beauty that thrills me with wonder,
> It's the stillness that fills me with peace.

I had thought about that line several times on the hike so far. It reminded me to enjoy the ride and to not solely focus on the destination. A day that started off in a mental low point, ended with my smiling and swelling with pride in my tent.

It isn't the gold that I'm wanting, so much as just finding the gold . . .

CHAPTER SIX:

Immersion

D ay Six on the trail started at 5:45 a.m. With Georgia Pass to get up and over, we decided we'd knock that out early in the morning before any chances of the summer Colorado thunderstorms rolling in on top of us. I was really getting proficient at breaking down my tent and packing my pack.

Because my "bed" goes on my back for the next evening's camping spot, I was forced to make it every day on the trail. I began to look forward to this task. It gave me a sense of accomplishment right at the start of the day, which in turn gives you more motivation to check off another task[14].

I was out of camp only 20 minutes after waking up. Tall Tale and Hairy Potter were still packing their gear when I left our campsite. I chowed on an apple, Pop-Tarts and a Honey Stinger as I started up the 2,000-foot climb to Georgia Pass.

I caught up with Bad Foot about two miles into the climb. He was always the first one up and out of camp. In my previous weekend backpacking trips, everyone would hike together, but I noticed that thru-hikers moving in a tramily could have different start times as long as they planned to reconvene later in the day.

We hiked together for a bit until we ran into a lone camper making his breakfast beside the trail.

He greeted us with a "Good morning!"

"Are you hiking the Colorado Trail?" I asked.

"I'm trying to do Segments One to Six before I move to California," he told us.

It was Saturday morning, and he had a flight to California to start a job at Apple on Monday. His plan was to get to Breckenridge that day — a big day that would require 25 miles and 4,000 feet of elevation gain.

"Wow, that's a monster day ahead of you," I said.

Our plan for the day was to camp near Swan River — a 14-mile day, which would leave us about 12 miles for Sunday.

"I'm Malcolm," he said.

"I'm Chr...I'm Chris." I said hesitantly.

"No, that's not it," Bad Foot chimed in.

"Oh, actually I'm Nugget!"

"Bad Foot," said Bad Foot.

"Nice to meet you both."

It was the first time I referred to myself with my trail name. It felt a bit foreign, like I wasn't quite sure if I was doing it right or something. Though I took more and more pride in it every time I used it.

Ever since seventh grade, when I found myself jealous of the nicknames of the guys in the friend circle one year ahead of me, I had desired one. I was envious of Lenny (whose real name was Zack). I hadn't a clue about the origin story of the name Lenny, but I wanted one similar.

Looking back on it now, I'm struggling to figure out why I was so envious of the other guys with nicknames like "Ham" or "Cabbage." "Ham" because the guy couldn't pronounce "jamon" in Spanish class and "Cabbage" on account of the flatulence that followed the consumption of said item. OK, I hear it now: they mostly aren't flattering, but still cool in my teenage eyes. I now realized on the trail that it wasn't necessarily the nickname per se, but the story that went with it. Or it was the way that using the alias felt like I was granted secret passage to an elite club — a part of the tribe.

After leaving Malcolm to his breakfast, I pushed ahead of Bad Foot as the trail crossed the Krummholz zone — the zone between the timberline and the wide-open alpine area in which the trees that can survive those harsh conditions take the form of dense shrubs. Krummholz is German, meaning "crooked wood." They are twisted, wind-shaped shrubs. Passing the Krummholz, you break into the trail's first stretch above the tree line, and you are rewarded with great views of Mt. Guyot (13,376').

The main thing to consider when deciding on a start date for the Colorado Trail is the lingering snow above the tree line. Many of the crests and ridges along the trail can be laden with snow through early July, especially on the north sides of the mountains where they get less direct sunlight. Those heading southbound from Denver will hike more than 80 miles before they top out above timberline at Georgia Pass. That's where we were at the time.

I spoke to my family while I admired the views.

I was able to find cell reception so I was able to ask my mom if she could make four reservations at the Bivouac Hostel in Breckenridge for the following evening. Like Ed, my mom delighted in aiding my adventure anyway she could. And I took the opportunity to do a favor for my trail family.

I was waiting for Bad Foot to reach the saddle so I could tell him a factoid about Mt. Guyot.

Interestingly a "guyot" is a geologic term for an underwater volcanic mound. But this mountain is neither a volcano nor is it underwater. It is named after the Princeton geography professor Arnold Guyot.

Eventually, I shared the high point of Segment Six with Bad Foot and Malcolm.

Bad Foot left the saddle before me as I was snacking and admiring the views. Bad Foot had an intelligent quietness to him that made you realize he chose his words intentionally and judiciously. He became to me someone I was proud to make proud.

We had another seven miles to get to Swan River, but most of it was downhill — losing 2,000 feet. Reaching the pass, we had gotten the hard part out of the way for the day. That felt reassuring. I felt a similar feeling once the trail dipped back into the trees — like the trees were beginning to feel like home.

After two miles of strolling by myself, I turned a switch-back in the trees and spotted Bad Foot in the middle of the trail interrogating a tall, thick, brown-bearded German hiker who looked like he could be a bouncer at the rowdiest club in the country. He was hiking the Continental Divide Trail (CDT), and his trail name, oddly enough, was "Cuddles." After hiking the Pacific Crest Trail last year, Bad Foot was acutely interested in the Continental Divide Trail. He'd been eager to get to a point where the CT and the CDT overlap. He had found his first hiker to question.

The two trails first begin to overlap just after Georgia Pass. This is why we suddenly began to see a small stream of northbound hikers trekking toward us on the Colorado Trail.

It can be easy to conflate the two trails — particularly as thru-hikers are speaking in acronyms. (Did she say C-T? or C-D-T?) The Colorado Trail spans 486 miles from Denver to Durango. While the Continental Divide Trail (CDT) travels through five states and covers 3,100 miles from Mexico to Canada. The two trails overlap for 314 miles.

It was June 26, and Cuddles had started at the U.S.-Mexico border near Hachita, New Mexico on May 3. He had started the trail alone but quickly met companions along the way. We learned that of the 50 days he had camped so far, he'd only spent three of them camped alone.

"That's a lot less days camped alone than I expected," he told us.

We also learned how injury-inducing hiking long stretches of flat desert road can be. It seems counterintuitive. You'd think that sloping, rocky, root-bearing terrain that you must negotiate would give you an increased chance at injuring yourself, but Cuddles told us that road walking is worse. For this reason: flat road walking requires hitting the same micro impacts on your feet step over and over.

"My bubble for the last three weeks has been with Caddyshack and Feeling Good," Cuddles said.

"That statement probably wouldn't have made any sense to me a month ago," I said.

A *bubble* is more thru-hiker jargon for a group of hikers headed in the same direction who generally remain within a few days' hiking mileage from each other. You might not see the hikers in your bubble each day, but they seem to sporadically show up. The social dynamics of thru-hiking were becoming a more and more appealing part of this quest.

That evening, I received a crash course on the social dynamics of a tramily as well.

I hadn't seen Hairy Potter or Tall Tale since I left camp this morning, but we reunited at that evening's camp spot just past Swan River and all cooked, ate our dinner together and discussed our day. Instead of poetry and trail name stories, we used our evening time together to do RAT No. 3. Hairy Potter joined Bad Foot and I this time. I brought along four copies of each quiz. We set the eight-minute timer, and each began our quiz.

I eked out a narrow victory over Bad Foot with five correct to his four. The victory wasn't, however, without a slight discrepancy. For the first line of clues "wild, man, fly," I guessed "horse" for "wild horse, horseman and horsefly." My aunt's answer key had "fire," so wildfire, fireman, firefly.

Bad Foot graciously accepted "horse." I was up two to one after three RAT tests. And it seemed I was improving my scores the more I was in nature.

The rain came through at 6:30 p.m. We had hiked 14 miles with 2,300 feet of elevation gain getting us to mile 91. I was looking forward to a town day.

I used that time to journal and listen to the patter of rain drops hitting my tent. Rain is great on the trail when you've already gotten to camp and set up your gear for the night. As I began to reminisce and savor my day, a major thought dawned on me: I realized I hadn't hit a mental low point. I battled anxiousness and doubt every day of the first five on the trail, but not today.

Maybe Nugget doesn't get depressed?

I made a mental tally of what was different on this day than the previous: I now had a new identity. I also had a shared purpose that was bigger than just getting myself down the trail. I had a trail family to help. I had found my tribe. I had found my element. I was Nugget. And my Ham, Cabbage and Lenny were Bad Foot, Tall Tale and Hairy Potter.

Clues to RAT Quiz #3:
wild, man, fly
down, dance, out
foot, pad, high
eight, bearing, park
game, dead, front
book, law, study
rise, five, mile
broken, time, book
under, zone, paper
apple, tomato, hot

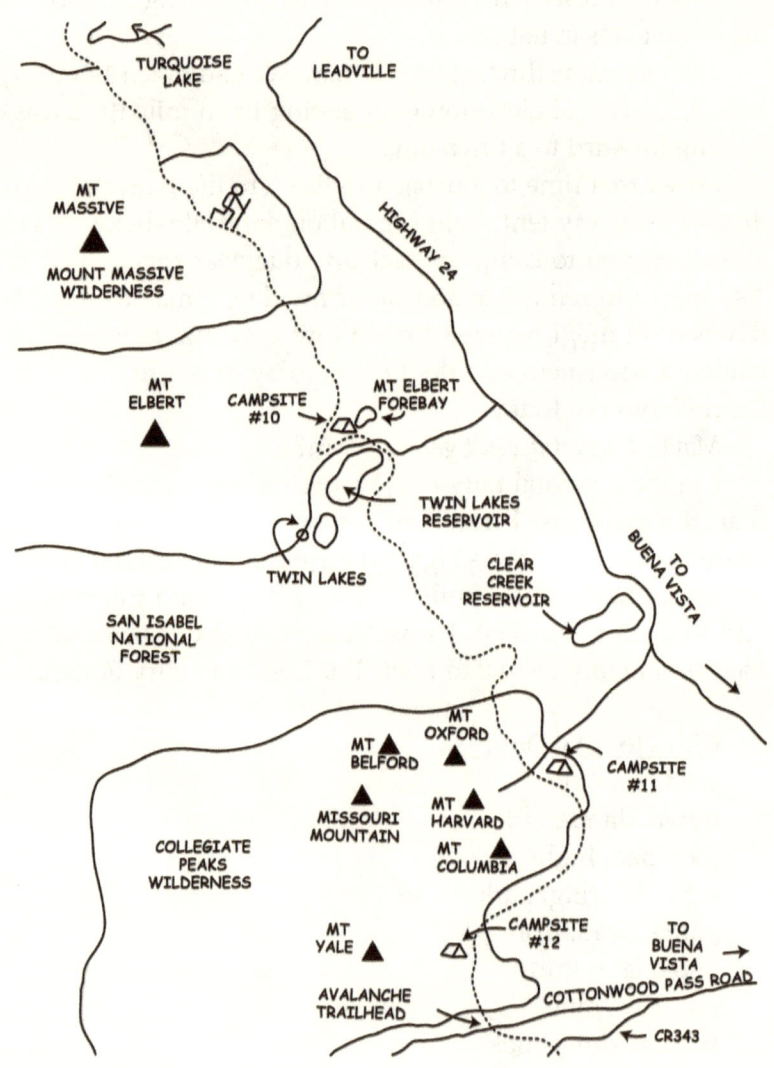

CHAPTER SEVEN:

Nugget

As I emerged from my tent on Day Seven on the trail, everyone was gone. All that was left was the packed-down grass and dirt of three tents, the evidence that someone had slept there. But those *someones* were already on the trail. I learned that people have more energy and get out of bed earlier on town days. Bad Foot, Tale Tall and Harry Potter were no different. Looked like Nugget had some catching up to do.

From the Swan River, the trail gains 1,200 feet over three miles to the day's highpoint of 11,169 feet. Then the next miles slowly drop to 9,200 feet where the trail intersects Highway 9.

After coffee and oatmeal, I packed up and hit the trail right at 7 a.m. I was getting up earlier and earlier as my body adjusted to thru-hiking and nature's lighting.

Aided by a mile walk and my morning coffee, I put my backpack down on the trail and headed into the trees for my morning routine. When I came back to the trail, there were two women hiking toward me.

I greeted them with "Good morning, are you hiking the whole Colorado Trail?"

And they were. Their names were Amy and Leslie. Both in their 50s.

"Oh, cool! I go by Nugget."

Is that how you say your trail name? I "go by?"

Walking everywhere with your shelter and food on your back allows you to start your day without set expectations. I started to feel a "why not" way to my hiking. When I was in that mode, I noticed something small like meeting fellow hikers made me feel warm and content.

There was something oddly familiar about Leslie, but I couldn't initially put my finger on it. Both were fast hikers. I learned that Amy was a cave explorer — as in stay-in-a-cave-for-several-weeks-at-a-time-for-scientific-research type stuff. Although we were high on the ridge with an expansive view of the Keystone Ski Resort, I felt claustrophobic hearing stories of living in caves with no natural light for a month. It sounded too close to hibernation to me.

About seven miles into our day, we met a CDT hiking couple gliding up the steep trail that made me think that the trail I was on suddenly overlapped with an iron man competition in progress. The small backpacks this tanned and toned couple carried seemed way too small for thru-hikers. They also moved up the trail as fast as I was moving downhill. They seemed like the type of people who say, "Which one?" when someone mentions they're training for a 50-mile race.

And unlike most of the CDT hikers headed north toward us on the Colorado Trail, they did not spend a night in Breckenridge.

"Too many people," the couple from Hawaii told me.

They had spent just enough time in town to resupply before heading back into the backcountry. Evidently, the refuge of the lonely woods was much more appealing to them than the crowded stores and streets of one of Colorado's busiest mountain towns. On my seventh day of hiking, having had yet to experience my first "town day," that didn't compute. I was craving a burger, beer and a shower.

The couple was friendly, but they also didn't want to dawdle. They were determined to hike another 15 more miles that day. I told them that they were true "big leaguers" as a compliment to their hike of the most challenging trails in the U.S. And even after learning they were CDT hikers, I still double-checked they didn't have the stenciled painted numbers of an iron man participant on their skin as they headed north. They were headed toward Gray's Peak — a Colorado 14er and the highest point on the CDT they would summit the following day.

Later in the day, I would learn each of the couple's trail names when we crossed paths with *Happy*, another CDT thru-hiker. Of all the people on the trail, the origin of her nickname was the easiest to surmise. A glow came from her beaming checks and flowing hair. She had an infectious smile and attitude.

"Are you moving with a couple from Hawaii?" I asked her.

"Oh, you mean *Sonic* and *Mud Slide?*" she responded.

The way she nonchalantly dropped their trail names was fascinating to me — as though it was completely normal to refer to a human being as *Mud Slide*. Happy had been moving in the couple's bubble for a few days.

Like a lot of subcultures, thru-hiking has its own vocabulary. So, once you submerse yourself into thru-hike culture, you find yourself saying sentences like "Oh you mean *Cuddles* and *Caddy Shack*? They are doing 30s with *Feeling Good* and *Onion*, *Worm* and *Gump* yogied a ride into town and took a zero." (Translation: Are you referring to Volker and Bryan? They are hiking 30-mile days with Rob, Jan, Andrew and Ankit who slyly mooched a ride into town and took a day off from hiking.)

As we ran into about a dozen CDT hikers over these miles, I started truly embracing my trail name. I was eager to run into more hikers, so I could tell them, "I'm Nugget."

Toward the end of the morning, I finally realized why Leslie looked so familiar. I had met her earlier on the trail. She was the woman at the end of Segment Two looking for her friend. That friend didn't continue, but fortunately Leslie met and had been moving with Amy for the past several days.

We crossed our first big milestone on the trail together: the 100-mile mark. We had a mountain biker take our photo at that spot. Amy was sticking her index finger in the air, and Leslie and I each made the sign language "O" with our fists to signify 1-0-0 together.

You got to celebrate the small achievements on the trail.

I shared the last 13 miles of Segment Six with those two. We arrived at the Gold Hill trailhead at 12:02 p.m. The rain arrived at 12:03 p.m, and my friend Rich and his fiancée, Heather, arrived at 12:04 p.m. The hail wasn't too far behind. Rich had been following my Garmin InReach, which pings my location every 10 minutes. He and Heather had enjoyed the weekend in Leadville and were on their way back to Denver. But before that, they'd resupply me and get a burger and beer.

I was 103 miles into the Colorado Trail. And I looked like, according to Heather, "I had just come home from a long beach vacation in the sun . . . and also didn't put deodorant on for that vacation week."

"Like a half-fermented, half-rotten piece of fruit?" I asked.

"That's a great description, you've had some time to pinpoint that odor, haven't you?" Heather said.

At a pub in Breckenridge, I was delighted with a cold IPA, nachos, a burger and sweet potato fries. I was, however, slightly jarred by the crowded racket of the pub.

Maybe Sonic and Mudslide were on to something?

We were seated next to a table of out-of-state tourist couples who, on account of their seats lacking direct eyesight of a television game broadcasting the Astros baseball game, were rude to the waitress.

I wanted to say, "You're going to worry about one baseball game in June? There's got to be 90 more games left in the season. It's not even the All-State break yet. Why don't you enjoy being present with your friends and family?"

But what Nugget actually said was nothing. I figured being in the general propinquity of me and my hiker odor was enough penance to pay for being rude to the waitress. I chuckled to myself thinking about that group looking around wondering if someone ordered spoiled fruit. Those types of worries were beginning to feel so frivolous to me. On the trail, as I was slowly discovering, it's so much easier to be fully present with people.

Your priorities crystallize: hike, camp, be.

After a late lunch, Rich and Heather drove me to Wal-Mart for some supplies. I decided to add some more sugary treats to my food bags. After a week seeing more chipmunks than people, the din of a crowded shopping super store was overwhelming and almost irritating.

After acquiring more candy, Rich and Heather dropped me off at the Bivouac Hostel at 3:30 p.m. The Bivouac Hostel (or Bivvi) was much nicer than the hostels I had stayed in before. It has a large high-ceiling lobby with a fireplace, couches, and a bar. It felt like a cozy ski lodge. I strolled into that lobby with my backpack to find Bad Foot sitting by the fire chatting with the pair I hiked with in the morning. Check-in wasn't until 4 p.m.

The weather of rain down here and hail higher up, drove a bunch of thru-hikers to this haven for the evening. The lobby was littered with the gear of CT hikers, CDT hikers and a bunch of road bikers who were biking across the country. I tallied people from six different counties in the lobby who were all united by the Colorado outdoors. It was filled with people like Blister, the Swiss Monkey and Flat Tire.

Once I got a key to our room, I headed straight for the shower. Since I made the reservations for my trail family, I got first dibs on the shower. I never realized how much dirt and grime accumulates on your legs while you are hiking. After a week without bathing, a long hot shower was like rain on parched earth, reviving every inch of me. My trail family shared a six-bunk room with two gals from the Czech Republic who had just arrived in Colorado to work for the summer.

After my decontamination, I mean a shower, I headed back to the lobby to absorb the hiker-enthusiasm-laced stories that were being shared. That's when I met the Wangler.

He was a 52-year-old brown-haired husband and father from Denver who was section hiking the trail. That summer's goal was to take a week to complete the mileage between Kenosha Pass and Twin Lakes. As I got to know Wangler, across the lobby, Leslie and Amy sat chatting with a lanky guy in glasses named Andrew. He had been biking across the country from Washington, D.C. When he got to Colorado, he liked it so much that he ditched his goal of California and decided to spend a few weeks biking the mountain passes of Colorado instead.

Little did we know at the time that we were chatting with the 2022 Summit County Adult Bacon Eating Champion.

"Hey, is there a brewery close?" Wangler asked.

"Looks like we are really close to spot called 'Broken something,' " said Leslie.

Broken Compass? That's the spot mentioned by the guy at Kenosha Pass.

The hostel is serendipitously a half mile walk from Broken Compass Brewery. It took no effort at all to convince the crew to head that direction. We had pizza, beer and watched the Avalanche win the Stanley Cup. Bad Foot, Hairy Potter and Tall Tale also joined us.

I knew that town days held the promise of a hot shower and food that isn't beef jerky nor had to be rehydrated, but I also learned something new about town days. A town day means laundry day — where you pool all your hiker clothes together with your trail family, and, while all your clothes are in the washing machine at the laundromat, you drink at a brewery wearing only your rain gear without any underwear. There was something immensely enjoyable in sharing the downtown of an expensive ski town with wealthy tourists, some of whom were seated at the bar stools next to me, as we were going commando — as in "Nugget airing out his nuggets," as Wangler suggested.

From the amount of laughter and camaraderie shared at our table, the other patrons in the brewery must've thought we were lifelong friends, but I'd only known half of them for less than 12 hours and the other half I only knew for four days.

It's like the bonds of thru-hiking fast forward a relationship.

Toward the end of the evening, Andrew pulled out a small trophy from the pocket of his down jacket. He had been carrying it the whole time. Instead of the ornament of a basketball player or softball player on the top, this trophy had a silver figurine of a big, fat pig. Engraved on the placard below the swine decoration was the words "2022 Keystone Adult Bacon Eating Champion."

The day before, he had biked into Keystone in the middle of a festival. He then somehow signed up for a chance to be drawn to compete in a bacon eating contest. His name was pulled to go on stage and compete.

"The secret to my victory was instead of eating the bacon strip by strip, I rolled the bacon into a burrito-shaped mass and inhaled it," Andrew proudly explained.

"The 'Andrew Technique' is probably banned for next year's contest by the Keystone bacon eating rules committee," I suggested.

The best part of the story was the additional value Andrew got out of that trophy. After being crowned champion, he spent the evening going from bar to bar telling each bartender that he was the 2022 bacon-eating champion of Keystone, and the victory came with the perk of one free drink at each bar in town. The strategy worked at three of the four bars he stopped in.

Everyone on the trail has a story . . .

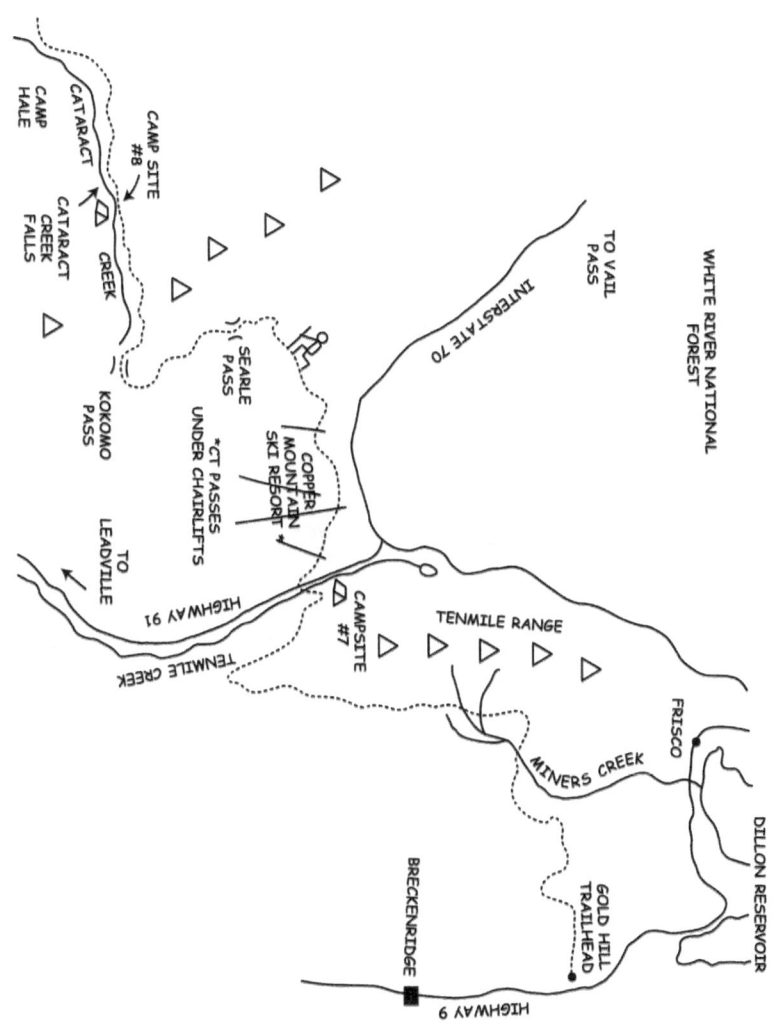

CHAPTER EIGHT:

Up is Correct

"There's something wrong with my pack," Hairy Potter said, straight-faced, as we were exiting our six-bunk hostel room the next morning. Thinking he'd needed some duct tape or something, I played right into his gag and asked, "What's wrong?"

"It's too heavy." he said with a smirk.

He got me.

I sensed that this line was a stale saying amongst veteran thru-hikers: like the equivalent of the old "Does your face hurt? . . because it's killing me!" line or the "It smells like up dog in here . . ." while waiting for person two to fall into the laid trap and ask, "What's up dog?!"

The gag made me feel like I was back in Boy Scouts playing similar pranks with my twin.

"Next you're going to tell me you forgot to bring your left-handed smoke shifter," I retorted.

The left-handed smoke shifter bit was a favorite of ours when we were young and in the scouts. I'd be adding more logs to our fire at a scout jamboree when I'd look displeased with the fire and turn to my twin.

"Hey Andrew, did you think this fire could use a smoke shifter?" I'd ask.

He'd pause, examine the fire, think for a moment, making a subtle display in front of the new and gullible scouts, then say, "Yeah . . . on that fire, I bet a left-handed smoke shifter would do the trick."

"Oh yeah, this fire could use a left-handed smoke shifter," I'd say, "Did we bring one?"

Turning to the newest and most naïve scout, Andrew would then say, "Hey, go ask the neighboring troop if we can borrow their left-handed smoke shifter."

And this is where the runaround would begin. The new scout would go ask the other troop. If the neighboring troop was clever, they'd say something like, "Oh yeah, we just gave our smoke shifter to troop 481, you should go ask them." And the poor young scout would be bounced between troops in a quest for a fictious device.

Games like this, while immature, made for fun memories, ones I savored most from my days in the scouts. I smiled knowing that the same dynamic was part of my experience on the trail.

The complimentary breakfast wasn't served until 7:30 a.m., which sounds early in the real world, but to hikers accustomed to hiking by 6:30 a.m., it meant waiting around for an extra hour.

And while waiting in the lobby, I glanced over at Tall Tale, who was laughing with her eyes closed.

"OK, try this one," Bacon-Champ Andrew said as he handed her a spoon that contained just a single piece of cereal.

Tall Tale was blind taste testing Fruit Loops to try to settle a bet that all the cereal bites, whether red, blue, green, orange, yellow or purple, all tasted the same. We discovered they don't. She was fairly accurate in guessing the correct color. It was child-like, but also hilarious. The breakfast hash was well worth the wait.

After breakfast and a ride on the free transit bus, I started up the trail from the Gold Hill Trailhead at 9:02 a.m. I would get to the night's camping spot by Copper Resort's parking lot at 5:03 p.m.: an eight-hour shift. It was a full day at the office, if your office was at 12,400 feet with an amazing view of the Mount of the Holy Cross, that is. (You know, all those pro skiers and yodelers out there.)

This was my eighth day on the trail; the start of my second week. It was also a Monday, the start of the normal work week.

I wonder how many people have read my automatic away message?

The task for the day was simple: up and over the Tenmile Range. But "simple" is different than "easy." Segment Seven is the steepest of any segment (mile for mile) on the Colorado Trail. It gains 3,300 feet over 8.2 miles and tops off at 12,495 feet. It's an up-and-over-and-then-back-down segment. Gold Hill Trailhead starts at 9,200 feet. We had some climbing to do with a fully re-supplied pack as well. We had re-supplied our packs with 4 days of food to get us to Leadville.

The first hikers I met on the day were Little Potato and Bill — a grandfather and granddaughter duo. I would leapfrog them a couple of times over the next few miles. The start of Segment Seven follows a single track west into an area where the trees have been cleared because of dead pines blighted by beetles. Then it moves through a couple of forest road junctions. At mile 3.6 into the segment, there is water and good camping for hikers who don't want to spring for the overnight room in town.

Four miles into the day as I was following the trail west headed for Peak 3, I came across a couple hiking toward me that gave me a hard stare as I approached.

Did I do something wrong?

The woman continued her stare as I got closer and closer. But the hard stare wasn't unfriendly, it was the exact opposite. The gaze was from the effort of determining if I was who they thought I was.

"I recognize you! Yeah, from your Bedford T-shirt in a photo on Facebook of you at Waterton!" the woman said.

"Oh, cool." I said, surprised.

The couple's names were Ann and Dave. They were day hiking Segment Seven north bound from Copper to Breckenridge. Ann recognized me from a photo my mom posted on the Colorado Trail Thru-Hike 2022 page that was me at the Waterton Canyon sign. In my mom's post, she mentioned that I didn't have a trail name yet.

"So, have you gotten a trail name yet?" Dave asked me.

I told them about "Nugget" and explained why. Then they wanted to grab a selfie photo with me, which was the second time on this trail that I felt like a celebrity. They were overflowing with enthusiasm and were an absolute motivation booster. They lived vicariously through thru-hikers.

What a blessing it was that I had the ability to do this, I thought.

I continued up the trail and made Miner's Creek my goal at mile 5.3 into Segment Seven. I'd fill up my water there and get a snack. As I turned the corner through the trees, I found myself suddenly and reflexively shouting out, "Mountain Goat!"

It was the Salida hiker whom I'd met on Segment One. I hadn't seen Mountain Goat since the previous Monday. This was a hard feeling to describe, but it was delightful. I had hiked with Mountain Goat for maybe 30 minutes a whole week ago and unexpectedly now seeing her again was like I was reunited with an old high school buddy at a class reunion.

She was refilling her water bottles at Miner's Creek with her good pal Sound FX, who had thru-hiked the Colorado

Trail 10 years prior with her husband. During that trip, Mountain Goat had helped re-supply Sound FX and hiked a few segments with her. Now the tables were flipped, and Sound FX was helping Mountain Goat. Sound FX was day hiking Segment Seven and planned to have her husband pick her up at Copper Resort. This also allowed her and Mountain Goat the ability to "slackpack."

The term or hiker expression "slackpack" originated with Appalachian Trail hikers. The term "slackpacker" describes a hiker who leaves their full pack at a hotel, hostel or with a friend and hikes a stretch of the trail with a lighter day pack. This option requires some transportation or rendezvous point to reclaim your full overnight gear. Or maybe a friend drops your extra gear to you farther on down the trail at the end of the day hike.

Segment Seven of the Colorado Trail is ideal for slackpacking since the distance of 14.5 miles makes for a good day hike and there are convenient access points at the start and finish of the segment. There is also the free bus system between Breckenridge and Copper Mountain. Many hikers will stay an extra night in a hotel around Breckenridge then slackpack over Segment Seven down to Copper and finally grab the bus back to their hotel and their gear — giving them an extra night in a comfy bed.

I tucked into their duo and chatted them up as we made our way past the 11,000-foot elevation mark. We eventually came to a spot with a long log that would accommodate all three of us as a seat for a snack break. Mountain Goat shared her avocado and cheese with me. After a nice rest and caloric input, Sound FX decided to use the tail end of our break to answer the call of nature. She wandered away from our snack spot as I decided this was a good time for me to head up the trail.

What we both didn't know, and that quickly became clear, was that our snack spot was right before a sharp hairpin turn in the trail. Hiking 30 yards, I had doubled back just above our snack spot — right back toward Sound FX's privy area. At the same time Little Potato and Bill came strolling up the trail. Instead of finding a discreet tree to pee behind, Sound FX positioned herself in an amphitheater. She had spectators in all directions, and she howled laughing.

Thru-hikers get thru-hikers.

As the trail made its way toward the top of the Tenmile Range, it got steeper, and the trail itself got lost under some snow fields. This made for some slippery snow crossings, which were the hardest obstacles of the day. The snow fields also covered up the moderate switchbacks, which forced us to head up hill in a more direct route.

"Which way?" Mountain Goat asked somewhat rhetorically.

"Up," I said.

"Yeah, 'Up' is correct," responded Sound FX.

As we entered the tundra, we ran into several more CDT hikers headed north. The names of the hikers I did remember and jotted down in my journal were: Spice, Mr. Fabulous, Pirate, Lady Bug, Storm Trooper and El Flaco.

I got slightly ahead of Mountain Goat and Sound FX through the maze of trees and snowfields, but they caught back up quickly when I stopped to chat with a CDT hiker from Britain.

"Are you hiking the CDT?" I asked the hiker headed toward me even though I knew the answer. You can tell a CDT hiker; they've been hiking for two months. I figured it was a polite way to start the conversation.

"Yes, I am," he responded.

"What's your name?" I asked.

"Buck Wild."

"I'm Nugget. Nice to meet you."

"Are you planning on stopping in Breckenridge?"

"Actually, I have an old friend who's driving up from Denver to pick me up. I'll spend a day in Denver."

Buck Wild then said, "I didn't much care for the city of Denver the last time I was there, to be honest." After a short pause he then asked, "Where are you from?"

"Denver."

"Oh I'm sorry, I didn't mean to disparage your city."

He genuinely seemed embarrassed. I just laughed. Plus, the use of the word "disparage" was the exact amount of pedantic vocabulary that I enjoy.

At that point Mountain Goat caught up to us. I introduced Buck Wild to Mountain Goat. Then we interrogated him about the CDT and what it was like to hike through the New Mexico dessert. As Buck Wild was facing Mountain Goat and me, Sound FX snuck up behind him and made some grunting mumble as she slipped on some snow. It was like this scene was perfectly scripted. This startled Buck Wild.

"Well, that's apropos. You just met Sound FX."

We bid him good luck and set our sights for what we thought was the top of the ridge. On this sunny June Colorado day, I was especially generous with my sunscreen application. I also wore my bandana under my hat to protect my neck and ears from the harsh Colorado sun above 12,000 feet. I soaked the bandana at each water source before putting it back under my hat and on my head. And every time I was amazed by how quickly the bandana became bone dry.

When we made it to the saddle of the ridge we had been heading toward as our destination for the last hour, we realized what appears initially to be the top of the segment, isn't. We still had another two miles on the backside of the ridge until the top of the Tenmile Range. The slight disappointment was made up for by the amazing views of Lake Dillion and Breckenridge below.

Two miles later, we were on the crest of the Tenmile Range, with views of Breckenridge on your left and the ski runs of Copper Mountain on your right. This is the first time the trail ascended above 12,000 feet.

The air at the top of the pass is much thinner than at 6,000 feet. Well, that's not 100% scientifically accurate. This all has to do with something you probably forgot from your high school chemistry class: Boyle's Law. The bit of chemistry also explains why your plastic water bottle that you drank from at the summit of a 14er, will be crushed when you get back to Denver if you don't open it after summiting.

At higher elevation there is a decrease in pressure. That means a given volume of air now has fewer molecules present. The percentage of those molecules that are oxygen is the same, it's just that there are fewer total molecules including oxygen molecules. Looking at an altitude-oxygen graph shows you what this means practically.

The effective oxygen percentage at 1,000 feet of elevation is 20.1%. At 5,000 feet, it drops to 17.3%. At 10,000 feet you're at 14.3%. Where we were at the high point of Segment Seven of the CT, the top of the ridge between Peak 5 and Peak 6, the effective oxygen percentage is 13%. That basically means that we have two-thirds of the oxygen that we'd get at 1,000 feet. At the top of Mt. Everest, the effective oxygen percentage is 6.9%, which means there's one-third of the oxygen on top of the highest peak in the world.

I immediately looked west toward the Sawatch Range and noticed the tiny white cross on the mountain horizon. After our battle with snowfields and 3,200 feet of elevation gain with a loaded pack, we were rewarded with a view that's hard to come by. It was a view of the namesake feature of one of Colorado magic 14ers: Mount of the Holy Cross. The 14er earned its moniker from the distinctive cross-shaped snowfield shining on its northeast face. It's hard to name a place where you can get a glimpse of the cross of snow without having to do some hiking. You must earn the view.

President Herbert Hoover made Holy Cross a national monument in 1929, but it lost its monument status in 1950 to waning visitor numbers. Ironically part of that had to do with a newly created national monument: Camp Hale, which was two days ahead of us down the trail. Because the soldiers at Camp Hale used part of the Holy Cross area for training during World War II, that area was shut out to the public. So inadvertently, Camp Hale (freshly made a national monument in 2022) helped strip Holy Cross of its status.

We took a long break on the top of the ridge. This also gave us time to chat with several more CDT thru-hikers. It also gave me ample opportunities to share the view of Holy Cross with everyone. Since the CDT hikers were headed east across the ridge, their backs were to Holy Cross.

Turn around and look there! You can see the snow couloir on Mount of the Holy Cross.

I felt a tug of obligation to let them in on the secret and to point out how rare this view was. I was reminded of the first person I met on the Colorado Trail who wanted to make sure I didn't miss out on seeing the mountain goats. Now I was the one making sure others didn't miss out on some of Colorado's magic mountain experiences. This would become a modus operandi of mine as I would meet out-of-staters farther along the trail, and I noticed my excitement in making sure they didn't miss out, either. One of the CDT hikers who really appreciated the view was Storm Trooper, whose thick Upper Midwest accent jumped right out.

"You from Minnesota?"

"Yep." Storm Trooper said.

I wasn't the only one doing some teaching above 12,000 that day. Sound FX taught me all about Colorado's wildflowers. On the tundra was a spread of alpine forget-me-nots and Old-Man-of-the-Mountain flowers. This yellow wildflower is hard to miss in the grey alpine tundra of the Rockies. It looks like a miniature sunflower. But unlike many sunflowers, which face toward and slowly follow the sun as it traces across the sky, the Old-Man-of-the-Mountain always faces east[15].

The descent from the top of the ridge is steep, which generally means some pain in my knees. Luckily the conversation between Mountain Goat, Sound FX and I distracted me from any joint pain. I learned all about wildflowers and the difference between introverts and extraverts. I had become curious about that topic particularly since the trail seemed to be turning me into an extrovert.

"I heard the best way to tell an introvert from an extrovert is to ask them what their ideal day looks like," Sound FX explained as we wove our way down the single-track trail. "Extroverts will say something like spending time with friends that emphasizes social interaction, but introverts tend to emphasize solo activities like reading," she explained.

Before the trail, a long conversation with someone I just met would send me into hiding for a few hours just to recharge. On the trail, the conversations were giving me energy.

About halfway down from the ridge top, Sound FX interjected "Did you see the pink elephants?"

"Uh? Are you okay?" I asked. "Are you feeling altitude sickness?"

"The pink flowers that look like tiny elephant faces?" she reiterated.

She was talking about the "Elephantella," a pinkish purple wildflower that resembles a miniature elephant head with ears and an upturned trunk.

A few moments later she pointed the flower out to me. Sure enough, it was a reed-like flower with a couple dozen miniature pink elephant trunks on it.

I was faster on the second half of the downhill, so I hiked the next mile by myself until about a mile from the Copper Mountain Parking Lot, I ran into a guy hiking toward me with two dogs. After chatting with him for a minute or so, he mentioned that he had done the trail 10 years ago and was hiking up to meet his wife.

"Wait, are you Mr. Sound FX?" I asked.

"I guess so, you must have been hiking with my wife today," he said.

I reached the parking lot of Copper Resort just after 5 p.m. Bad Foot, Hairy Potter, and Tall Tale showed up about 30 minutes later.

Making dinner together, Bad Foot said, "I had a very enjoyable day and partially because you were up ahead securing a camp site, that it took some pressure off me. This allowed me to better soak up the day."

That made me feel more and more like part of the team.

I had a dehydrated meal as an appetizer followed up with Ramen Noodles and two chicken pouches as a second dish with Swedish fish candy for dessert.

I thought meals tasted so good in the backcountry because you've been burning so many calories all day. I also learned that nature helps us relax, and when we are relaxed, our parasympathetic system — often called the "rest and digest" branch — starts kicking in. Modern life in the city tends to trigger the sympathetic nervous system — the "fight or flight" behaviors[16]. Therefore, the same food doesn't taste as good at home as it does seated in the dirt among the trees.

Camping is prohibited on the first four miles of Segment Eight because it runs through the Copper Mountain Resort's property. Therefore, camping where we were was common. There were six of us who shared the campsite that evening: the four in my tramily and two gals in their early 20s from Oregon.

Before we went to our tents, we decided to camp near Cataract Creek the next night. The plans allowed the tramily to get up in the morning at their own pace because we'd re-unite eventually the next day.

I enjoyed sleepy time tea as a night cap while I journaled.

We camped next to West Parking lot of Copper Ski Resort next to the river Tenmile Creek, not too far from Highway 91. Heading south on Highway 91 by car you can be in Leadville in about 30 minutes. It would take us another 2.5 days. We'd get to Leadville, but the Colorado Trail takes a different route. We first had to get over Searle and Kokomo Pass, through Camp Hale and the Holy Cross Wilderness.

CHAPTER NINE:

How Far are You Going?

O n Day Nine, I woke up to a photo text from my mom: a screen shot from her iPhone of the 2022 Colorado Trail Facebook Group page.

The caption read: "We had a great time hiking Segment Seven today, Copper to Breck, and met quite a few CDT & CT hikers. I recognized 'Nugget' from the pic his mom had posted at his start, so had to get a pic to put here. He was doing great & lots of fun to talk with!"

It was posted by Ann, whom I'd met with her husband the day before.

As I was making my coffee, I was startled by Mountain Goat wishing me a good morning as she hiked past my campsite. The same thing happened five minutes later as I was boiling water for my breakfast when I heard, "Good Morning, Nugget." It was Wangler getting my attention as he hiked past. He had camped about a half mile back.

I set my sights on the first goal of the day: catching up to Mountain Goat and Wangler. I was the last of my group to leave the campsite that morning.

The Brad Paisley song "Celebrity" popped into my head as I was loading my backpack because of the joy that Ann's Facebook post brought to me. So, I found that song on my iMusic and listened to it on repeat for the first mile of my day using my trekking pole as my air guitar as I skipped up the trail. With some peppy music and great attitude (and altitude) to start the day, I figured I'd catch up with Wangler in no time.

Segment Eight of the CT starts by crossing Highway 91, then does a few switchbacks as it crosses under powerlines, lift lines, and skirts a golf course. You pass the closest to the Copper Ski Resort at 1.6 miles into the segment as you duck under the American Eagle Ski lift. This puts you just uphill from Copper's Center Village. It's an easy detour for a hot meal. From Copper's Center Village the trail climbs 2,500 feet over the next eight miles. The resort looks a lot different in summer compared to the typical views covered in snow during ski season.

Just past Center Village, about two miles into my day, I caught up with Mountain Goat. She mentioned that Wangler had passed her a couple of minutes prior. Busting with energy, I pushed uphill in search of my next target of the day. But I never found him.

As it happened, Wangler, just after passing Mountain Goat, followed a trail that turned out not to be the Colorado Trail. He realized his mistake when the path dead-ended onto a back porch of a Copper Mountain Resort condo.

"I don't remember this in the guidebook." he blurted out.

Retracing his steps, he realized his error from another hiker's post on the FarOut app. The advice was sound: it was a confusing intersection; what Wangler didn't realize was it was posted by a Northbound hiker. We were southbound. So, the advice "to stay left" from a NOBO hiker would mean "stay right" for a SOBO hiker — the exact opposite.

During Wangler's detour, I had come through correctly turning right at the intersection about the same time Wangler was turning around from his back porch dead-end.

Just past five miles into Segment Eight, the trail comes to Jacque Creek which is followed by Guller Creek. This area holds some good camping sites, particularly since camping isn't permitted in the first four miles of the segment through the ski resort.

As the trail heads up the valley, it crosses some gorgeous beaver ponds. This was a great spot to take a break for a snack and look back down the valley at all the distance I had gained that morning. I peered at the mountain range that we went up and over the day before.

The biggest waypoints of the day were getting up and over Searle Pass (12,034') and Kokomo Pass (12,027').

Above tree line and two miles from Searle Pass, I stopped for a snack with a couple in their 60s named Margaret and "Hazy" who had recently moved to Colorado Springs from North Carolina. They were working on the CT in segments. Margaret had given her husband the nickname due to his affinity for hazy IPAs. They were sweet. They shared some peanut butter crackers with me.

As you approach Searle Pass, you get views of the Climax Molybdenum Mine (pronounced *moh-LIB-dih-num*) and the byproducts of that mine in the large ponds. Besides the molybdenum, the mine produces waste called "tailings" that are tiny pieces of left-over rock from those mining operations. They can cause toxic concentrations of metal in the water. The ponds act as a water treatment function of sorts as they separate out the solid particles.

The five miles of trail prior to Searle Pass have you hiking due south. At Searle, you make a right turn and the CT charges due west toward the Sawatch Range. Around 2.7 miles and about 570 feet of elevation gain separate Searle Pass from Kokomo Pass.

Kokomo Pass has a beautiful 6-foot tall, three-slab sign in yellow writing announcing the pass and the elevation. It also bears the CT and CDT logo and informed us that Copper Mountain was 11.2 miles behind us and Tennessee Pass was 12.5 miles ahead of us.

The pass derives its name from a mining boom town in the area from the late 1870s and apparently some of those miners came from the town of Kokomo in Indiana. During Colorado's silver boom, the town of Kokomo, Colorado, had more than 10,000 residents, but little remains today because the Kokomo town site became the dumpsite for the Climax mine.

The hike down from Kokomo heads straight for Mount of the Holy Cross. The views leaving Kokomo Pass are scenic, stunning and serene. The single-track brown trail winds through the green tundra and the snowcapped Sawatch Range looms ahead. For a mile or so the views headed west somehow, it seemed, naturally follow the rule of thirds in photography. In your view is the first third of the trail meandering through the green tundra; the middle third is the green forest with a layer of gray-striped, snowy Sawatch Mountains on top; and the top third were the puffy rain clouds building and the blue sky. The darker rain clouds with sunshine fighting through created a stunning effect. I stopped several times in awe; like my eyes couldn't fully absorb and grasp how beautiful this was.

We made camp in a spot on the right side of the trail a third of a mile above Cataract Falls. A great spot with access to water and plenty of space for several tents — which we needed because six of us shared that spot that night. Mountain Goat and Wangler joined Bad Foot, Tall Tale, Hairy Potter and me.

As Wangler and Bad Foot arrived together at camp, Bad Foot said, "Hey, we had to give a couple on the trail $5 for the peanut butter crackers you stole from them."

Ha, they must have met Margaret and Hazy.

Then Bad Foot continued with a compliment that made me swell with happiness, "Boy, am I sick of meeting people on the trail today that said, 'Oh are you hiking with Nugget? He was super friendly.'"

Hearing that caused my stomach to swell with a ball of pride. The comment also set in motion a snowball that helped shape my identity as a friendly thru-hiker.

That's because believing in your identity can be self-fulfilling. The ignition of such an identify can even be a fluke, but those moments lead us to say something like "this is who I want to be[17]." They mold your judgments, world view, beliefs and self-image.

The trail was changing me into someone more friendly, more patient, a better listener and a positive force. (Which, come to think of it, was everything my exes wished I'd been.) That seemingly insignificant comment and idea that "I am super-friendly" catapulted me to spend the next few days trying to tally votes in the yes column that reaffirmed that identity. Enough votes and your identity forms habits and those repeated habits strengthen even further your identity.

In the book *Atomic Habits* by James Clear, one of the first lessons to improving habits is to stop focusing on the outcome and instead establish an identity[18]. The reason: because actions that are incongruent with your identity won't last long. James Clear uses the example of two people trying to resist smoking. When offered a cigarette, the first person says, "No thanks, I'm trying to quit." The second person says, "No thanks, I'm not a smoker." It's a subtle difference, but extremely meaningful. The first person still believes they are a smoker while the second person's words exhibit a shift in identity.

I figured, don't focus on finishing the trail, *focus on becoming a thru-hiker.*

I have a good friend, Rob, from my softball team that got the trail name *Brew* when he successfully hiked the Appalachian Trail. As I was preparing for my Colorado Trail hike, he told me a story that he describes as some of the best hiking advice and life advice he's ever heard.

On his fourth day on the Appalachian Trail (AT), Rob ran into a hiker named Eagle who was doing the AT for the third time. Rob and some fellow hikers peppered the veteran hiker Eagle with questions. Eventually the big question came out, "What's one piece of advice you'd give to other AT hikers to help them make it through?"

Eagle thought for a brief second, sipped his beer, and then said, "When you ask hikers starting the trail how far they are going, they answer in one of two ways: One group says, 'I am going to the end. To Maine. To Katahdin.' The other group says something along the lines of 'I am going as far as I can' or 'I'll see how far I can make it.' "

Eagle's point was that the first group is the one that by and large makes it to the end. Because they have the end destination as their goal, things that come up — blisters or weather or $5 peanut butter crackers — are just part of the journey. Their identity is solidified as someone getting to Katahdin. The other group doesn't have thru-hiker as an identity. They more readily let those barriers turn into the ending point. They come up against a difficult stretch and stop their hike because, in their minds, this is as far as they can make it.

"I pretty much credit this advice with getting me through the rest of the trail. I still use that thinking all of the time. I've found it helpful with almost everything in life," Rob told me, "And to think, it was given to me from a guy with 20 teeth, tops!"

With this advice in my mind, I started to pick up on the words people choose, like when someone says "I'm trying to write a book" versus "I am writing a book." I notice the subtle difference right away.

I only saw the other five sharing my campsite for a few minutes each over the day, but we all shared dinnertime together. We had stories to tell each other of our day and we all enjoyed hearing them because we had also crossed the same mileage and elevation separately, yet somehow together. I really enjoyed that.

Yet, despite the documented benefits like higher self-esteem, better academic performance and more confidence, only about 30 percent of families regularly eat dinner together[19].

In a 2003 study, solders fighting in the Iraq War said their top motivation was the deep emotional bond they established between fellow soldiers[20]. It wasn't the training time that mattered most to building that bond, but the down time that soldiers had together. The hours of noncombat time, shared boredom and sharing meals was what created authentic connections.

On the trail, it seemed my tramily was prioritizing tramily dinner.

After dinner, I had some first aid to perform. The half-dollar-sized blister on the sole of my left foot popped open as I was filtering water out of Cataract Creek. Bad Foot shared his first-aid materials as well as his story of a similar blister he had on the PCT that was responsible for his trail name.

The day's mileage was 17 miles and 3,300 feet of elevation gain and, like yesterday, quite a bit of time again above tree line. After two back-to-back days going up and over mountain ranges, we all sought our sleeping bags well before the sun was down. I laid in my tent yards away from 5 fellow thru-hikers that evening, exhausted and proud of another big day. I drifted to sleep hearing in my mind: "When they say I've gone insane, I'll blame it on the fame. And the pressures that go with, being a celebrity."

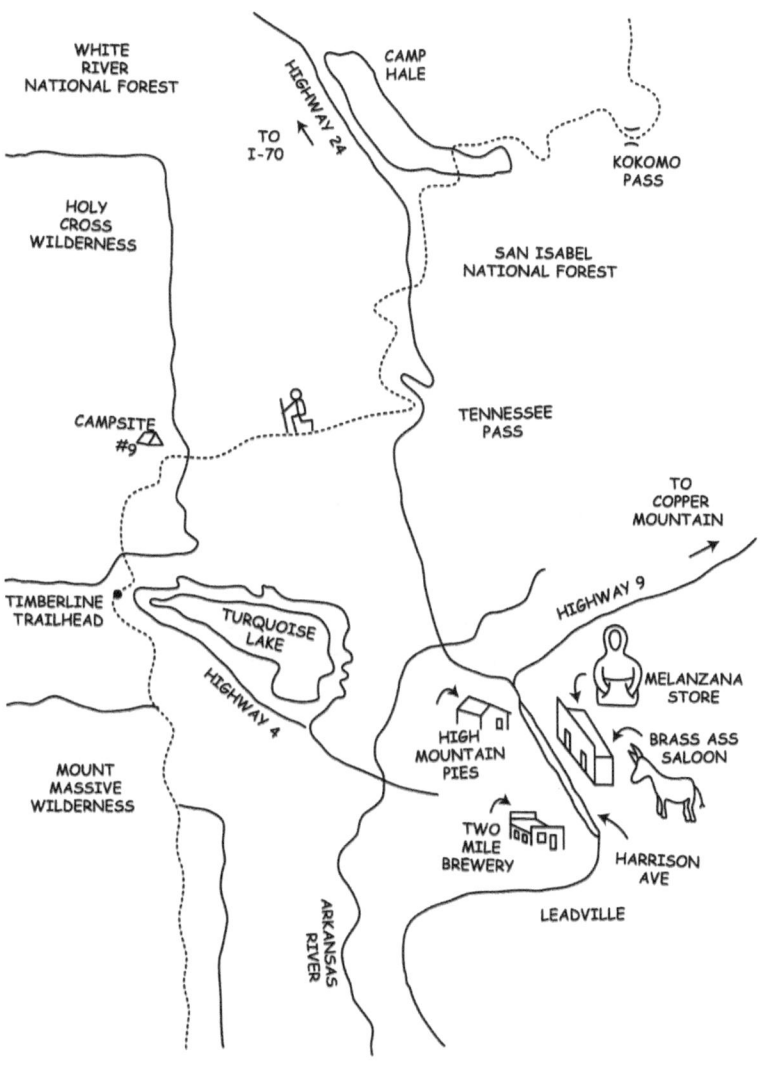

CHAPTER TEN:

Stillness and Presence

Appropriately, I'd hike through the 10th Mountain Division's Camp Hale on the 10th day on the Colorado Trail. (Counting that required fingers and toes).

I wasn't the last one to leave camp the next morning. Mountain Goat was still enjoying her breakfast and the morning air as I departed down the trail toward Colorado's World War II army training facility. The other four had packed up and hit the trail before me. Tennessee Pass and the Holy Cross Wilderness were also on tap for the day.

After dropping down a steep section to Cataract Falls, I entered an expansive valley not too long after the morning sun had. I was greeted with a warning sign: Danger Explosive Hazard Do NOT touch!

Camping isn't permitted over the next several miles because of explosion hazards. Fair enough. If I wanted to make it to Durango, I'd need my limbs and all those digits I was bragging about earlier. I'd stay on the path. Kokomo Pass was five miles behind me and Tennessee Pass six miles ahead.

I had the whole valley to myself: still, quiet, uninhabited and only just waking up to the morning. I had a hard time imagining that if it were 80 years ago, the valley would have been bustling with the sounds of army M1 rifles and marching cadences as 10,000 mountain troops trained for cold-weather mountain warfare during World War II.

Eventually the trail passes what looked like concrete bunkers built into a mound of earth. I learned from interviewing David R. Witte, Army Chaplin, 14er finisher and author of *World War II at Camp Hale: Blazing a New Trail in the Rockies* that those bunkers were the firing range where the soldiers changing the targets would hide out.

I also learned from Witte's book that if it wasn't for the nearly extinct trumpeter swan, Camp Hale might not exist. The war department initially identified West Yellowstone, Montana, as the best choice for such a cantonment site, but the Wildlife Conservation Committee led a fight to protect the environment of the trumpeter swan — the heaviest living bird native to North America with a wingspan of six to ten feet (and I'm guessing an excellent hugger).

Camp Hale was unique. Never before had the army needed a location big enough for an entire division to do daily training as well as including basic training for a unique group of soldiers called ski or mountain troopers. The perfect location would need highway access, railroad access, water, elevation, room for barracks, significant snowfall, mountains and a friendly community nearby in which troops could enjoy leave.

The War Department was sure this valley had all of that except the friendly community nearby to act as a social outlet for troops. One report warned that Leadville "affords little recreation conducive to the morale of command. The morals of Leadville are said to be on a rather low plane[21]." According to the army, for the troops preparing to fight Nazis, a rough western mining town where brothels once outnumbered churches nine-to-one, Leadville apparently wasn't the best for soldier morale.

About three miles shy of Tennessee Pass, I caught up with Hairy Potter and Wangler. When we crossed some railroad tracks, I couldn't resist but tell the only train joke I know. I felt a pull to continually add value to my tramily. Wangler and Hairy Potter were strolling behind me on the single-track trail when I launched into it.

"So, there were these two blondes walking along in the forest when they spotted some tracks on the ground. The first one says, 'Hey look, there's some deer tracks.' The second blonde interrupts and says, 'No I think they are moose tracks.' They were still arguing when they were hit by a train."

That got a mild chuckle out of each of them.

We passed the miles to where the trail meets Highway 24 by swapping jokes. Hairy Potter told several jokes — all of which are unfit to publish here (or in the 1940s army lingo, "were on a rather low plane.") Tall Tale was waiting for us at Tennessee Pass. Bad Foot had already pushed ahead into the next segment. Hairy Potter and Tall Tale caught a car ride into Leadville with Mountain Goat and her husband and Wangler, and I set off toward the Holy Cross Wilderness to catch up with Bad Foot.

At Tennessee Pass, the trail enters the Sawatch Range and heads toward Durango on the Range's eastern flank. The range is home to 15 peaks about 14,000 feet from Mt. of the Holy Cross in the northern end to Mt. Shavano in the south. It also holds Colorado's highest peak in Mt. Elbert (14,438') and the second highest peak in Mt. Massive (14,427').

I spent the next seven miles chatting with Wangler about breweries, books and the biography of his nickname.

Wangler's alias was earned during a fruitless day of fishing. After hours of staring at a still fishing string, he decided to go skinny dipping. But just as he submerged his naked body in the lake, the fishing line began to dance. In both a panic and his birthday suit, Wangler reeled in the first catch of the day buck naked. He told this story to thru-hikers the previous summer, and those hikers gave him the nickname. As sophomoric as *Wang-ler* sounds, it does have several levels and layers of creativity.

Now hear me out.

It plays off the pun "Wrangler" (a person that herds wildlife) and the term "angler" (a person who fishes with a hook) and of course the reproductive organ-related slang term "wang." Right there, that's three levels of comedic sophistication.

Later down the trail I did ask for clarification on whether it was "*The* Wangler" (which I thought gave it more gravitas and movie-hero-like weight) or simply "Wangler." He told me that it was just "Wangler, no 'the.'" That didn't stop me, however. I still referred to him as "*The* Wangler." And I also heard (in my own head) the sound of a whip cracking and the old, whistling-filled soundtrack of a spaghetti western play each time I articulated "*The* Wangler!"

After lunch, we ran into a trail adopter named "Yard Sale" who had completed the CT two years earlier. She had timed her thru-hike to conclude in Durango on the day of her 40th birthday. She was walking with a Colorado Trail Foundation employee named Darin to scout out the section of the trail she was taking under her wing. I got to learn how the Colorado Trail Foundation mobilizes their army of trail adopters. I also learned that the hiker jargon "yard sale" refers to when you empty all the contents of your pack onto a surface to sort, resupply and re-pack it.

The army of trail adopters are different from the trail crews. The Colorado Trail Foundation has the trail divided into 83 Adopt-A-Trail sections. Adopters are responsible of keeping the trail passable and reporting the trail conditions back to the foundation each year. This means assessing the trail's signage and a lot of clearing of fallen trees and digging, raking and hoeing the trail for water diversions to prevent erosion. To get an idea of what it takes to maintain 567 miles of trail, you can check out the Colorado Trail Foundation's CT Adopters notes. In 2022, they cleared over 600 trees from across the trail among a lot of other projects.

"There's a few sections open for adoption this year, but they are pretty remote," Darin told us, "One is available close to Denver, but they allow current adopters first dibs on it."

Becoming a trail adopter, something to think about.

The CT bisects the southern corner of the Holy Cross Wilderness area. If the wilderness area was a page in a book and you folded it along the CT, it would create a small dog ear in the bottom right corner of the page.

I'd spent a few trips in this wilderness area. One climbing the 14er with my friend Rich and one to make it to Notch Mountain Shelter with my friend Heidi to experience the sunrise on the couloir that forms the namesake cross.

Wangler and I took each other's photos in front of the Holy Cross Wilderness Boundary Sign. It wasn't 300 yards into the wilderness area that we saw Bad Foot filtering water. We had been waiting to run into him for an hour. You see, we had devised a bit of a prank.

We elbowed each other as we slowly approached making sure everyone was ready to deliver their lines. You see, Bad Food divided thru-hiking into two distinct geographical places: 1) environments where there were Diet Coke and cheeseburgers and 2) environments where there weren't.

"Yeah, I think I'd get the bacon on my buffalo burger next time," I said.

"I was happy with my Swiss and mushroom burger," Wangler casually replied.

Our idea was to pretend that we got a hitch into Leadville from Tennessee Pass and had cheeseburgers for lunch.

"Oh, hey Bad Foot! Did you find us a good camping spot?" I asked.

"You jerks! Did you guys get burgers in Leadville?" Bad Foot asked in a fear-of-missing-out tone.

We paused as he stared at us with the saddest face.

Then we burst out laughing.

"No! We just wanted to tease you! We will get burgers tomorrow when we get to Leadville."

Bad Foot shook his head in relief and led us toward the camp spotting he'd found. Bad Foot had settled on an amazing camping spot just inside the Holy Cross Wilderness in an open dell with amazing views of the Continental Divide.

We got to camp at 3:30 p.m. — admittedly still early in the day. We had done 16 miles, and it put us within seven miles of the Turquoise Lake trailhead where'd we'd get a ride in Leadville. We made plans to get there at 10:15 a.m. the next day.

I sensed some uneasiness in Bad Foot. So, I sat down and tried to connect with him. Slowly the source of his anxiety revealed itself. He hated ending a hiking day before 5 p.m. Bad Foot was accustomed to the constant hurry-mentality and pressure of the Pacific Crest Trail from the year prior.

As I learned from Bad Foot, that mentality is unfortunately pervasive on the PCT. Hikers starting at the southern terminus of the PCT continuously have a ticking clock in the back of their minds. Like Cinderella constantly racing against midnight, every day. And although PCT hikers' backpacks don't turn into pumpkins in the fall, the trail crossing Washington transforms into winter wilderness in October. Add to that the remoteness and dearth of roads and places to bail in case of an emergency and you get an idea of why you need to get through there before the snow does. Washington is constantly on your mind. That weather window locks you into a strict schedule. And locks you out of the ability to slow down and let the experience come to you.

"You might be in California, and Washington is still months away, but in the back of your head the weather in Washington is always lingering," Bad Foot told me.

I realized how this nagging thought made it hard for Bad Foot the prior year on the PCT to take long lunches, or just sit and be still for an hour with a good trail friend. He always felt that he had to be on the move — always trying to knock out big mile days. It took away his ability to savor the day. Constantly pressing devastates our ability to find *stillness*.

Bad Foot had begun the Colorado Trail in 2022 with that same mentality. He had carried it for miles on the Colorado Trail, like a pebble in his shoe — unwanted, nagging, but hard to shake.

Bad Foot told me about a fast-moving pair of hikers they came across in the Sierra Nevada range of California. The pair was trying to link the CDT with the PCT in one huge loop. But with such a crazy goal, they had no time to slow down and enjoy the trail. The views from the Sierras are some of the best in the country. PCT hikers long look forward to reaching them.

Then Bad Foot told me the part of the story that made me cringe.

He continued, "The speed hikers even articulated their circumstance. The one speedy hiker said to the other, 'Boy, we should come back here again when we can enjoy it . . . '"

They were *rushing through* and not *experiencing* the trail. "How depressing," I thought.

What if we hiked with the same philosophy as the drunken, overly-enthusiastic dancer at a wedding who embodies the mantra that the best dancer is the one having the most fun?

Forget the destination — enjoy the ride.

Hiking isn't a competition. Hiking isn't about conquering. Hiking doesn't require that you earn your spot on the trail. Hiking is about fellowship and support. Hiking is about *being*. Hiking is about presence. But you won't get that message from social media, which constantly pushes lighter gear and continuously celebrates fastest known times on every path and peak.

About a month before I started my thru-hike, there was a post on the Facebook Colorado Trail 2022 group page that asked, "For those of you who have already completed the CT, what would you do differently if you were to do it again?"

If Bad Foot had written an entry relating to this Facebook Post, he might tell you to bring a pack rain cover and also plan on re-supply at some grocery stores with what you are craving. It's likely you'll grow sick of the same food you'd be eating over and over. Bad Foot had learned that the hard way on the PCT when he ordered a case of Ramen Noodles in bulk to save money. The flaw in his plan to buy-in-bulk Ramen Noodles was the fact that they were Ramen Noodles. Bad Foot quickly discovered that he didn't like Ramen Noodles.

In the 45 comments that were on Facebook, the most common answers had a similar theme, which was simple: slow down. There were people who had hiked the entire trail in 27 days that recommended taking closer to 35 days. There was also recurring advice like: take more time, try an on-trail zero (a day when you don't hike any miles), relax more, camp in beautiful spots instead of having set mileage to accomplish, and finally: hike slower.

If the advice wasn't about slowing down and enjoying the ride, it included some helpful hacks. The one I thought was clever was to include a single Tide pod in your resupply shipment. That way you can do your laundry in your resupply town without having to buy over-priced detergent at the laundromat. Another piece of advice was for people mailing re-supply packages to thru-hikers that a recommended handwritten note mixed in with their Ramen is a great way to boost a thru-hiker's spirit. Even a quick, "You got this!" or "You can do a 20-mile day." Or "Embracing the stink yet?" goes a long way.

Soaking and savoring was a different mentality to the peak-bagging, 14er-list-finishing mindset. I completed the Colorado 14ers in September 2019, nine years after I climbed Grays Peak as my first 14er. But for nine years, the summit was my only focus. Which means I missed a lot. I passed up hiking trips to alpine lakes because they didn't have a 14er to check off my list.

When you wake up without the pressure of getting to a summit, your mind changes. You make the walk the journey. You enjoy the ride more. Your shoulders relax. You take more in. I was starting to understand the difference here on the Colorado Trail. I thought back to my fifth day on the trail just past Kenosha Pass when I was still Chris and when I couldn't find stillness and just relax at 4 p.m. at a campsite. Now I feel Nugget trying harder to enjoy the ride.

Around 4:30 p.m. we sat relaxing and bathing in the Colorado sun staring at the Continental Divide when Wangler asked, "What's your five minutes of fame?"

"I've been on the cover of Sports Illustrated" Wangler coolly boasted. "Now admittedly, I don't get stopped in the streets as often as you might think because of it." He wasn't lying. Wangler was in the stands of a Broncos game when the Sports Illustrated cover photo was taken of quarterback Tim Tebow. If you blow up the cover photo (and use a magnifying glass) you can make out Wangler and his father in the Mile High stands.

We learned that Bad Foot had a brief stretch as a briefs model in his youth. I told them that I had gone through a six-month professional wrestling training school in Golden, Colorado. They didn't fully believe me until I hoisted the Wangler into a body slam position. They were believers after that. Professor Bedford, my wrestling persona, showed them body slam form. That was the biggest laugh I had witnessed from Bad Foot up to that point. And a photo of me body slamming Wangler was used in Bad Foot's hiker blog.

Bad Foot maintained an online trail journal, so every evening he'd retreat to his tent and scribble about the day's thoughts, adventures, mileage, trail conditions and elevation gain. He mentioned to us that Wangler would be featured on this day's post.

To which I quickly asked, "When do I get a featured day?"

"Oh, you're already a fixture on my blog along with Tall Tale and Hairy Potter," he responded.

I got a little sentimental upon hearing that.

I even sent a message with my Garmin Inreach to Ed about Bad Foot's blog. I also asked Ed if Lake County had a fire ban. He graciously called the sheriff's office and delivered some good news: no fire ban. So, we built a small fire in the ring just beside the meadow with hopes that the smoke would ward off the mosquitoes as we cooked our dinner.

The fire didn't help. I fed a platoon of bloodsuckers who left dozens of bites on my limbs. And no tip. The tiny spear of a mouth on the mosquitoes easily went through my leggings. This was why Bad Foot put on his rain gear as we told stories around our campfire.

"Will the rest of the trail be this buggy?" asked Bad Foot.

"In all my backpacking and 14er hiking trips," I said, "I've only experienced mosquitoes like this when I was camped by Cross Creek when I was climbing Mount of the . . ."

Then I had a realization. ". . . Well, the last time I was in the Holy Cross Wilderness," I said. "Exactly where we are now."

Five years ago, it was my friend Rich and I swatting mosquitos in the same area, I remembered.

These mountains are more enjoyable with company.

Tonight's meal was a first for me. It was a thru-hiker tradition, a carbohydrate overload: the Ramen Bomb. A traditional Ramen Bomb recipe combines instant mash potatoes with a package of Ramen then throws in other random sauces, proteins, gravies and extras. My recipe consisted of one chicken ramen packet, one bag of four-cheese instant potatoes and two pouches of buffalo chicken.

We also set our eight-minute timer and did another remote association test. The Wangler was the third participant this time.

Bad Foot and I tied — getting five out of 10 correct.

After the RAT test, I recited some more poetry, and we told more stories. We eventually sought the protection of our tent's bug screen a bit earlier than need be. We were glad we did since the heavy rain came not much later.

We fell asleep in our tents at 10,900 feet of elevation and exactly 150 trail miles from the start of the Colorado Trail. We had done 16 miles this day. We finished up Segment Eight, that runs from Copper Mountain to Tennessee Pass and knocked out seven miles of Segment Nine, which ends ahead of us at Timberline Lake Trailhead (Turquoise Lake). We were in great position for a town day the next day. Up to this point on the trail, this campsite was the most picturesque.

But that was a placeholder that wouldn't last long.

The clues to RAT Quiz #4:
kin, flag, shape
fall, chill, law
play, under, water
air, knife, watch
chip, sweet, salad
moral, rose, reading
stool, first, dance
open, work, trip
phone, sick, work
shoe, elbow, game

CHAPTER ELEVEN:

Deaf Zero

I began Day 11 on the CT inhaling the cool, crisp morning air, with a reminder to myself of why I loved being out here. It really wasn't too hard at all digging for that reminder when I was waking up to the beauty of the Holy Cross Wilderness. The smell of rain and lingering fog slowly yielded to the morning mountain sunshine. I thought about Bad Foot's story of hikers who were speeding through the Sierras and took another luxurious huff of mountainous air.

Like usual, Bad Foot was up and out of camp 45 minutes before I was. Wangler was out 15 minutes ahead of me.

I had about seven miles to knock out to meet my pick-up spot at Turquoise Lake for a ride into Leadville from my friend Noah. Those seven miles passed by enjoyably, which had a large part to do with the good conversation I had hiking with the Wangler. I strolled into the parking lot at 10:14 a.m. (a minute to spare) to find Bad Foot chatting with Noah.

We had completed just over 156 miles on the Colorado Trail up to this point.

The Wangler would continue down the trail toward Twin Lakes, where his wife would pick him up the next afternoon. We hopped into Noah's car reeking of pickled armpits and headed for a well-needed shower. It would be the Wangler who got the shower first: a large rain shower.

I had only "met" Noah two weeks earlier on a Zoom call for work. He was looking for some data on housing costs and wages in Leadville for his work. Noah's goal was to bring down the costs of expenses like food, housing and childcare for the folks that live in Leadville. Like many mountain towns, the workers who keep the town running can't afford to live there. Noah works for a non-profit that believes health goes well beyond just healthcare — it includes housing, transportation, education and healthy foods and physical activity.

At the end of our virtual meeting, Noah extended an offer, "Hey if you're up in Leadville, let's get together."

I suspect, seeing that we had just met, that his offer was half-hearted, and he didn't expect me to take him up on it.

Well, I did.

I quickly and maybe too boldly responded, "Hey, I'm headed your way in two weeks. Would you be able to pick me up at Turquoise Lake?" Nothing like asking a stranger to help you move.

Noah then half-laughed and said, "Ha, yeah sure."

Then my coworker Caitlin jumped in and said, "No, he's not kidding with you, Noah. He's hiking the Colorado Trail and could use the ride."

Fortunately, Noah had done his share of hiking and had received help from strangers while doing it. He was also planning and training for something much crazier than a thru-hiker: the Leadville 100-mile race. Known as the "Race Across the Sky," the grueling ultra-marathon was dreamt up by a miner who is famous for the saying, "Make friends with pain, and you'll never be alone." The pain Ken Chlouber is talking about is exertion discomfort. Ken advocates for a shift in mindset — from dreading the pain of pushing your body to the limit, to embracing it. The race is nearly four full marathons, half of them by head lamp, with two 2,600 feet climbs in the middle. You start at 10,000 feet and only go up from there. It's crazy. But complete that craziness in under 25 hours and earn yourself a large Leadville 100 belt buckle.

Noah graciously opened his house, his washer/dryer and his shower to us. Once our laundry was done and a long hot shower was taken, we strolled up town to the Golden Burro and Brass Ass Saloon in the heart of Leadville.

As we walked into town, I shared a bit of Leadville's history with Bad Foot.

"With four shots and a fire, that's how the town of Leadville got its start," I said.

In this area 162 years earlier, a miner named Abe Lee dipped his gold pan in a creek 100 miles from Denver City. Lee and some fellow gold seekers spread out across the Arkansas Valley agreeing that if anyone hit a "strike," they would signal the others with four gunshots and a huge bonfire. When Abe Lee found gold nuggets in his pan, the story goes, he shouted, "I've got California in this here pan!" Hence the area near Leadville is called California Gulch and why Leadville began with four shots and a fire.

There, at the Brass Ass Saloon, I was doing a slight twist to "four shots and a fire," I was doing one shot of Fireball Whiskey. Doctor's orders.

Back when Lee was cashing in on his bonanza, Leadville was known as Bough Town; this would be one of several monikers given to the settlement that sprang up around California Gulch. It was also called Oro City after the Spanish word for gold. Five years after Abe Lee's discovery, the gold was few and far between. The 1860s saw the town's first boom and bust. Then 1876 began a new boom for Oro City when William Stevens and Alvinius Wood realized that the black sand in their sluice boxes, though devoid of gold, was lead carbonate filled with silver. By 1877, word of the silver strike was out and the rush to the area was back on.

The town was renamed to Leadville and nicknamed Cloud City. A sleepy town of several hundred in 1877 suddenly ballooned to over 10,000 by 1879 — more people than the town's feet of elevation above sea level. According to the Leadville City Directory, those 10,000 residents were served by 120 saloons, 19 beer halls and 118 gambling houses/private clubs as well as four churches and four banks. At one point, Leadville was the second largest city in Colorado. The population of Leadville in 2021 was 2,613, which hasn't much changed from the population in 1990 of 2,696. Now it is a town of workers of the Climax mine and a bedroom community to workers who make the commute over Fremont Pass and Tennessee Pass to labor in the ski towns of Vail and Breckenridge.

On two of my 11 days on the Colorado Trail by that point, I had experienced torrential rain downpours. But both times I beat the rain to the bar. The first time I beat the rain to the pub in Breckenridge. This time, I was happily in the Brass Ass Saloon while thunder shook the windows, and a deluge of rainwater washed down the main street in Leadville. I felt a slight pang of sadness for Wangler out there alone in the Sawatch Range Mountains getting pelted with water, but the whiskey shot and the Voodoo Ranger IPA effectively washed over me and splashed away any sadness I had for *the* Wangler (whip crack).

The Golden Burro Café had recently changed owners who drastically changed the menu — to all plant-based. The staff is quick to correct your assumed meatless displeasure and disappointment with a few "just try its." Boy, were they right. They know how to make plant-based dishes taste delicious. What they lack in animal protein, they compensate for with fried breading. I devoured the fried buffalo cauliflower and a plate of sweet potato gnocchi. Noah joined us for lunch, which allowed Bad Foot and me a chance to ask him a bunch of questions about his training for the Leadville 100. Hint: a LOT of running and pain.

After lunch and once the rain had stopped, we strolled down the streets of Leadville toward a sports outfitter shop. Bad Foot and I each modified our gear in Leadville. I purchased a new stove to better fit my boil pot/coffee mug. Bad Foot bought a pack rain cover.

After our gear buying, we again set out to wander around the streets of Leadville when we ran into a bearded, burly guy that looked like he'd fit right in as an extra in a Lord of the Rings movie

"CT or CDT?" he asked looking at our backpacks slung messily over only one of our shoulders.

"We're hiking the Colorado Trail," I told him. "I'm Nugget."

"Bad Foot."

"You can call me King Arthur," he told us.

"Why King Arthur?"

"Because I'm a legend." he declared, "but actually it's because I helped pull out a tent stake from a tree root."

He earned his trail name when hiking the Pacific Crest Trail. Early in his trek, he was camping with a fellow hiker who had pounded her tent stake deep into the ground and deep into a tree root. When she couldn't pull the stake free the next day, she asked for help. After several hikers had no success liberating the tent stake, he — in Arthurian-legend fashion as though he were a young boy drawing free Excalibur from the stone in which it had been magically fixed — had been able to pull the stake free.

After seeing our backpacks, he'd purposefully crossed Harrison Avenue to chat with us.

The Continental Divide Trail and the Colorado Trail overlap during this portion outside Leadville, so it's a guess as to what backpack-laden folks are hiking when you see them on the street. Although, to me, CDT hikers are easier to spot. They've spent about two months on the trail getting to Leadville. Whereas CT hikers can get to Leadville in less than two weeks. CDT hikers have endured the suns of the deserts of New Mexico and look like they have. They are already too weathered, too sun-kissed, too shaggy and too emaciated to have been on the trail for only 11 days like we had been. And if you talk to them, they too rapidly turn the conversation toward food. Thru-hikers have a super-sized gratitude for free food.

I thought it was a huge compliment that people would mistake us for CDTers.

This was one of the first instances that made me notice the deep tribal nature of the thru-hiker community. The only thing similar I can compare it to was when my family and I were in Cincinnati for the opening day of MLB baseball season at Great American Ball Park. Among the sea of red, Reds fans and "free Pete" T-shirts stood me, my twin, my older brother and my dad and mom, all of us decked out in the black and yellow of Pittsburgh Pirates gear and sticking out like a sore thumb. We were part of the tiny minority of Pirates fans in Cincinnati that day. As we walked the streets, we had other fellow Pirates fans cross the street to talk to us. They saw us as fellow members of their tribe and went out of their way to speak with us. The experience in Cincinnati was a small glimpse into what it would be like on the trail.

King Arthur even offered to buy us a beer while he killed time waiting for his friends to arrive. It was like we were old friends who hadn't seen each other for years. Except we weren't. We were complete strangers — almost interchangeable from the hundreds of Texas tourists in Leadville for the July 4th weekend. But we shared a common bond: we were thru-hikers.

As Bad Foot explained to me as we strolled down the streets of Leadville, "Hiking the PCT is a big deal. To many, it's arguably the biggest accomplishment of their lives, so you can see why people like that want to revel and savor their accomplishment with fellow thru-hikers."

I was still trying to grasp the deep connections and the instant camaraderie that the thru-hiker community shared.

Bad Foot continued, "If we were at a restaurant and a fellow thru-hiker walked in the room, who was a complete stranger, it wouldn't be uncommon for us to invite them to join us for dinner, straight away."

As someone who requires a lot of time before I allow someone behind my introvert armor, I was astonished and excited at how quickly I liked fellow long-distance hikers. And how little time needed to pass before my spirit brightened when I saw that same hiker later on down the trail.

Ed and Julie got to Leadville in the afternoon, and we spent the evening eating pizza, doing triage to the silver-dollar-sized blister on my left foot, and staring at Mt. Massive from the Airbnb's hot tub.

Day 12 on the trail would be my first zero day (hiker lingo for a rest day when you hike zero miles). It would also be the first day on the trail I woke up in a bed that wasn't a triple-decker bunk bed. Julie had found an Airbnb rental complete with a hot tub and mountain views. I soaked in that rejuvenating water as I sipped my morning coffee.

I then borrowed Ed's car in the morning and drove to the Colorado Trail Hostel to pick up Bad Foot, Tall Tale and Harry Potter. I shuttled them back by Turquoise Lake to the

Timberline Lake Trailhead and the start of Segment Ten of the CT.

"We plan to hike about 12 miles each over the next two days," Bad Foot says, "So you should be able to catch back up to us pretty quickly."

I had plans to take a day off in Leadville with Ed and Julie then do two big-mile days to reunite with the tramily.

On my drive back to Leadville, I spotted a weather-worn backpacker around 30 years-old walking the road around Turquois Lake.

I slowed down beside him and asked, "Are you headed into Leadville?"

"I am."

"Me too, hop in."

"I'm taking a zero today, I've been hiking the Colorado Trail," I said trying to signal my trail bona fides, "my trail name is Nugget."

"I'm hiking the CDT. I go by Rattler."

So these big league hikers do say "I go by . . ."

"Why Rattler?"

"I got that trail name the very first day. I plopped myself and my pack down for a break then quickly realized I sat down right next to a rattle snake."

Luckily it only gave him a scare and not teeth marks.

During our short drive, I gave him suggestions on the best places to get food and a beverage. It felt rewarding to pay it forward and help another hiker as I had been relying on the kindness of others as well.

The trail is like that; it'll conjure in you a desire to give back.

I enjoyed a relaxing day exploring the shops of Leadville, reading, journaling and chatting with Ed, Julie and tourists. In the off-trail world, days like this don't seem to happen very often. There are always tasks, chores, distractions, to-dos and the next thing to plan and execute that disables us from having lazy, still, and slowed-down days. After 11 days of thru-hiking, I was more readily able to find peace and stillness. I relished the down time.

The only thing on my calendar was to meet up with the Wangler and his wife Mary for a beer at Two Mile Brewing Company in the afternoon.

I was on the patio as they drove up. The Wangler's week on the CT would end at Twin Lakes, where he'd pick up the trail next summer.

"I can only stay for one pint because we are headed back to Denver," Wangler told me.

His wife suggested we find a table outside so as not to expose her husband's week-old hiker stench to the other brewery patrons who had noses.

"You'd better not sit too close to Scott, he doesn't smell pleasant," Mary said.

Who is Scott? I know him only by his trail name.

"Nugget's a thru-hiker, he understands the hiker stink," Wangler said.

We toasted cheers with our IPA-filled glasses as the Wangler told us, "It's hard being a segment hiker because I'm just starting to get my stride and I've found a great group of hikers to share the trail with and I have to stop."

"Keep going. What's stopping you?" I ask.

"Oh, just a couple of important things: his job, his family, his wife, you know," Mary says.

"You should think about joining me next summer for a week," he suggests.

"I doubt you'll have to twist my arm very hard to get me to join next year," I say, "You'll be missed for the rest of this trip though. Are you sure you can't continue? We're guaranteed to make more great stories to tell."

"You're right about that," Wangler said, "but those stories won't sound too good being told at my divorce proceedings."

After Wanger and his wife hit the road, I then had an experience that would make my second-grade teacher swell with pride. Out of the corner of my eye, I noticed the brewery patron two seats down had the three middle fingers of his right hand pointed in a "w" shape as he was moving his hand back and forth in front of his mouth. From a few classes that I took on American Sign Language, I reckoned that the patron was asking the bartender for a glass of water.

Normally in a situation like this I'd have to summon up courage to approach a stranger — if I even did at all. But Nugget, he didn't need to think. I went right over to this bearded grizzly-looking guy in a Tennessee Volunteers hat and signed, "Hello, my name is Chris, I know a little Sign Language." And I really stressed the "little."

I quickly learned that he went by "Silent Nomad," a trail name he earned when hiking several hundred miles of the Appalachian Trail.

I have a suspicion that my confidence in my signing ability was heavily influenced by the consumption of alcohol. (I also think I'm a good dancer when I drink). Maybe I was properly remembering the correct hand gestures, and maybe I just thought I was, and Silent Nomad was too polite to tell me otherwise. Either way I had a wonderful time. We drank for the next two hours together. I briefly thought back to my first day on the trail out of water, slowly drawing closer to the Platte River and fantasizing about my best beer experiences. This one with Silent Nomad makes the Top 5.

As we were approaching our third beer together, the brewery worker stormed off in the direction of the bathroom. I clumsily signed to Silent Nomad that the backpackers again stole all the toilet paper.

This, I learned, was a common occurrence here in Leadville with the confluence of CDT and CT hikers.

"Who would do that?" I ask.

You should know that in my hiking shorts pocket was a two-day wad of toilet paper I had stashed from the previous trip to the restroom.

"I can't believe they took the whole roll!" I tell the bartender in feigned disbelief.

When I couldn't understand a sign, Silent Nomad would write it in text on his iPhone. Silent Nomad was extremely patient. I'd finger spell a word and he'd graciously show me the sign. I told him about the CDT hiker King Arthur and the origin of that trail name. He reminded me that the sign for "king" was taking the "K" hand sign and moving it from top left shoulder down to right hip like you are tracing a royal sash.

I paid my tab and stood up from my stool, I was headed to meet Julie, Ed and my friend Tim at High Mountain Pies for dinner. I invited Silent Nomad to join us. He was waffling because he had plans to eat at the Tennessee Pass Café (he was a big Tennessee Volunteers fan, hence the hat). So, I tried to make High Mountain Pies more appealing.

"I had the pizza yesterday and it was great . . . also last night on the back patio there was fantastic live Irish music."

Silent Nomad smiled and signed, "Remember, I'm deaf!" Then laughed at me.

Oh Geez! I did remember the signs for "sorry" and "I'm stupid."

I was successful in recruiting him to join us for pizza, however.

While ordering at the cash register in a crowded Mountain High Pies, I heard someone call out from a table, "Hey Chris!"

It was Chris and Cory from Colorado Mountain Expeditions, the group I hiked and camped with on Day Two and Day Four at Kenosha Pass. They had just finished their 2nd week of their CT expeditions. They were excited that I had made it to Leadville and was doing well.

Seeing them made me realize how much more confidence I had built since I first met them on my second day on the trail. I was beginning to realize that these serendipitous run ins with people you share the trail with were a delightful feature of thru-hiking.

While waiting for our pizza at a table on the patio, Ed left the table to take a phone call then came back and said, "We are getting kicked out of our Airbnb."

"Huh?"

"Yeah, we goofed up and only booked it for one night, not two like we thought. We need to stuff everything into the car and get out of the rental property for the next guests," Ed said.

Ed was embarrassed, flustered and nervous.

I was buzzed, relaxed and learning the ASL sign for *toilet paper*.

I responded with, "It'll eventually become a good story!"

And that became my new motto.

CHAPTER TWELVE:

Go Weast Young Man

I blinked open my eyes on the 13th day without immediately recognizing my surroundings.

No tent, bird sounds, or trees, so not outside. Nor is it the Leadville Airbnb . . .

Then it clicked.

We were in the Columbine Inn just outside downtown Leadville. After our accidental overstay at the Airbnb, Ed and Julie had scrambled to find the last two available rooms at the hotel. Ed and Julie shared a room, while I bunked with my friend Tim. He would take in and enjoy Leadville today, then camp with me near Twin Lakes that night. Which meant I would be up against about 22 miles today, from the Timberline Lake Trailhead to where the Colorado Trail crossed Highway 82 near the small town of Twin Lakes.

After a decidedly less frantic checkout than at the Airbnb, Ed, Julie and I had a delicious breakfast at the Silver Llama restaurant on main street. (Get the Eggs Benedict, trust me.) As we sipped coffee on the outdoor patio, Ed observed, "Your shoes seem to be holding up quite nicely."

"Yeah, 150 miles in, I'm glad I went with a half-size up," I told him.

Fittingly enough, Leadville helped me dial in my footwear for this hike. That is, it was Leadville, donkeys and a tradition nearly 75 years old.

In 1949, a challenge went out to anyone who dared race alongside a donkey from Leadville to Fairplay for the chance to win $500. It was the first-ever pack burro race.

The origins of the sport come from the 19th century, when gold miners kept donkeys around to carry supplies. Two miners once raced each other to stake ownership of the area where gold was found. Nowadays, runners mimic that same competition (except with more selfies).

In 2012, the Colorado General Assembly designated pack burro racing as the official state summer heritage sport (over rock climbing and sitting in traffic on I-70). Today's burro racers must get across the finish line with a donkey carrying a pick, gold pan and shovel.

Like most major sports, burro racing has its own ruling body: the Western Pack Burro ASSociation (that name wrote itself, didn't it?). The ASSociation, by the way, has its own registered trademark, lest it be confused with another similar organization like, say, Congress.

On Memorial Day Weekend, several weeks before I started on the CT, I ran in the eight-mile Georgetown Burro Race with my rented running partner Einstein, a sandy brown donkey with floppy Bugs Bunny ears. When the endorphins of the run wore off, I realized I had two pea-sized blisters on each of the tips of my second toes. Despite walking the stair climber and running on the treadmill with these same trail runners with no problems, running this race had caused my feet to swell.

That week, I ordered a pair of trail runners in size 12.5. Long distance hikers often order their footwear a half-size larger to account for swelling, a piece of knowledge my little piggies will forever be grateful for.

After breakfast, I shuttled back around Turquoise Lake to the Timberline Lake Trailhead and the start of Segment 10. Ed and Julie joined me for the first 100 yards on the trail before returning to their car. The trail over the next 13 miles has several climbs and descents keeping hikers at between 10,000 and 11,000 feet before finishing at the Mt. Massive Trailhead.

My plan for the day was to hike the entirety of Segment 10 and another eight miles of Segment 11. The ending point offered a good access point for Tim to meet me with his car, and a big mile day would help me catch up to my tramily.

Three miles into my hiking day and about an hour after I departed ways from Ed and Julie, I entered into the Mount Massive Wilderness Area. For the next 10 miles, the trail runs through the third of its six wilderness areas.

When the Colorado Trail was first proposed in the mid-1970s, the Mount Massive Wilderness Area didn't exist yet. In fact, four out of the trail's six wilderness areas didn't yet have that designation.

The original Wilderness Act of 1964 is the closest you can get to poetry in federal law. It enshrines "wilderness" as "where the Earth and its community of like are untrammeled by man, where man himself is a visitor who does not remain . . . undeveloped Federal land retaining its primeval character and influence." Wilderness can't be used for timber, mining or any other extraction or development purpose.

The original Act established 9.1 million acres of land across the U.S, comprising a handful of designated areas in Colorado including the Maroon Bells (near Aspen), Mount Zirkel (near Steamboat Springs), La Garita (near Gunnison) and the Rawah (near Fort Collins). The Colorado Trail runs through only one of the original Wilderness Areas from 1964. The Weminuche was added in 1975, and the other four that the trail winds through (Mount Massive Wilderness Area,

Collegiate Peaks Wilderness, Holy Cross Wilderness and Lost Creek Wilderness area) were designated by Congress in 1980.

Midway through the Mount Massive Wilderness Area, I began to belly laugh as I noticed Mountain Goat. This was my second surprise encounter with her, just three days since we camped together at Cascade Creek. She had met her husband at Tennessee Pass and helped shuttle Tall Tale and Hairy Potter into Leadville. Then she went home to Salida for a night to accommodate visiting relatives. After her day off in Salida and mine in Leadville, we were back on a similar schedule.

We spent the next couple of miles hiking together. Then we shared a snack spot next to Halfmoon Creek before we parted ways. The start of Segment 11 begins with a rather steep 500-foot climb. Mountain Goat wasn't planning on going as far as I was that day, so she told me to speed ahead.

As I started Segment 11, I received a text message from Bad Foot telling me where they planned to camp that night. It was farther down the trail than Bad Foot told me when I dropped him off at the trail the day before. This would make it much harder to catch back up to my group in one day. I felt a bit abandoned.

Was I merely an honorary tramily member or a real one?

Segment 11 shares the trail with a common route up Mt. Elbert, Colorado's highest peak. I ran into a few exhausted day hikers coming downhill from the summit. I also saw several thru-hikers' packs abandoned for the afternoon on the trail as they side-tripped up Mt. Elbert.

I had been on this part of the Colorado Trail before, but it was in snowshoes. In 2010, my climbing buddy Shawn and I outlasted a blustery day on this mountain to get to a November summit. I had only conquered three 14ers at that point and had been in Colorado for as many months. We hit the Elbert Trailhead at 7 a.m. and didn't return to the car until

6 p.m. At that point in my mountaineering career, this was a push-the-comfort-zone experience. Never had I been in the mountains for 11 straight hours.

As I hiked along this section, it made me realize how much my comfort bubble had been expanded since 2010.

The trail is like that.

As I subtly pushed my comfort bubble each day, it might've been hard to notice how much strength and confidence I'd built up. Incremental gains are trickier to notice. It's not until I paused, looked back and took stock of how far I'd come both physically and figuratively when I could really spot the difference — like looking at a photo of myself five years ago. One way to better appreciate progress is to ask what your past self would think of your current accomplishments.[22] Only two years earlier, I considered a seven-mile backpacking day a big day. Now I was doing three times that mileage without thinking much of it.

I met a bunch of CDT hikers headed north to Canada, each with a colorful trail name: Peaches, Hot Rod, Sour Patch, Dog Bite, Plus 1 and Velveeta.

I got to the culvert that crosses under Highway 82 around 6 p.m. where Tim picked me up, and we drove to a dispersed camping spot around the Mt. Elbert Trailhead. Our plan to cook a high-caloric meal over the campfire was foiled by thunderstorms, so we decided to drive into the small town of Twin Lakes for dinner.

As we walked into the Twin Lakes Inn and Saloon, I noticed two familiar hikers — it was the women from Oregon who had camped with us near Copper Mountain. They were now soaked by the rain, yet they still hadn't decided if they were taking the west or east route.

"You have to make a decision tomorrow, are you going east or west?" I inquired.

"We are going '*weast*,'" they responded. The same combination of east/west reply they had been giving anyone who asked their Collegiate Peaks strategy. They still hadn't made up their minds.

"You gotta decide by tomorrow," I said.

The thunderstorms hadn't abated after we paid our check. Luckily, the restaurant is connected to the lobby of the hotel. The manager allowed us to hang out in the lobby and even served us some beers. We chatted with a part-time Twin Lakes resident and chemistry teacher who we learned frequently wanders into the lobby to sip on a glass of Merlot and use the wireless internet.

We were getting the locals' treatment.

Waking up the next day, it was as if our campsite had been transported to the summit of a nearby peak. Looking around we could only see fog and clouds. Our camping spot was just above the South Mount Elbert Trailhead and 450 feet above the lakes below. But the lakes were visible below because of the persistent clouds.

We paid the costs with rain the night before, but the rewards the next morning were worth it.

As the sun worked its magic to break apart the lingering clouds, we were offered stunning views of the whole valley: Twin Lakes hugged by Mt. Elbert and Mt. Hope and veiled in clouds, pierced by the morning sunshine.

Tim shuttled me back to trail as I chowed down some Pop-tarts. I was hiking by 7:30 a.m.

Because my tramily had camped five miles ahead of me, I needed a monster day to catch back up — whatever miles they were planning plus five. But despite my goal of big miles, I spent a good portion of the first two miles of the day slowed down as I was looking over my shoulder and photographing the lake, Colorado's tallest peak, and the ever-changing cloud cover that continued to say, "Here, take a picture of me in this pose . . . now one in this pose here."

I caught up with Mountain Goat after about three miles into my 14th day on the trail. This would be the third time I surreptitiously ran into Mountain Goat. She had camped a mile or so before the spot where I started my day hiking, but she had started earlier and had leaped-frogged me.

If Twin Lakes were shaped like a clock (instead of a kidney bean), the CT would split apart around five o'clock. This meant my first five miles of the day were spent on flat trail circling around clock-wise from noon to five o'clock. The sandy, single-track trail marches through sagebrush. With no shade, this is a good section to knock off in the early morning.

After crossing the dam, we took a snack break and pulled out our wet tents to let the Colorado sun dry them out. Mountain Goat decided to take a longer break than I wanted to, so I wished her good luck and told her I hoped we met up again in Lake City. We didn't have much trail left to share anyway. The Colorado Trail splits a mile or so ahead and she was going the other route.

Are you turning right or left at the sign? Are you taking the Collegiate East route or the Collegiate West?

It's the one direction decision that each CT thru-hiker must make on their way to Durango. The whole Collegiate loop is 160 miles, which some people do as a thru-hike. Doing the CT requires you to pick one side of that loop, a decision point. Mileage and elevation gain aren't as much of a separating factor. The routes are comparable in distance (about 80 miles each), although the West route is about five miles longer. The Eastern route gains 17,800 feet over those 80 miles while the Collegiate West gains 19,800. There's a couple extra miles and 2,000 more vertical gain if you go west.

The College East was the original route when the CT was linked in 1987. There's a list of tradeoffs in taking each. The West trail stays higher for longer which means you're more susceptible to thunderstorms. The West trail also has the challenging yet amazing climb up Hope Pass, great views of Lake Ann (generally described as a jewel along the Collegiate West), a chance to camp by Lost Lake (for those willing to make the off-trail diversion and descent) and striking views of the Three Apostles (a group of rugged 13ers that contains two of the top 100 tallest mountains in Colorado. They are craggier than the rest of the Sawatch Mountains that surround them.) Re-supply is also much harder on the West trail. You can climb 14ers from both routes.

The East trail offers the Princeton Hot Springs but also requires several miles of highway road walking. The East also allows access to Buena Vista and an Airbnb rental occupied by my mom, aunt who were visiting from Pennsylvania and Ed and Julie for three nights. My decision was made for me.

Right before the turnoff, I ran into my first NOBO (North-Bound) Colorado Trail hikers. They were hiking from Durango to Denver. Their trail names were Zee and Shepherd. Zee recognized the Pennsylvania town name of "Bedford" on my shirt because she had lived in that area for seven years.

Small world.

The Collegiate West Alternative Junction and the Avalanche Trailhead (which gives easy access to Buena Vista) are both right around 9,300 feet in elevation. There's 33 miles of trail between them. If there weren't multiple ridges and valleys to get up and over between them, those 33 miles wouldn't be difficult. But there are four different up-and-overs, and quite a bit of elevation to be gained, lost, gained, lost, gained and lost between Twin Lakes and Buena Vista. In total, it's 8,200 feet of elevation to gain and lose. Hikers must get up and over into the Clear Creek Valley, then up and over into the Pine Creek Valley, then up and over into the Silver Creek Valley and finally up and over into the Cottonwood Creek drainage. Like a slow-motion roller coaster.

My plan for the day was to knock out two of those big up-over-and-into-another-valley obstacles.

The beginning of the Collegiate East turns sharply to the left and climbs up away from the lake. Six miles later, I was on top of the first big ridge of the day looking down over a descent into the Clear Creek drainage. The end of Segment 11 of the CT ends at Clear Creek Road. Shortly into Segment 12, the trail enters the Collegiate Peaks Wilderness.

The 14ers Harvard, Columbia, Yale and Princeton are collectively referred to as the Collegiate Peaks, which sit inside the Sawatch Range. It shares ties with a 14er in California (Mount Whitney) because these mountains were first surveyed by Harvard professor Josiah Dwight Whitney.

Looking at a map of the Collegiate Peaks Wilderness, you'll notice some odd boundaries and some pockets of non-designated wilderness surrounded by wilderness. This leaves the College Peaks Wilderness map looking like a bunch of gerrymandered boundaries. (That is, if mountain goats could vote.)

There are several indentations known as "cherry stems." Since logging, mining and road building are prohibited in Wilderness Areas, Congress drew the wilderness boundary to avoid historic mining remnants, roads and private mining claims. The Collegiate Peaks Wilderness Area is one of Colorado's 10 largest, but because of the "cherry stems," you're never more than five miles away from a road while in the Wilderness Area.[23]

After hiking 14 miles, the biggest part of my day was still in front of me. I had a much bigger up-over-and-into-another-valley maneuver to accomplish. Segment 12 goes from 9,000 feet to the top of a ridge off Waverly Mountain at 11,653 feet in about four miles before it drops into the Pine Creek valley.

If you statistically look at all 28 segments of the Colorado Trail, Segment 12's ratio of elevation gain to mileage was the second highest after Segment 7's up-and-over of the Tenmile Range from Breckenridge to Copper.

About halfway through the climb, a slight rain started. Through the drizzle, I saw a Forrest Gump look-a-like setting up his tarp. It was Hairy Potter setting up his sleeping gear. He had fallen behind Tall Tale and Bad Foot and had enough for the day.

That's odd.

That was the first time since knowing them that the three-some didn't camp together.

It was rejuvenating to see a familiar face. But the spike in energy didn't last too long. I still had another 1,000 feet to gain to get up, over and into the Pine Creek drainage. I slowly plodded upward. Still among tall trees, it was harder to gauge where the trail reached the top of the ridge. This made that section particularly mentally challenging, so I tried to daydream about my last visit to the Pine Creek area.

I had been in that valley on two separate occasions, both on 14er climbing trips to climb Mt. Oxford, Mt. Belford and Mt. Harvard. That was back when a seven-mile backpack day seemed so monumental.

Now, after two weeks of hiking, my mind thought of seven miles as easy. I mean, seven is just a little longer than five miles, and five miles quickly turns into three, which gets to two and then one mile, and one mile, at this point, felt like it was just around the corner.

But mileage was going by slowly at the tail end of my day.

At the top of the ridge, I was exhausted but relieved. The trail then quickly descends 1,200 feet to cross Pine Creek. I started to feel a sense of giddiness and excitement — a feeling I get when I notice a friend whom I'm about to surprise. That excitement to surprise Bad Foot was what motivated me while I was low on energy.

I stumbled across the bridge over Pine Creek where an orangish-red tent was set up next to another strange tent. Outside the tent I didn't recognize was, I later learned, a remedial English teacher. She had done Segments 1-11 of the CT last year before back pain forced her to quit. She was back this year for redemption.

Oh crap! Maybe this isn't Bad Foot in the other tent?

"Is that Bad Foot?" I announced, not quite certain if that was really the tent of a member of my trail family.

Then silence.

This must have been an odd scene for the woman: a stranger appearing in the wilderness, whose first words aren't hello, but as instead a strange nickname like *Bad Foot*.

There's no way I can continue any further today.

Then I heard it.

"Nugget?"

The genuine happiness a thru-hiker experiences when they reconnect with a trail friend is hard to describe. It's an amazing aspect of thru-hiking.

"I'm really glad you were able to catch up," Bad Foot admitted.

It's a great thing to feel cherished — to feel like I was part of something bigger than just myself.

"Where's Tall Tale?" I asked.

"The three of us had a tough conversation about what we should do. Hairy Potter wants to get off the trail at the next town. Tall Tale wants to continue to do big mile days, which if I'm forced to do, I won't enjoy the trip," Bad Foot informed me.

It seemed like our group was scattered to the wind. Tall Tale had pushed even further ahead. She had a strict schedule to keep. Her next adventure after walking across Colorado was to bike across Iowa in an event called Ragbrai. Not only that, after biking across Iowa, the plan was to drive up to Minnesota to the headwaters of the Mississippi and buy a used canoe, then row that canoe to the Gulf of Mexico — the entirety of the Mississippi River!

Up to this point, our trail family's decisions were all in unison. Now the goal of staying together conflicted with everyone's individual goals. Tall Tale wouldn't be able to make the bike across Iowa if she matched the slower pace of Hairy Potter. Bad Foot wouldn't find stillness if he was forced to do big mile days to match Tall Tale.

I had been naïve in assuming the trail family would remain the same the whole time. There's a tough tradeoff when each individual's goals conflict with the ability to stay together as a unit. I felt a pang of sadness when I realized that trail families sometimes must disband. But I was also glad to have caught back up with Bad Foot. The gloom from dissolving the band, combined with the steep climb and the rain, had sapped my positivity. Any day with over 4,000 feet of elevation gain is an energy-draining day. Fortunately, I had been training my brain to be better at recognizing the positive. Which isn't easy, since we humans are biased to the negative.

Blame this on evolution and survival. Is that a mountain lion? Was that a snake? Paying attention to dangers to a caveman was literally a matter of life and death. Our brain, particularly the amygdala, is programed to keep us safe, which means sifting and staying alert for threats. We no longer need to be on high alert like cavemen to survive, yet that negativity bias still controls how we think.[24]

I notice it when I ruminate on an insult or dwell on a mistake. To me as a college professor, it seems one bad teaching evaluation outweighs 10 glowing ones.

On this hike, however, I had been training myself to see the positive, which meant reflecting on my memories through an upbeat lens. Depressed people tend to do the opposite: when they formulate memories, they code them by recalling the unpleasant aspects. I learned that my capacity for joy is like a muscle — it can be trained. One proven technique that works to counteract this negative mode of thinking: gratitude.[25]

Gratitude experts also recommend writing down 10 things you're grateful for. But don't just write them down and move on — you should savor each of the items you write down. Recall them and how they make you feel in your head, gut and heart. Basically, you train your amygdala, that part of your brain that is responsible for that fight/flight reaction, to filter more positive information.

Do this for a month and the benefits will start to show. The research shows that three weeks of doing a daily gratitude practice is enough to start rewiring your brain to help you notice the positive,[26] to more easily delight in the ordinary, and to sharpen the capacity to notice each day as a gift. Gratitude practice is a firewall — it builds a protective cloak around you that helps fend off negativity, resentment, envy and anger. People who practice gratitude also report sleeping better. So, when our heads hit the pillow, we should be counting fewer sheep and more blessings.

Lying next to some beavers' handiwork and the singing ripples of Pine Creek, I finished my journal answering two questions: What are you grateful for today and what are you proud of so far in the trip?

1. Getting my tent up before the rain
2. Airheads' sugar boost
3. Music to listen to
4. Accomplishing big gains
5. Setting a new bar
6. Beaver ponds
7. Latrines
8. 5-Hour Energies
9. plus 20-mile hiking days
10. back-to-back 20s
11. friends who support my hike
12. reconnecting with trail friends
13. returning to hiking trails I've been on before
14. easy spot to hang my bear bag

I had been doing this practice since Night One camped next to the Platte River.

In my journal at the end of Day One, still facing 470 miles of hiking Colorado mountain passes, I wrote down: "I'm grateful for my support circle: Ed, my mom and her friends sending me words of encouragement. I'm grateful for Airheads, Gatorade and fighting the bonk. I'm also grateful for people like Kyle, whom I met on the trail today and who wanted to make sure I enjoyed the mountain goats."

The section in my journal dedicated to gratitude began to get longer and longer the more I was on the trail and the more I performed my gratitude practice.

Not long after my journaling and gratitude practice was complete for the day, fatigue was setting in after 20 miles and 4,500 feet of gain. I felt my sore knees and shoulders melting into my sleeping pad and I began to fade into sleep.

I don't know how long I had been sleeping, but the next thing I remember was a sudden yell from out of the darkness.

"Magic!"

Huh?

I rustled around my sleeping bag wondering if I was dreaming. I was in the space where you're almost asleep, so you don't know if what you heard is real. Then again through the cool mountain darkness I heard it again.

"It's Magic . . . Magic . . . Magic Carpet, Magic Hat and Black Magic. Magic!" It was Bad Foot from inside his tent. He couldn't turn off his brain and fall asleep until he came up with the answer to the RAT question "Hat, Black, Carpet."

I smiled. There's something about the Pine Creek drainage that feels like home. I was also happy to be camped with a part of my tramily again.

Clues to RAT Quiz #5
camp, seat, fire
grass, blood, moon
drain, window, thunder
gray, ground, wheel
bill, book, ground
will, back, last
black, carpet, hat
hand, smoke, turn
box, hung, duty
light, natural, station

CHAPTER THIRTEEN:

200

The start of my third week included the 200-mile marker. This was my 15th day on the trail, my third Monday and the Fourth of July. Pine Creek crosses the CT at mile 198, leaving us two miles in the morning to hit the 200 milestone. Immediately from our campsite beside the river, the trail ascends up switch backs and tops off at an elevation of 11,847 feet. There were no warm-up miles today, it's straight up from the get-go: 1,400 feet of gain in the first 2.5 miles of the morning.

Hi Ho, Hi Ho, it's up the hill we go.

After Bad Foot's morning head start, I was pleased to catch up with him about a quarter mile from the 200-mile spot. When we reached that mark, I headed off the path for my morning ritual. In my previous backpacking adventures, I had tried my hardest to avoid the forest squat. So much so that I have an intricate knowledge of the restroom stalls in the Walmarts of Montrose and Salida from many backpacking trips. But after about 10 days out on the trail, I began to enjoy it. It would normally occur about one or two miles into my day when I'd drop the pack and head into the trees with my trowel. I later learned that a regular walking plan can help improve digestion. Put simply, movement causes our digestive systems to move more quickly. As food moves faster through the large intestine, the body absorbs less water from the stool, which means it is passed through easier. So, the advice for anyone who's plugged up is to do more walking. This adds to the list of the myriad ways your body adapts to the natural rhythm of hiking every day.

When I came back to the trail, Bad Foot was finishing up the last touches of his pebble creation. He had gathered a bunch of rocks and used them to write out "200" in the dirt beside the trail.

You got to celebrate the small achievements on the trail.

I was glad I was able to share this moment with Bad Foot.

After topping off on the ridge, the trail has a pleasurable nine-mile descent to the end of Segment 12 at the Silver Creek Trailhead. In the late morning, near Harvard Lakes, we ran into a pair of hikers coming toward us on the trail.

"Happy Fourth of July," I cheerfully greeted them.

And then I waved, but the first hiker didn't wave back. Then I heard the second hiker telling the first, "OK, you have two people on your left, some rocks in the middle of the trail, and a cliff on your right."

The hiker was giving detailed instructions of the trail and the surroundings because the first hiker couldn't see those features. He was a blind hiker.

They both eventually wished us a "Happy Independence Day" and continued up the trail.

"Can you imagine what it would be like to not being able to see anything and hear your hiking partner say, 'There's a cliff on your right!?' " I asked Bad Foot.

I was impressed. It also made me reflect on how blessed I was to be out here on July 4, healthy and hiking. In my 15 days on the trail, I had now met a blind hiker and a deaf hiker. I smiled at the amazing people I had walked into and how things kept working out for me on the trail.

As I hiked, I couldn't help but reminisce about all the lucky events I had encountered so far: I thought about the dinners I had with Colorado Mountain Expedition, my friends Ed and Julie who resupplied me at Kenosha, another friend who picked me up in Breckenridge, the fun I had with fellow bikers and hikers in the Bivvi Hostel, hiking with Sound FX and Mountain Goat all day to Copper, the generosity of Noah picking us up at Turquoise Lake and letting us shower at his house, the time drinking with Silent Nomad, Julie scrambling around and booking us a room at the Columbine Inn in Leadville, drinking after hours in the Twin Lakes hotel lobby out of the rain with the restaurant manager and camping with my friend Tim at the Elbert trailhead.

It got me thinking. I had a bunch of questions swirling in my head as we strolled toward the end of Segment 12. *Is this only happening because of the trail? What is it about the trail that allows all these fortuitous events to occur? How do I bring this trail luck back to the real world? Am I purposely putting myself in situations to create lasting memories? Maybe thru-hikers are luckier than other people?*

Then I remembered the academic research on luck and the famous newspaper experiment done by Dr. Richard Wiseman. He started by placing advertisements in newspapers recruiting people who considered themselves exceptionally lucky or unlucky[27]. He then had the lucky and unlucky people read a newspaper and asked them to look through it and tell the experimenters how many photographs were inside. The people who identified as unlucky on average took about two minutes to count the photos while the lucky people took just seconds.

Why?

Because on the second page contained a message that read, "Stop counting — There are 43 photographs in this newspaper." It wasn't even subtle. The message took up half the page, but the unlucky people tended to miss it.

Later on in the newspaper, a second large message announced, "Stop counting, tell the experimenter you have seen this and win $250." The unlucky folks were still focused on counting the photographs and missed the opportunity. Unlucky people are more anxious and that anxiety goofs with people's ability to notice the unexpected. The difference between lucky and unlucky people is simply where they are looking; that is, their attention spotlight. Anxious people tend to have a narrower focus, and thus fail to notice opportunities for luck. Self-identified lucky people are looking for opportunities. The unlucky miss them. The way the lucky behave simply makes them more likely to create, detect and act upon opportunities.

Maybe thru-hikers are like the people who think of themselves as lucky?

They are more aware of the chances to receive luck. This also means that if we are in a pessimistic mindset, we could be missing amazing opportunities. Like the hiker who is so focused on the destination and the difficult hike ahead and doesn't see a chance for luck.

It helped that I now had a goal of writing a book about my Colorado Trail experience and I was always on the lookout for a good story. But what if I weren't on the lookout? What if I didn't approach Silent Nomad at the brewery? I wouldn't have that part of the story. I wouldn't have gotten lucky (Not in that way, get your mind out of the gutter). I was really feeling proud of all the times I purposefully placed myself in situations to make memories. The literature on luck guides you to be more open to new experiences, be more extroverted, and initiate more opportunities for lucky encounters.

My proud feeling of gratitude was short lived and was turned into laughter shortly after what Bad Foot said next.

"You have a cliff on your right and an asshole on your left! That's what the guide should have said." Bad Foot joked. Referring, of course, to me as the asshole on the left.

After meeting the blind hiker, I got to learn a lot more about Bad Foot's life, as this was a rare occasion where we hiked together for that nine-mile stretch. He was an Iron Man. Back when Bad Foot was swimming the open Hawaiian ocean in an Iron Man Race in the 1980s, the etiquette was to forego wearing the Iron Man Finisher T-shirt because it separated you from the ones who weren't able to complete the race.

"Back then it was about everyone finishing together and everyone motivating each other to finish the race. Today you have people viewing their fellow racers as adversaries — trying to finish 1,121st instead of 1,122nd. Now it's a lot more about *me, me, me,*" Bad Foot lamented, "It seems like much more of a competitive zero-sum mentality today."

I had a similar feeling each time I go skiing in Colorado. It's all a race to get the first groomed turns or ski the fresh powder. Even parking seems to be an anxiety-producing endeavor. Parking lots fill up. The scarcity mindset takes hold. People fight over who will be the first in the lift line.

There's no first chair on the trail. There isn't a scarcity mindset. No first tracks. In my experience, there wasn't even a race to get the best camp spots since it was understood you'd share your site with the fellow thru-hikers.

"Seems like the opposite ethos of thru-hiking?" I asked. "Everyone out here seems to be on the same team?"

"Yes, that's one of the most important aspects of thru-hiking," Bad Foot told me.

"It's not about chopping down your competition. It's about togetherness. And also, there are no castes in thru-hiking. No divisions. A thru-hiker is a thru-hiker, it doesn't matter their age, their income or their religion."

I realized thru-hiking was the great equalizer. Sure, some people invested in lighter and more expensive gear, but at the end of the day, we all shit in the woods.

After realizing how important that casteless culture was to Bad Foot — how a 22-year-old college student was just the same as a 66-year-old retiree — I couldn't help it! "Hurry up old man!" I blurted out.

"I stand by that asshole joke I made earlier," Bad Foot countered.

When we made it to the end of Segment 12, we crossed the bridge over North Cottonwood Creek into the start of Segment 13 and took a break to cook a dehydrated meal beside the river. Our plan was to "calorie up" before the big climb ahead. We also sipped half of a 5-Hour Energy. This was the fourth and last big up-and-over left before the town of Buena Vista.

Mileage-wise, we only had another two miles to knock out, but those two included nearly 1,700 feet of elevation gain. The trail gains 1,000 in a mile at one point on this stretch. It's no coincidence this segment is unlucky 13. That's quad-toasting. There's no room for the trail to switch back as it climbs up a steep gorge. So straight up it goes. There are steep drop-offs on your left side up this section.

I wonder how that blind hiker would handle this stretch?

"Remember how I raved about the angelic trail designer who gave the trails relatively gentle climbs on earlier parts of the CT? Evidently, he died before the Colorado Trail was finished and his evil twin stepped in for him," lamented Bad Foot when commenting about this stretch of the trail in his blog.

After hiking for most of the day together, Bad Foot told me to go on ahead so he could hike at his own pace up this steep section. I would power up about 40 yards of that stretch, then be forced to sit down in the pine straw along the steep trail. About the third round of burst-and-sit, I noticed the butt indentations of previous hikers left in the pine needles; someone else had the same strategy.

I was glad when the trail flattened out into a nice meadow bisected by Silver Creek. We found a great campsite on the right side of the trail, complete with a rock fire ring and a tiny log cabin, albeit missing one minor architectural feature: a roof. It also provided stunning views of Mt. Yale's (14,200') east ridge — part of that ridge we could gain the next morning. We'd camped above 11,000 feet that night. This was a 15-mile day with 3,500 feet of elevation gain.

Around a campfire, Bad Foot and I did the sixth RAT.

I was curious if we would be able to see or hear fireworks that night. But I never found out. That had to be the earliest I've ever been asleep on a July Fourth.

I woke up at 6:09 a.m. on my 16th day on the trail. This was the first time that I "hit the snooze." I pulled my quilt over my eyes — now accustomed to my hiker stench — and slept in until my 7:15 a.m. alarm went off. We had a short mile day today and were in no hurry since my support crew, i.e., Doris (my mom), Nancy (my aunt), Ed and Julie, wouldn't get into Buena Vista until the afternoon.

Bad Foot had been squirming in his sleeping bag since 6 a.m. like a child on Christmas morning. I didn't start hiking until 8:27 a.m. that morning, the latest start from a tent I had since the second day on the trail.

Our biggest challenge of the day was gaining the 800 feet to the top of the ridge on Mt. Yale's east side. Then it was downhill to the Buena Vista and an Airbnb to sleep in for a few days.

After breakfast and water filtering, I admired the views of Mt. Yale, basking in the morning sunshine for several moments before I motored up Yale's east ridge. The view is extra special since I had stood on the peak's summit more than a decade before.

This was the third time I had been on this section of the CT on Yale's east ridge. I used this route to obtain my first "snowflake," or calendar winter 14er summit. After a failed attempt earlier in the month, my hiking companion Shawn and I successfully summited Mt. Yale in January 2011. I learned that day how the most rewarding summits are often the ones where we had been unsuccessful in a prior attempt.

As I was reminiscing about our Yale snow climb and working my way up the climb, I suddenly got my first dose of a term Bad Foot had been casually mentioning for the past several days:

Testosterone Poisoning.

The term is used to describe behaviors that are excessively masculine. Bad Foot used it in situations when he tried to exceed his desired pace to keep up with a younger hiker.

Up until now, I had been that younger hiker. But the tables were turned on the steep climb up Yale's east ridge. A kid came charging up my back. I had thought I was maintaining a good pace. This kid was flying. If he didn't have a trail name, I was going to call him Pheidippides after the Greek runner who ran from Marathon to Athens delivering the news of the Battle of Marathon. He was hiking 25 to 30 per day and had started a full week after I did from Waterton.

"Wait, that means you covered in only eight days the same mileage I had done in 15?" I said.

I gathered this information as we shared a snack break on the top of the ridge together. He was munching on a Honey Stinger Waffle. I had the exact same snack in my pack, so I also ate a Honey Stinger Waffle. I think it was a Freudian move on my part to signal that I measured up to him. I controlled myself from blurting out loud, "My Honey Stinger is bigger than yours."

I did take solace in the fact that I was really soaking up that trail experience. Going at that fast of a pace alone, I was wondering if he was savoring the trail. It also got me thinking about Bad Foot's perspective.

Hike your own hike, I guess.

He took off down the trail before he fully noticed my sour grapes.

From atop the ridge, the trail drops about 2,500 feet down to the Avalanche Trailhead — the trailhead I had parked at in January 2011. Once again, the last time I was on this section of trail, it was in snowshoes.

Just before the Avalanche Trailhead, we met a friendly female solo hiker.

"I'm Nugget and this is Bad Foot," I told her.

"They call me *Sketcher.*"

Hearing this, my eyes looked down at her feet expecting to see the name brand shoes. But they weren't there. Then I saw her drawing book.

Sketcher was on the Colorado Trail on her 65th year on the planet. She had a welcoming smile that made her feel instantly like a part of our tribe. Now living in Moab, she had spent a portion of her life running and climbing these mountains. She gained her trail name because she carried watercolors in her pack which she used to draw in her sketch book/journal each day.

My initial plan was to meet my support crew at the Avalanche Trailhead because of its easy access right beside Cottonwood Pass Road (Chaffee County Rd 306). That's when I learned my support crew had stopped at Kenosha Pass as they drove Highway 285 to Buena Vista.

My mom texted me a photo of my signature at the Kenosha Pass trail registry penned 11 days earlier. I realized that was the last trail register that I signed "Chris."

My support crew then hiked a half mile of Segment Six admiring the aspen trees. They weren't expected for another hour, so Bad Foot and I continued another three miles until the point where the CT crosses the dirt County Road 343. It ended up being about seven miles and 1,000 feet of gain on this day.

Parked right beside the trail on Co Rd 343 was a big white pick-up truck with green lettering that spelled "Colorado Mountain Expeditions." It was the group that offered me trail magic on my second and fourth day on the trail. The same group I bumped into in Leadville. They were on their third expedition of the CT with a fresh group of hikers for the week.

I was excited to catch up with my guide friends.

The guide that showed up, however, I hadn't met before, a tiny let down. Though I got another favor from them. We were able to *Yogi* a ride in the back of the truck back to Cottonwood Pass Road where it would be easier for my crew to pick us up. (Yogi is a thru-hiker verb — after Yogi the Bear — for when you solicit food, rides or assistance from strangers, typically without directly asking them).

Bad Foot first taught me the term.

"You just hang about looking needy around non-hikers," Bad Foot informed me, "until they offer you food that you wanted them to give you in the first place. Hairy Potter is the king of Yogi-ing."

It's a learned skill. Day One on the trail, I would have been pretty sheepish to ask strangers for help. After thru-hiking for a week or so, it comes naturally. It's like the trail subliminally whispers, "Hey, that anxiety ingrained in your brain about social norms, forget it."

We had 220 miles down, which meant 266 miles left to get to Durango.

But Durango wasn't on our minds. We were craving conversations with friends and family, K's burgers and beers from Eddyline Brewery. Not necessarily in that order.

Clues for RAT Quiz #6
think, drunk, dunk
one, phone, line
through, side, board
mixed, road, car
sound, book, hat
man, arm, lift
line, piece, event
TV, light, airplane
play, fold, board
over, mark, end

CHAPTER FOURTEEN:

Family

Being on the trail for 16 days and riding the sun's rhythm, our bodies were used to waking up before 6 a.m. But that wasn't the case for Ed. Yet true to his pledge to help with my hike in any way that he could, Ed was up early at our Airbnb rental in Buena Vista to shuttle Bad Foot and me back to where we left the trail the day before. This was the start of my 17th day on the Colorado Trail.

The starting elevation of the day was 8,890, and the geographical high point of the day on the ridge would be just over 10,000 feet, but the figurative high point of the day was what was waiting for us just 10 miles down the trail at mile 230: the Mount Princeton Hot Springs. The trail goes right beside it.

We were hiking through the Sawatch Range, whose features were carved by glaciers. Once they melted, all that snowmelt poured loads of silt that now form "alluvial fans" at the peak's edges. It's the reason why the peaks in this valley seem to have sloping toes, so it felt like we were hiking around Mt. Princeton's bare feet for several miles in dry forests.

Three miles before the hot springs, the CT joins a dirt road that is familiar to 14er hikers — it's the road to climb the standard route up Mt. Princeton. For the next 5.7 miles, the

CT follows roads to avoid private land. The official trail is on a paved road for a bit leading into the hot springs.

When building the Colorado Trail in the 1980s, this was an easy section to find volunteers to work the trail crews. Volunteers, after being released by trail crew leaders after building trail all day, would happily reconvene in the hot springs. The hiking day was 10 miles and 1,400 feet of gain in total.

So far, I'd been sharing hiking days with fellow thru-hikers. It was extra special to see the faces of the people who had been supporting me for years. My mom, aunt, Ed and Julie joined us for lunch and a soak.

While Bad Foot and I knocked out another 10 miles of the Colorado Trail, those four hiked to Agnes Vaille Falls whose trailhead is very close to Mt. Princeton Hot Springs. Like the Godmother of the Colorado Trail, Agnes Vaille was also a legendary female Colorado mountaineer.

My time doing light days around Buena Vista helped us rejuvenate, restore, recover and prepare for the second half of the trail. It also helped me view the idea of rest through a different lens.

In today's fast-paced world, it's easy to find yourself viewing days off or down time as weakness. There seems to always be something else you should be doing. But sometimes rest is more beneficial. It can be an antidote to burnout. The reason it's hard to see rest days as a boost to performance is partly to do with a psychological quirk that behavioral scientists call *commission bias*. Basically, humans have a tendency toward action even though inaction might lead to a better outcome.

I learned I needed to reframe rest as an active part of high-level performance[28]. It shouldn't be viewed as "not training." Rest allows me to go harder in the future. If we never take an easy period, we won't be able to go all out during the hard periods.

I try to remind myself to view rest as an active process that revitalizes me and gives me the ability to push harder in the future. Take a rest day, give myself permission to recover, get great sleep and come back with full energy on the next workout.

But not all rest is equal. Beer and television don't have the same recovery benefits as Epsom salt baths and reading. Scrolling through social media isn't as restorative as a quiet walk.

That's why, as we all soaked in the Mt. Princeton Hot Springs that afternoon, I left my cell phone in the truck.

My 18th day on the CT began with some trail magic. But this time we were playing the role of trail angel. We loaded up my truck at our Airbnb rental in Buena Vista with eggs, bacon, cheese, English muffins, soda, and chocolate chip cookies and drove up to the top of Cottonwood pass, where the CDT and Collegiate West route of the CT cross the highway.

In preparing to come to Colorado and help hikers, my mom reached out to the CT Facebook group seeking ideas on how to be the best trail angel. Providing fresh fruit, cold drinks and a place to throw out garbage were recurring comments from people familiar with thru-hiking. After my experience thru-hiking, I agree. When you spend your days eating beef jerky and dehydrated meals and constantly seeking water, your body craves things like juicy grapes or watermelon. It's also quite nice to declutter your pack of wrappers and used meal pouches.

We spent three hours between 9:30 a.m. and 12:30 p.m. waiting for thru-hikers. Disappointingly, we only got one. He was a military guy named Mike from Colorado Springs who was hiking the 160-mile Collegiate Loop. It wasn't the trail angel experience my mom and I envisioned, but Mike's smile enjoying a cold diet coke, cookies and bacon-egg-and-cheese sandwich made it worth it.

While we were trying to conjure up thru-hikers to feed on Cottonwood Pass, Bad Foot used the morning to catch up on his trail blog. Once we got back to the BV, we loaded up our day packs and hopped back into the car as my mom and aunt shuttled us back to the Mt. Princeton Hot Springs where we got back on the trail to knock out five miles in the afternoon.

From the hot springs, there are still 2.5 miles left of Segment 13 before the trail crosses a nice bridge over Chalk Creek and the start of the next segment. Those 2.5 miles are easy road walking by cabins along the river. As you gain elevation at the start of Segment 14, you get a better understanding about why Mt. Princeton was originally named Chalk Mountain. The trail gives you great views of the Chalk Cliffs. While in reality the cliffs were granite altered to white clay by the water from the hot springs, I was struck by how it really looked like a bunch of white chalk.

Doris and Aunt Nancy then drove around to an access point five miles down the trail, parked the car and started hiking backward (not physically backward as I had been doing to strengthen my knees) on the trail toward us. We ran into them about a mile from the car. They turned around and strolled together, so they could officially say they hiked one mile of the 486 of the Colorado Trail with us.

We then drove south to the Salida post office to pick up a re-supply package that Bad Foot had mailed. Because the last post office resupply at Jefferson was a calamity, we held our breath as Bad Foot ran into the post office. We celebrated the package's safe arrival with a beer at Brown's Canyon Brewing Company on the way back to Buena Vista.

The bartenders and owners were a friendly couple who originally owned a raft guiding company. Now they have a raft guiding shop that has a brewery in the back.

"Why did you decide to connect it with a brewery?" I asked.

"Well, we realized that after you finish an awesome day of rafting, you want to relive it and chat about it over a beer. So, we figured, 'why don't we add a place to drink that beer and connect it to our rafting operation?'" the friendly couple told us.

While we were performing trail magic, hiking and drinking, we had roast beef in the crockpot cooking all day long. With our beef, we added mashed potatoes, corn and bread and butter. The exact meal my Grandma Marker (which we called her because her first grandchild couldn't pronounce "Mary") would make about every week. There's nothing better than the taste and memory of Grandma's house. That night, Bad Foot and I got back some of the calorie deficit we had been running for the past two weeks.

Bad Foot and I got back on the trail where we left off the day before at mile marker 235 at 8:30 a.m., but not before caching some extra calories with the pancakes, sausage and eggs my mom made for us. The plan for Day 19 was to hike 12 miles to the Angel of Shavano Trailhead, where my mom and aunt would meet us with six days of food for our big push to Lake City, then hike an additional five miles to camp next to Cree Creek at mile 252.

Four miles into my time back on the trail, I had a sudden feeling of deja vu. I realized this wasn't the first time I had set foot on this section of the Colorado Trail.

But when was that?

Then I came across the sign for Little Browns Creek headed west toward the 14er. I had a brief stint on it when hiking Mt. Antero in 2019. We had parked at the Browns Creek Trailhead back in the summer of 2019. I had started that summer with nine 14ers left to finish before I completed all 58 of them. Mt. Antero was the last one remaining for me to check off the Sawatch Range.

The peak is named in honor of Chief Antero of the Uintah tribe. Mount Antero is also the continent's top source of aquamarine, a pale blue cousin of emeralds. Mt. Antero has been attracting gemologists in search of aquamarine since the 1880s. The prized gem's presence on Antero is the reason there's a Jeep trail to just shy of 14,000 feet. And avoiding that Jeep trail is also why we'd decided to take a non-standard route to this peak. Our approach from Little Browns Creek added an extra six miles to bag Antero compared to the standard route.

I had heard of the stories of amateur rockhounds finding lucrative crystals of aquamarine on this mountain. I wasn't greedy, I just wanted to find one tiny speck of aquamarine that I could turn into homemade cuff links.

My pal Patrick, who finished the 14ers the year prior, and I didn't leave Denver until after 5 p.m., which got us hiking around 7:30 p.m. from the trailhead. But night hiking didn't bother us, we'd do a couple of miles, set up camp and be that much closer to finishing the Sawatch Range the next day. About 30 minutes after turning on our headlamps, we noticed an auburn glow shining on our backs as we hiked west. We must have missed another group camped near the trail with a campfire giving off a warm, orange glow. We hiked five more minutes, and I turned around again. The campfire was somehow getting bigger. But it wasn't a campfire at all. It was a giant full moon cresting the horizon and casting those long San Isabel National Forest shadows. We were soon able to turn off our headlamps and hike by full moon light. We briefly discussed hiking the whole 14er at night instead of setting up a tent, but after stopping for dinner, our muscles stiffened, and we decided to pitch the tent and get up at 4 a.m. to enjoy the tail end of the full moon.

I spent most of the hike staring at my feet scanning the rock for any blue sparkles. We made the summit by 8 a.m. and after a nice summit nap, I continued my search for aquamarine on the descent. Then around 11,200 feet, I found some blue!

I had already envisioned how the aquamarine would fit into customized stainless steel cuff links!

My heart beating even harder than it normally beats at elevation, I turned to show Pat.

But he didn't give me the look I was hoping for. He paused with a smirky smile. He didn't want to hurt my feelings, but he also couldn't stop himself from laughing at me. Patrick then collected himself and delicately informed me, "that's just a piece of an old tire."

Dang it!

The rubbery feel and tire tread were dead giveaways, but it did have a blue tint to it. Therefore, I wasn't completely crazy. I blame the lack of sleep on my mental blunder.

No 14er gem cufflinks to wear at the next wedding for me. The real gem was the laughter and memory of thinking the tire piece was a rare jewel. This experience wasn't just about the physical accomplishment, but rather, the people and connections. I noticed the Colorado Trail was similar.

Another four miles after the Little Brown's Creek Trail Junction was the official halfway point at mile 243. I kept a close eye on the FarOut app as we approached that milestone, but tucked in the trees it wasn't really a picturesque spot. Still, I was now officially closer to Durango than I was to Denver.

We knocked out the 12 miles to the Angel of Shavano Trailhead by midafternoon.

The day before my family were trail angels at Cottonwood Pass. Now we were waiting for our trail angels at the Angel of Shavano Trailhead.

"Trail Angel of Shavano" would be a before-and-after, which is a Jeopardy category that has players mash up two terms, with the end of the first answer starting the beginning of the second. For example, clue: Harry Potter's godfather's power tool company would be Sirius Black and Decker (Sirius Black plus Black and Decker).

In this case the clue would be "Thru-hiker helper and Sawatch 14er Snow feature."

The Angel of Shavano refers to the snow feature on the 14er Mt. Shavano's southeast slopes that looks like an angel with arms and wings. The tale goes that a Ute princess went to the base of the mountain to pray for water to deal with the drought and help her starving people. Responding to the prayer, the god demanded she make a sacrifice. Her body appears every spring upon the mountain slowly melting and providing the valley with the much-needed water.

We often make up before-and-after questions to distract us on long 14er backpacking trips. It's a great way to pass the mileage. Often, we require one of the answers be a Colorado 14er name.

So "Highest 14er and Sesame Street pair" would be "Mt. Elbert and Ernie." It's another example of how your hiking partners can make the hike. The title of this book is a before-and-after.

We had timed a meeting with my mom and aunt perfectly — had they driven to the Angel of Shavano Trailhead instead of the Shavano Trailhead.

I had sketched a map of Highway 285 and the appropriate turn offs to get to the Angel of Shavano Trailhead for my mom to follow. Although the Shavano Trailhead and Angel of Shavano Trailhead are two miles apart, it takes about an hour on the slow-traveling, circuitous dirt roads.

"Didn't you follow the map I made you?" I said in a tone that might well have been "What are you, an idiot?"

"OK, I'll see you in an hour." I snapped.

As we sat in the shade waiting for my mom and aunt to arrive, we did our seventh RAT.

As we were finishing up our RAT in the shade spot, the trail delivered an instantaneous reminder of the empathetic person it was molding me into and how I didn't measure up to that with the irritation I showed my mom. Right then, a gal hiked by who quickly put things into perspective.

"Do you know which way I go for the Shavano Falls?" she asked.

She was there that day to spread the ashes of her mother at a spot on the trail where they had memories together. We learned that the north fork of the Arkansas River makes a sharp turn through a canyon and creates a picturesque waterfall not too far from where we sat.

Holy Shit Karma, that was right on the nose.

I had no deadline, I had no rush, I had no need to snap at my mom on the phone and make her feel bad for not following my directions. I was in default mode from my pre-trail world in which I was overly judgmental of someone not following my detailed instructions.

We had a great "half time" during our days in Buena Vista. It was time to put those full packs on with a week's worth of food and began the second half. We wouldn't get resupplied until we reached Lake City — 95 miles down the trail.

After saying goodbye to our trail crew, we slowed our pace in the late afternoon. As the trail leaves the trailhead, it climbs 600 feet over the next 1.5 miles. It was slow-going, but we had no reason to hurry. I got reacquainted with the thoughts in my head.

In a world full of distractions, where tech companies actively mine for our attention, people are losing their ability to be alone with their thoughts. Researchers found that people would rather inflict pain on themselves than explore their own thoughts. A study put participants in a room with no phones, no other people, no devices to distract them. There was only a chair, table and a button that, when pressed, delivered a painful shock to the participant. You had two choices: face down boredom and spend time thinking or inflict pain on yourself through a shock to kill time. Two-thirds of men and one-fourth of women chose to shock themselves rather than sit with their thoughts for 15 minutes[29].

I notice this when I need to half listen to a podcast to fall asleep. On the trail I never once needed a podcast to fall asleep. My thoughts and I were friends before sleep on the trail. Long distance endurance athletes purposefully are now training without headphones so they can train their capacity to be alone in their own heads while they simultaneously train their legs.

A long distance thru-hike will force you to come to terms with your inner voice. Which is what I was doing in the afternoon on Segment 14 of the CT.

What was I doing snapping at Mom on the phone? She flew across the country to help my hike, and I yelled at her for taking a wrong turn?

I wondered if my town days had reverted a part of me back to my pre-trail self. I had very few regrets on this adventure, but that interaction was one of them. I realize I avoid my feelings in my off-trail life. On the trail I have all day to get acquainted with them.

Why was it so hard to look my mom in the eyes and tell her how much her being in Colorado meant to me?

My mom was the reason I had the strength to do something like the Colorado Trail. Whether it was sewing a beret to dress as a mime for spirit week at High school or building a speaker box for my subwoofers for my first car, my mom instilled in me a notion that I could do anything with enough research and perseverance.

Our destination was another five miles down the trail to Cree Creek which would cap off a 17-mile day with 2,900 feet of elevation gain.

It felt good to get back into the aloneness of the trees. I had hours of alone time on the trail each day, but in BV, back in town, I didn't. Like an iPhone that didn't get plugged in overnight, I felt like I was on low battery. Returning to my hours of solitude, strolling through the trees, my mind began to resettle. I began to recharge. I felt more like Nugget again. Soaking my feet in the chilly water of Cree Creek that evening, I began to understand what Mud Slide and Sonic (the CDT couple that eschewed a night in Breckenridge) meant by how they felt more at home in the forest than in town.

<u>Clues for RAT Quiz #7</u>
Eye, tickled, slip
Wind, puppet, monkey
Pillow, town, fall
Coffee, bag, magic
Note, food, river

Fishing, flat, line
Fall, second, trade
Line, floor, hall
Night, mother, house
Boat, knot, up

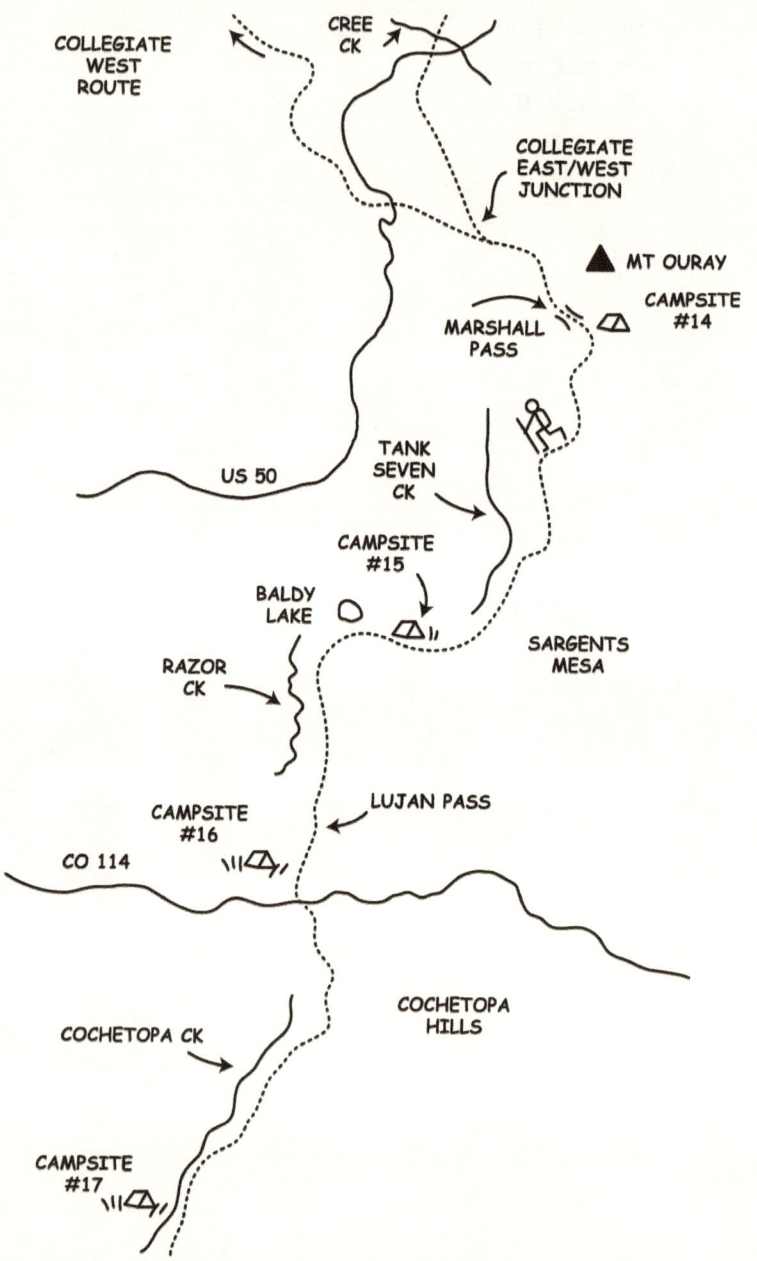

COLLEGIATE
WEST
ROUTE

CREE
CK

COLLEGIATE
EAST/WEST
JUNCTION

▲ MT OURAY

CAMPSITE
#14

MARSHALL
PASS

US 50

TANK
SEVEN
CK

CAMPSITE
#15

BALDY
LAKE

SARGENTS
MESA

RAZOR
CK

CAMPSITE
#16

LUJAN PASS

CO 114

COCHETOPA
HILLS

COCHETOPA CK

CAMPSITE
#17

CHAPTER FIFTEEN:

Blue Light

W aking up next to Cree Creek, I knew that Marshall Pass was the goal for my 20th day on the trail. From the campsite, Bad Foot and I had a mile to finish up in Segment 14, which ends as the trail crosses Highway 50. Segment 15 then runs for 14.3 miles while gaining 3,500 feet between Highway 50 and the Marshall Pass trailhead.

As usual, Bad Foot was up and out of camp ahead of me. With a steep climb on itinerary, I'd be able to catch up quickly.

Less than a mile into my day, I ran into a couple hiking toward me.

"Are you hiking the CT?" I asked.

"Yes we are."

"Northbound?"

"Well . . . kinda."

"Kinda?"

"We got on the trail on Segment 2 and hiked south to Marshall Pass, then we decided to turn around and head back north toward Breckenridge," they told me.

They were the walking definition of "enjoying the ride," I learned. The married couple were triple crowners of thru-hiking — they had completed the Appalachian Trail, the Pacific Crest Trail and the Continental Divide Trail — an accomplishment that I found so very impressive. They went by "No Trace" and "Unbreakable."

What was most striking about them was their lack of goals or a discernable destination. Their objective was to enjoy the trail, whether that was hiking north or south or doubling back over the parts of the CT that they had been on several times.

Hiking for the hiking's sake without external goals seems anathema to the culture I see today. It seems everything is done for the social media likes now.

It changes how we experience the outdoors.[30] I found a 2018 study that drove home the point for me. In the study, participants were divided into three groups: one group was asked to document an experience to share on social media, one group was assigned to document for themselves, and the third group didn't make any documentation.

The results were clear. Both groups that had to document the experience were much worse at remembering details of the event. Put differently: using social media to preserve the events hinders our ability to remember the very events we are trying to preserve.

Is a photo worth it if we can't actually remember the experience?

Where the study got more interesting was when they tested engagement and enjoyment. If the documenters were curating the experience for others — which meant viewing it as a source of connection and community, that enhanced their experience and their enjoyment. The negative side of documentation occurred when subjects worried about what others would think of their posts. Worrying about being compared to others on social media harmed their enjoyment.

So doing something to promote yourself on social media hurts your experience. Doing something like an update on the trail's conditions or a trip report to offer information to the hiking community helps your experience. Doing it for the "gram" is bad, doing it to share beta with other hikers is good use of technology in nature.

So as a social media user I've learned to ask myself, "Am I doing it to promote myself? For the likes and dopamine? Am I solely focused on the final destination instead of the journey?"

In other words, "What would Unbreakable and No Trace do (WWUANTD)?"

After saying goodbye to the triple crowners, I made my way to the top of the ridge as the trail crosses under a powerline. The view from there felt like a watershed moment, a momentous dividing point, where land divides the flow of different rivers.

The day before we crossed the halfway point of the CT, but that spot didn't have any striking transition like the view I had now, delineating the next phase of the trail. Here, you have 500 feet to drop to reach Highway 50 which revealed great views to my right of the highway as it snakes up Monarch Pass among the powerful round ridges and alluvial fan toes like broad gravel aprons that are characteristic of the Sawatch Range.

Twenty days into my hike, I stood under those powerlines and looked at the trail ahead of me, marveling at the notion that 252 miles behind me was the trailhead. Behind me was Twin Lakes, Leadville, Breckenridge, Copper Mountain. I'd come over the Kenosha, Georgia, Searle and Kokomo Passes already. Ahead of me were the rugged San Juan Mountains and the Weminuche Wilderness and the most remote and isolated stretch of the Colorado Trail. Ahead of me, 234 miles, was Durango.

Looking across the highway, the views intimidate you with the 3,400 feet of gain between the Highway 50 crossing and the top of the ridge at 11,922 feet. You could walk every stair to the top floor of the Empire State Building twice and you'd still be 900 feet short of the elevation I had in front of me.

The stroll downhill was very pleasant, but in the back of my head I knew that every easy downhill step must be re-traced uphill only a few miles later. The trail follows roads for about three miles before crossing South Fooses Creek where it turns back into single-track. The elevation plot for this seg-ment goes from up to up and upper — 8.6 miles of steady uphill slogging to reach the crest of the Continental Divide.

And the steepest grade is saved for the very end of the climb. That last mile gains 800 feet — twice as steep as my 400-foot-per-mile rule of thumb. That's a 15% grade.

You know those bright yellow roadsides warning trucks about the steep grade ahead? Those signs typically mark highways when they reach a grade of only 5%. So, the march up this section is basically three times steeper than the limit that warns drivers imposed by the U.S. Interstate Highway system.

I wonder what a trail grade warning sign would look like?

Instead of smoking a truck's brakes, this was smoking my quads. And even worse, a total of 668 feet of that vertical gain comes in the last half mile — one of the steepest half-mile stretches on the CT.

In addition to the steepness, there was also the heaviness of my pack. This being the longest stretch between resupply points, I had six days of food weighing it down.

At the top of the climb up Fooses Creek is a route that Bi-cycling Magazine named as one of the top five mountain bike rides in the country: the Monarch Crest. Mountain bikers can get a shuttle to its top and drop 3,000 feet headed back to Poncha Springs. It's an extremely popular route, especially on weekends. And today was Saturday, so I saw dozens of cyclists.

The same crazy steep 668 feet of vertical gain I was struggling to come up, the mountain bikers about to drop down Fooses were struggling to start. Each of the bikers had to psych themselves up to drop in — like children who stalled on the edge of their first attempt to jump from the highest diving board at the neighborhood pool.

Gaining the top of the divide was the most satisfying moment of the day. The joke that Bad Foot had told me earlier fully made sense on the top of the ridge.

"A man comes across a guy banging his head on a brick wall. When asked why he's banging his head, the other guy responds, 'Because it feels so good when I stop.'"

Stopping here for a break and taking in the views is a must. You are given unobstructed views in every direction with three mountain ranges in sight — the Sawatch, San Juan and Sangre de Cristo.

While having a snack, two CDT hikers joined me on the ridge, Baby Grand and Rex. They were still talking about their first-place trivia victory from their night at the Lake City Brewery Company.

"I still am amazed you knew that Betty White and Drew Barrymore were the oldest and youngest hosts of SNL," Rex said.

Baby Grand and Rex wouldn't drop down the steep section I just came up — that was part of the Collegiate East Route. The CDT shares the trail with the Collegiate West Route. The top of this ridge was the junction. This was also the first instance where dirt bikes were allowed to share the trail.

With all the elevation gain out of the way in the morning, the next six miles to Marshall Pass and the end of the segment was extremely picturesque and enjoyable. The trail provides multiple stunning angles of Mount Ouray (named after the

Ute Chief) and two neighboring peaks: Chipeta Mountain (Ouray's wife) and Pahlone Peak (Ouray's son). At 13,961 feet, Mount Ouray is one of the tallest 100 mountains in Colorado (but not a 14er, so it doesn't get the love that it deserves). It's a cool mountain. The broad side of Mount Ouray's hump provides a wide canvas for the setting Colorado sun to cast its glow. And from our campsite that night, it felt like we had front row seats for the show.

It was like I was at a drive-in movie theater with my family, except the big screen was replaced with the broad side of Mount Ouray. "The Terminator" (last movie I can remember seeing in a drive-in) was replaced with the tremendous rosy light of the setting Colorado sun, and my family was replaced with my tramily.

First there was Connie whose originally solo truck-camping site soon had an extra five inhabitants. Bad Foot, Sketcher, Nugget, Miss Fit and Miss Fit's friend, Chris, all enjoyed the view.

We'd first met Sketcher four days earlier near the Avalanche Trailhead outside of Buena Vista. We'd met Miss Fit earlier that day. She was segment hiking a portion of the trail. Her friend Chris drove up Marshall Pass to camp with her for the night. Chris provided us with a charging station to fully power up our electric devices for the five-day stretch we had ahead of us.

We sat in a circle, the hikers leaning up against tree trunks and Connie sitting on her Toyota Tacoma tailgate.

Connie, excited to hear trail stories, was like a conversation maestro, giving everyone in the circle a chance to contribute.

"What about you, Bad Foot?"

"What do you think about that, Sketcher?"

"How has your week on the trail been, Miss Fit?"

An additional testament to the instant camaraderie granted to you on the trail was how quickly everyone at the camp site that night became best buds. Bad Foot was telling us about his plans to canoe down the entirety of the Mississippi River after he finished the Colorado Trail, when Chris (whom we'd only known for about 47 minutes) decided she would try to join Bad Foot for a week canoeing the Big Muddy. *Where else but the trail would something like that happen?*

It reminded me of the confusion and awe that you see on people's faces in towns when they are shocked to learn that they are in the company of hikers who've only just recently met.

"Wait, you didn't start the trail together?" they'd ask.

"Nope, we actually just met two days ago," I'd say.

"Really? You act like you are lifelong friends."

"Yep! That's the magic of the trail."

Since Connie had hiked the Colorado Trail back in 1996, I was keen on asking for her best advice for thru-hikers.

"Process your feelings about finishing the trail a day or two before the final day," Connie said as her eyes filled with memories from 16 years before, "You'll get more clarity and inspiration if you do it before then."

After a day of 16 miles of hiking and 3,600 feet of elevation gain, I was barely able to make a note of Connie's bit of wisdom, how intentional she bad been about pulling everyone into conversation, and how I wanted to be more like her in my journal before I fell asleep under a cloudless sky.

Sketcher and Bad Foot were already gone when I emerged from my tent to start heating up the water for my coffee on my 21st day on the trail. I ate my oatmeal while admiring the view of Mt. Ouray and charted out the water sources for the day. The next stretch would be the driest segments of the entire trail. I filled my water bottles to the brim from the jugs that Chris drove up to the Marshall Pass Trailhead. The next available water source was 11 miles down the trail where it crossed Tank Seven Creek.

The morning's sun seemed hotter than usual as I tried to conserve my limited water.

About halfway to that creek and five miles into my day, I caught up with Sketcher. True to her trail name, she was sitting along the path with her sketch book spread out. She used her pad as a journal to deposit a daily drawing and hai-ku poetry.

Looking over her shoulder, I could see her sketch of the most prominent feature on the trail that morning, which was the beauty of a Sawatch Range 13er called Antora Peak.

I was able to catch up with Bad Foot just before lunch at Tank Seven Creek — named after the railroad steam engine fill spot. Because this was the last fully reliable water source for another 15 miles, we decided to cook our dehydrated meals for the day while we had access to water instead of saving them for dinner. Our plan for the evening was a new one for me: dry camping, making camp away from a water source. Which necessitated a big lunch and eating the water-less lunch supplies for dinner.

While digging into some teriyaki chicken dehydrated meal, a mountain biker with a thick Southern accent hopped off his bike to enjoy a rest beside us. He was from Virginia and went by the trail name *Shade Patch*.

"Why do they call you Shade Patch?" I inquired.

"Because I like to take frequent breaks along the trail. I bike through the sunny parts and rest at all the shady ones."

I like that philosophy: enjoy the ride and take full advantage of every shade patch.

While we were eating our lunch, Sketcher arrived at the river crossing. With a long dry stretch ahead of her, Sketcher decided to camp near Tank Seven Creek for the evening.

Bad Foot and I said our goodbyes as we made our way up the trail toward Sargents Mesa and the start of Segment 17 of the CT.

As if on cue, some rain clouds moved in on us in the afternoon. The light drizzle was a small price to pay for the cloud's shade on this arid stretch.

Bad Foot and I made camp in a flat spot where the CT meets the Big Bend Trail. That completed three full weeks on the trail. The day's effort was 18 miles and 3,300 feet of elevation gain.

I journaled in the last bit of daylight I had left. One of the ideas I listed in my gratitude section of the daily journal was "cloud cover on a dry section" and "rain clouds provide awesome pictures."

As I was journaling, I sipped my sleepy time tea. I had budgeted eight ounces of water at dry camp for my evening tea. This still left me a liter of water for the morning and the eight miles to cover before the next water source.

Then like clockwork, it got dark, and my body said, "It's time for sleep." At this point in my hike, I was on a natural caveman-like sleep rhythm: up at sunrise, down at sunset, which helps explain why "hiker midnight" is around 9 p.m.

You'd think that after sleeping on the ground and waking up at 5:45 a.m, I'd be waking up feeling groggy. But I wasn't. The reason I was waking up feeling alert, optimistic and grogginess-free had a lot to do with when and how much light my eyeballs were absorbing each day. On the trail I was absorbing direct sunlight as soon as I woke and avoiding artificial light after dark. Too much artificial light at night tricks our brains into thinking it's day light, screwing up our sleep-wake cycle.

Most days off the trail, I don't get direct sunlight right when waking. But what's worse is all the artificial light I absorb, particularly from screens, after the sun goes down[31]. And that screws up the sleep chemicals in your body: adenosine and melatonin.

Adenosine induces sleep and accumulates in the brain the longer you are awake — the more of it that builds up, and the greater the need is to sleep. Physical activity, like walking 18 miles a day, increases adenosine.[32] A good workout is a prescription for insomnia.

The other chemical, melatonin — the hormone that makes us sleep — is produced in conditions of darkness. Light is the top cue for the circadian rhythm. Light regulates the production of melatonin.

But too much artificial light before bedtime explains why I wake up feeling groggy off the trail even though I'm waking much later. All the artificial light we flood our eyeballs with after dark causes a delay in our melatonin production. As this production starts later, it lasts longer in the morning. When your melatonin production is still going when your alarm sounds at 7:30 a.m., you feel groggy. Simply put, stop watching Netflix at 1 a.m. if you want to stop waking up groggy.

I wasn't messing with screens at night on the trail, which meant my body started producing the sleep chemical much earlier, and it was out of my system before I woke up at sunrise[33].

The good news is that a couple days camping can help you get on a healthy sleep cycle[34]. So, a weekend camping trip can reset you closer to a natural circadian rhythm and promote sleep (as long as your nose isn't in your phone in the tent Googling, "ways to enjoy nature.")[35].

What's the takeaway for when you're off the trail? First, get outside early in the morning, which increases your natural light exposure during the day, particularly in the morning (five minutes right away can do the trick[36]). And second, limit the amount of artificial light you absorb after the sun goes down. This means avoid looking at screens one to two hours before bed. Both of which were much easier to do on the trail[37].

It can also help produce melatonin by diming the lights in your home as it approaches bedtime to avoid the amount of energy your eyes absorb. This is why you should use your red light setting on your headlamp at night when you're ready to nod off. Red light has long wavelengths around 670 nanometers. Blue light, on the other hand, has shorter wavelengths around 450 nanometers. Red light has a lower frequency, longer wavelength and less energy than blue light. Off the trail, I read for at least 30 minutes most nights to the red light of my headlamp. It seems like a hack because my body is getting ready for sleep but I'm also productive. Reading a traditional book instead of an e-book helps sleep as well.[38]

If you want to fix your sleep problems, you could do worse than trying a thru-hike. The routine, the natural light, the lack of service and with it the inability to watch shows on your phone, the exercise — they all increase your ability to sleep. Your list of problems might include blisters, but it likely won't include trouble dozing off. In the off-trail world I complain of restless sleep because I can't "turn my mind off." Blue light tricks your body into staying in alert mode, but the natural light of the setting sun gives a different message. It says, "the day is over, it is time to rest." In my tent on the trail, I had no trouble welcoming sleep.

I was surprised how little I used my head lamp on the trail. On weekend 14er trips, I'm not going to bed until after 11 p.m., and we're hiking before the sun rises to be off the summit before the afternoon thunderstorms roll in. This means there are plenty of hours of headlamp usage. Once I got on the caveman rhythm — up and down with the sun — I hardly used my light. Most nights, I'd use the last remaining daylight to write in my journal before I closed my eyelids.

Which I did that night.

CHAPTER SIXTEEN:

Between Cathedrals

As the beginning of my fourth week on the Colorado Trail began, the first task of the day was to make it the eight miles from our dry camp location to Razor Creek. This was best done in the cool morning hour. I was packed up and moving down the trail by 6:20 a.m. Bad Foot had a 30-minute head start on me that morning.

Sipping my coffee completely alone in the remote woods, I realized I was oddly calm. At the start of the trail, I was worried about being alone in the woods. Now, I was used to it. Fear of the unknown subsides as you gain confidence on the trail.

Several miles into my morning, I crossed an intersection where the trail detours off down to Baldy Lake. An alternative to dry camping through this section like we did, is side tracking down to Baldy. The lake is a half mile and 400 feet of elevation below the trail. Some hikers take the detour to pitch their tents around Baldy Lake. And some thru-hikers opt to camp right at the junction and hike their water bottles down to the lake without a full pack on their shoulders, which was what the group of three female hikers had done the previous night. They were eating their breakfast when I passed through at 7:20 a.m.

Three hours of strolling later and I got to Razor Creek. The water source crosses the CT at a clearing in the trees. There was a slight trickle of water meandering through the green grass tufts. Thirty yards up the hill in the dell, I was able to find a small flow of water no wider than the mouth opening on my Smartwater bottle.

I ran the water through my Sawyer Squeeze Filter. Water filters work by pushing dirty water through micro-tubes that are smaller than 0.1 microns. They prevent 99.9% of bad stuff from getting through. Hence, they are super effective, but only if the water goes through the filter.

But.

The white O-ring on my filter had been falling off as I had been filtering water throughout the past week. The leaky O-ring allowed a few droplets to bypass the filter. And that's exactly what happened here on Day 22 of my journey. I can't quite say "unknowingly" because I had a sneaking suspicion based on the smell and taste of the water (it smelled like a barn yard), but I had lit the fuse to a ticking time bomb in my gut that would begin to cause havoc the next day.

As I was eating an early lunch, breaking through the trees and joining me at Razor Creek were two female hikers: "Legs" and "Bangs." Appropriately, Legs was the tall one and Bangs, well, was the one with bangs. They were two of the three women I had seen at the Baldy Lake trail junction three hours earlier. Bad Foot also caught up to us and joined us for an early lunch.

After lunch and the story of how they had met teaching for AmeriCorps, I packed up my gear and said, "I'll see you at Lujan Creek!" as I departed down the trail away from Bad Foot, Bangs and Legs.

Bangs and Legs were puzzled by what seemed to them as me ditching Bad Foot, my hiking companion. They spent every moment together on the trail. They shared meals and a tent. They walked six feet apart on the trail and slept about a foot apart. The thought of not having my own space, not having hours of solitude for myself each day on the trail made me cringe.

If you told most people that you hike the trail with so-and-so, they would assume that you spent every waking moment with that hiker. But this is way off. A tramily moves together each day but might spend eight hours separate from each other. This was the dynamic that I experienced on the trail.

For example, Bad Foot would get up about 45 minutes before I did; he'd be packed up and leaving camp by 6 a.m., while I would emerge from my tent at the time he was departing. I'd make coffee and enjoy the morning air. You can have solitude for hours and hours on the trail, but you know you'll reconnect with your trail family before day's end. Each evening you have someone to share dinner with, chat about your day, and complain about the dearth of switchbacks (If you are like Bad Foot.)

Several miles will come between your tramily members throughout the day, but by dinner time, hikers will find themselves back in the company of their Trail Family. If you ever feel disconnected, your tramily knows what you're going through. This dynamic gives thru-hikers tremendous amounts of solitude, but also the safety of a group at night.

With Bad Foot's morning head starts, I'd usually catch him before lunch. Then I'd spend the afternoon ahead of him on the trail. When he would catch up to me, he would always ask, "How long have you been waiting?" and every time I'd say, "Oh about five minutes," whether it had actually been five minutes or 50.

This dynamic also highlights the uniqueness of the thru-hiking. In what other scenario is it appropriate to completely ditch your traveling partner for half a day? But with thru-hiking, you know they are headed on the same trail in the same direction, and you'll find them eventually but you don't know when. So, each day your hours of solitude might surprisingly end with seeing your good hiking buddy filtering water at the next river around the corner of the trail. It's a welcomed surprise every time.

Bad Foot and I developed a bit of a schtick each night as we looked at the FarOut map to plan the next day's camp site and mileage.

"Hey, Bad Foot," I'd ask, "What are you thinking we should do the next day?"

"I think I'll wake up and walk in a southwesterly direction tomorrow," he'd say.

"I think that's a good idea. How else will we get to Durango?"

At five minutes before noon, I started jogging up the trail. I was trying to get exactly 11 miles before noon, but I came up just short. My GPS had me at 10.9 miles when the clock hit noon. Bad Foot and I had a goal of getting 10 miles by noon each day. It was our "10 by 12" goal. I learned that such a goal was common among thru-hikers. When we asked one CDT hiker how he hikes 30 miles a day over and over, he told us, "If you can get 10 by 10 a.m., then anything is possible for your day."

In the early afternoon at the last high point of my day, I took a rest when a hiker appeared from the other direction on the trail. He had no phone and one book in his possession.

"Are you hiking the Colorado Trail?" I asked. "I'm Nugget."

"I'm Santiago, and yes, I'm using the Colorado Trail as part of my pilgrimage," he tells me.

He was using the Colorado Trail for part of a journey that had started at a cathedral in Santa Fe and would end at a cathedral in Denver. The sole book he carried was the Bible. Sincerity and authenticity seemed to pour out of him.

That encounter with Santiago left a deep impression on me. Santiago was like a social magnet, effortlessly drawing me in with his warm demeanor and inviting presence. His body language was open and relaxed, making me feel instantly welcomed. He maintained steady eye contact, listening attentively to every word I shared about my hike. In those moments, I felt genuinely valued and heard.

Reflecting on that brief interaction, I realize the profound lesson Santiago taught me about the power of presence in conversations. It's about more than just words — it's about adopting an open posture, uncrossing your arms, making sincere eye contact and truly listening without thinking ahead to what I would say next. These small gestures create a meaningful connection that goes beyond superficial interactions.

Those 10 minutes with Santiago linger in my memory. I found myself wishing we could have talked longer, sharing more stories as we both journeyed towards our destinations. I was happy to offer him advice about the upcoming trail conditions as he headed north toward Denver's cathedral.

Santiago's presence reminded me of the importance of slowing down, engaging authentically with others, and treasuring those moments of genuine connection. His quiet magnetism and genuine interest in people are qualities I strive to cultivate in my own interactions, hoping to make others feel as valued and heard as he made me feel that day.

The last four miles of Segment 17 of the CT go downhill, giving my afternoon a pleasant stroll. I also stopped along this section of the trail and gathered small rocks to spell out "300" where the trail was officially 300 miles from the start.

That evening, Bad Foot and I shared our camp site with Legs, Bangs and German Mountain Goat — not to be confused with the Mountain Goat who lived in Salida from earlier on the trial. Around the campfire, we introduced the women to our Remote Association Tests.

Before bed, I gave our camping companions a warning before they headed back to their tents: "If you suddenly hear someone yell out in the middle of the night a seemingly random word, it's just Bad Foot excited that he came up with the RAT answer that we haven't been able to solve. This happened the other night when my head popped off my pillow to Bad Foot yelling 'Magic! Magic Carpet!' "

"Don't be ruining my sleep over a RAT game," Bangs joked.

I felt much more relaxed on my third day back in the wilderness after my town days in Buena Vista. In the gratitude section of my nightly journal, the list of things I was thankful for that day concluded with "people like the priest I met today who are fully present."

The following morning, I was the last one out of camp. Bad Foot, Bangs, Legs and German Mountain Goat had already set off down the dirt road toward Highway 114 which marks the end of Segment 17. The night downhill stroll starting off the day was a good warm up to a big mile day ahead of me.

The character of the trail of the last two days of ridges above 11,000 feet shifts into the gentle Cochetopa Hills between 9,000 and 10,000 feet.

Opening the gate into the pasture by the highway, I was immediately put on notice that I was entering cattle country. Dozens of cows were within a stone's throw from the trail . . . and one cantankerous and attentive bull. Had I been in an open field that close to a bull, I would have made a retreat, but since the Colorado Trail went through there (I checked to make sure) it somehow made it all right to trudge into the bull's territory. And since I didn't see Bad Foot's jabbed body anywhere, I figured he'd progressed un-gored. Several cows were right on top of the trail that languidly arose and waddled 20 yards away as I passed through.

The bovine made me think back to my third day on the trail hearing cow jokes from Lilly about why cows don't drink milk . . . *because they lactose!*

I wondered how Lilly and her mother were doing. It also made me realize how hiking the trail with new groups every couple of days was like distinct phases, like the trail was conveniently partitioned in chapters. Hiking with Tall Tale and Hairy Potter felt like a few chapters back. Now I was moving with a different bubble of folks, whom I was trying to catch on these flat roads by making killer time on the relatively flat roads of Segment 18.

The first four miles of the segment I covered in an hour. These are dry, flat and expansive miles on jeep roads. Eight miles into my day I caught up with Bangs and Legs. Another mile ahead I leap frogged German Mountain Goat. And 10 miles into my day, I caught up with Bad Foot.

I wonder if 4 mph is too fast for John Muir?

John Muir, co-founder of the Sierra Club and early advocate for the preservation of wilderness in America, used the term "saunter" instead of hike. He even describes the holy etymology of the word: "People ought to saunter in the mountains — not 'hike!' Do you know the origin of the word saunter? . . . Away back in the Middle Ages, people used to go on pilgrimages to the Holy Land, and when people in the villages through which they passed asked where they were going, they would reply, 'A la sainte terre' — 'To the Holy Land.' . . . Now these mountains are our Holy Land, and we ought to saunter through them reverently . . . [39]

Whether I was ambulating, speed walking or sauntering, it was the first day on the trail we got 12 by 12 — that is 12 miles before noon, at which point we diverted off the Jeep roads into a welcome patch of trees to give us a reprieve from the hot Colorado sun. Though this section is lower in elevation, there isn't much tree cover.

"I think we should pull a Shade Patch," I said referencing our southern mountain biker friend we met two days prior, as Bad Foot and I positioned our backpacks as pillows and reclined in the shade.

"Lazy lunches like these were rare on the PCT because you are always trying to do big miles," Bad Foot told me, "But I'm getting better at taking them on this trail."

Bad Foot was slowly erasing that hurry mentality that was too pervasive on his PCT hike. The plan which we devised around the campfire the night before had us camp six miles ahead at what might be a water source. Through this arid section of the CT, streams weren't guaranteed. We got to that spot around 4 p.m. and realized there were no flat spots to camp in.

The next best option was to push another five miles and another 600 feet of elevation and drop down into the valley to camp next to Cochetopa Creek. That's what we decided to do.

Two miles later our pace really slowed in the early evening. It's like our bodies knew we had crossed the 20-mile mark for the day. Luckily the last three miles dropped 700 feet of elevation. At this point the trail makes a swooping left turn, and the valley floor below comes into view along with the snaking Cochetopa river shimmering in the 6 p.m. sunlight. After two days of scarce water sources, the flowing river looked like the Mississippi compared to the rivulets, which required us to use our boil pots to scoop water from.

We set up camp next to a big bend in the Cochetopa Creek. Cochetopa pronounced ko-che-*toh*-puh is the Ute word meaning "pass of the buffalo." It's one of the many features along the Colorado Trail that honors the legacy of the Native American Indian tribes from the area. Those tribes include the Apache, Navajo, Ute, Shoshone, Comanche, Cheyenne, Pawnee, Kiowa and Lakota Sioux. The day before we camped at Marshall Pass in view of Mt. Ouray — named after Chief Ouray of the Tabeguache band of the Ute Tribe.

We'd already hiked by Mt. Antero, named after the chief of the Uintah band of Ute Indians and passed Mt. Shavano, named for the chief of the Tabeguache band of Ute Indians. The 14er Tabeguache Peak isn't too far from the CT as well. Ahead of us, the trail heads through the Weminuche Wilderness (pronounced weh-mih-*noo*-chi, which means "canyon people.") The trail cuts through the La Garita Wilderness. La Garita (la gar-*ee*-tuh) means "look out." Legend says that Indians would use smoke signals across the San Luis Valley, and hence the name was given to a 13er in Saguache County and later the wilderness area.

In addition to Native Americans, the names of the towns, creeks, rivers, mountains, mountain passes, gulches, counties, forests and wilderness areas in Colorado and along the Colorado Trail comes from a handful of unique influences: the Spanish, miners, mountain men, politicians, railroads, ranchers, geological features and the post office[40]!

With their reliance on religious reference, the Spanish Empire, and in turn Mexico, had considerable naming impact in Colorado. The Colorado Trail crosses the Animas River near Silverton. It was initially referred to as the *Rio de las Animas.* ("River of the Souls" in Spanish). We would soon get to San Luis Pass and Molas Pass. Oh yeah, and Colorado comes from Spanish, referring to a reddish-brown color.

The early explorers of Colorado claimed much of the naming rights in Colorado. This category includes surveyors, soldiers, mountain men, ranchers and trappers. Keen to connect the coasts of America via railroads, Congress encouraged and incentivized explorers to head west. You'll most likely recognize the names of the people in charge of the early expeditions. Zebulon Pike led an early trip in 1806. Then you had Major Stephen H. Long leading a trip in 1820, followed by excursions by John C. Fremont and John W. Gunnison. In addition, there were four federally funded exploring and mapping tours occurring between 1869-1879. Many of Colorado's names were first recorded by the likes of the Hayden Survey and the Wheeler Survey. Hayden got his version of a trail name from the Plains Indians who, seeing Hayden digging in the soil, gave him a name that translates as "man who picks up stones running." I like Nugget better.

Many of the early explorers of the remote parts of Colorado territory were drawn in search of beaver pelts, which were sold and used to make felt hats. Luckily for the Colorado beavers, European fashion trends changed from beaver felt hats to silk, likely saving the beaver population. We already hiked by Camp Hale, named after Brigadier Gen. Irving Hale (1861-1930) and camped at Marshall Pass, named after Lieutenant William L. Marshall — a member of the Wheeler Survey.

Prospectors and miners get their own unique influence on the etymology of Colorado. The town of Creede, a trail town, comes from Nicholas C. Creede (1843-1897), a highly successful prospector who found pay dirt in the Holy Moses mine. The town of Fairplay gets its name from the mining community. Legend has it the early miners of Colorado's gold rush in Park County were mistreated by the tricks and deceit of a nearby mining operation. So, they moved down the valley to find another mining camp where there could be, you guessed it, fair play!

Politicians weren't shy to get their names on Colorado features, either, nor was there a shortage of brownnosers ready to curry favor with politicians by suggesting those politicians claim naming rights. For example, Breckenridge was named after John Cable Breckinridge (1821-1975). Well, sort of. Note the different spellings of the name.

When the town was founded by a bunch of miners led by Gen. George E. Spencer, who was from Alabama and wanted to honor another politician from the south, suggested they name the town after the then vice-president, Breckinridge. This was also a subtle move to get a post office in the remote mountain location. Every tiny new up-and-coming town wanted to get an official U.S. Post Office designation, which meant the postal service had considerable say on the names that went on new post offices.

But then the Civil War broke out, and Breckinridge joined and fought for the confederacy. The inhabitants of Breck, who were Unionists, petitioned to change the name. So, they changed one letter. Breckinridge became Breckenridge.

Chaffee County is named after Jerome B. Chaffee (1825-1886), one of the state's first U.S. senators. Mt. Elbert, to which many CT hikers take a detour to climb — being the highest 14er in Colorado — was named after Samuel Hitt Elbert (1833-1899), governor of the Colorado territory and later a Colorado Supreme Court justice.

Namers also drew inspiration from geological features. Although this wasn't always without considerable redundancy. For example, in Colorado there are 72 different Willow Creeks, 49 Bear Creeks, 49 Beaver Creeks and 49 Dry Creeks — the Colorado Trail crosses one of the Dry Creeks and two Pine Creeks (and one Porcu*pine* Creek.)

We ended our day at the only Cochetopa Creek in Colorado after hiking 23 miles. Bangs and Legs also pushed to our spot by the crook in the river. They joined for the second night in a row at our camp site. I recited some cowboy poetry to my mesmerized audience before we crawled into our tents.

"Boy, this valley is spectacular," Bad Foot mentioned. "If it were easily accessible, it would be crawling with campers."

This was the biggest hiking mileage day that the four of us had done so far.

Clues for RAT Quiz #8
False, slide, ladder
Boxing, diamond, leader
Super, cereal, over
Glass, country, fine
Blood, cast, writer
Prime, dance, line
Rope, start, high
Office, hitching, card
Greeting, flash, punch
Plug, elephant, worm

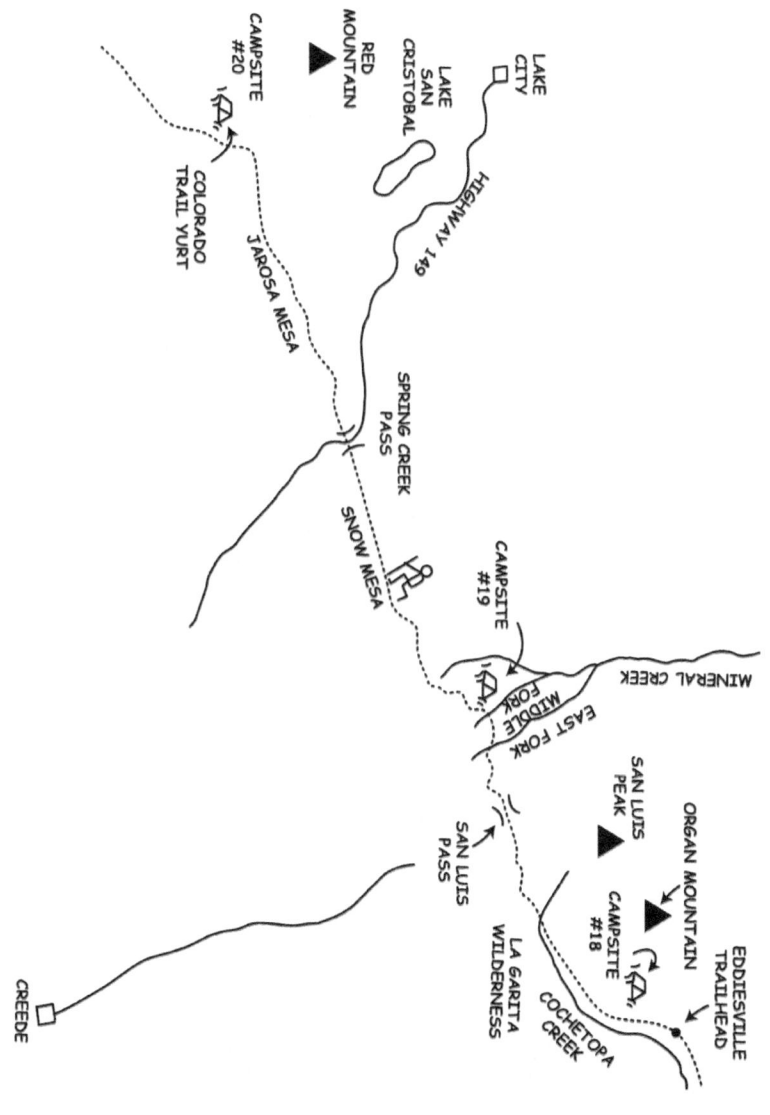

CHAPTER SEVENTEEN:

Beaver Fever

My 24th day on the CT began with a six-mile stroll just east of the Cochetopa through a grassy meadow. It was the type of low-exertion mileage where day-dreaming comes naturally to me, where I'd fall into a trance-like rhythm. It was the perfect start to my morning. Hovering around 10,000 feet, the trail through this section reminded me a bit of the high alpine meadow in the Lost Creek Wilderness from my fourth day.

Come to think it, I realized that part of the trail was a full 20 days and 270 trail miles ago. In that period, I had traversed four other wilderness areas and was about to enter the fifth: the La Garita Wilderness.

I caught up to Bangs and Legs several miles into my morning right about the time when the trail crosses the Co-chetopa. We forded the river together on some shaky logs — only partially soaking our trail runners.

We finished the remaining six miles of Segment 19 by late morning, which put us at the Eddiesville Trailhead. Strolling into the dusty dirt parking circle, we found Bad Foot pulling a "Shade Patch." He was reclining on a boulder under a tree's shadow in the oasis-like patch of grass in the middle of the parking circle.

"Shade-patching sounds like a good idea," I told Bad Foot.

After I availed myself of the latrine at the trailhead, I positioned my backpack under the tree and reclined next to Bad Foot. Because of the extra five miles we had knocked out the day before, we had a light mileage afternoon in front of us. We planned to camp right at tree line where the trail crossed the last water source before heading up to the saddle of San Luis Peak. This meant we only had about seven more miles to hike for the rest of the day to get to that spot.

About 20 minutes into our lounging session, a cloud of dust appeared on the road. It was a pickup truck pulling a horse trailer that deftly negotiated the Eddiesville Trailhead parking lot.

Out jumped a wiry guy in a straw hat with a button snap shirt tucked into wranglers tucked into cowboy boots. He hopped out of the truck, looked us over and introduced himself as Clayton. If we couldn't tell right away that he was a true cowboy from his boots and hat, we could by the bull he had in his trailer.

I liked his style; it declared he was a cowboy. He liked that people knew it, which I could agree with. I like it when people know I am a thru-hiker. No bull, just muddy trail runners.

His job for the day was transporting a bull from one herd to another. At this point in the day, he had completed half of his tasks. He spent the morning corralling that bull. The next step was to drive that bull into the herd that was grazing on public lands that ran alongside Segment 20 of the Colorado Trail. It seemed like a complicated task for one person. Then we got to meet his secret weapons: Brodie and Skinner, his dogs. They, we learned, did most of the corralling.

As Bad Foot described Clayton, "most folks when they wear the cowboy regalia look like Halloween costume-wearing imposters of the Village People, but Clayton . . . he pulled that look off." Maybe it was his lanky, confident, but slow strut.

We had a wonderfully present conversation with Clayton. We asked about life as a cowboy.

"It's long hours for not great pay," Clayton told us, "but look around you: this is my office."

He asked us about life on the trail. He was jealous of our ability to hike for weeks on end. We were jealous of his "office."

Who else gets to saddle a horse, drive a bull into another pasture, deposit some salt licks for the cattle and call it a day?

"How could we help a cowboy out?" we asked, only slightly revealing how much we wanted to be a part of this. Clayton graciously allowed us to assist. He saddled his horse ready to direct the angry bull toward the gate opening. I got to unlatch the gate of the trailer as the bull came charging out.

Right before I swung open the trailer gate, Clayton paused and said, "Hey, if things go sideways with this bull, jump into the bed of my truck — for cover."

Wait, what?

The lumbering bull stormed out of the trailer, but my nerves quickly subsided as it was immediately flanked by Brodie and Skinner. Those dogs had that bull toeing the line straight to the gate that an uneasy (and yet un-gored from yesterday's cattle mingling) Bad Foot held opened. Once through, Bad Foot put the chain back on the big nail to close the gate.

After our brief stint as honorary cowboys, I swear there was extra confidence in our strut — like every step was destined for the horizon (said in cowboy poetry twang) — as we started the next segment of the CT. The start of Segment 20 leaves the Eddiesville Trailhead, crosses Stewart Creek and boomerangs south of Organ Mountain along the Cochetopa

River. I met two CDT hikers headed north this afternoon: Tammy and Toucan, who earned his trail name on the Pacific Crest Trail because he was carrying not one, but two bear canisters (two cans).

Comparatively, the grade of the trail over the next several miles is gentle, particularly compared to some of the terrain we had already come over. But I was zapped. I felt as though someone had Velcroed five-pound weights to each of my ankles. I struggled to choke down any calories. My stomach was rejecting food like a bouncer at a college-town bar during freshman orientation week.

A mile from the trailhead, the trail crosses into the La Garita Wilderness. Sardonically, my friend Pat referred to it as the "La Giardia" Wilderness because the trail's few and far between water sources are also between cow patties. I was acutely aware of that moniker, as my suspicion that I had the gut parasite became more and more likely. The ticking time bomb in my stomach exploded in the early afternoon. It took two full days before the giardia symptoms showed up full bore.

Damn you, Razor Creek!

The next miles felt like some of the toughest of my entire trip even though it was an easy low-grade trail. They were slow miles, and I was the last one to get to our camp spot that night — an open space next to the last stream crossing at 11,747 feet. This was about two miles before the trail climbed to 12,618 feet on the saddle of one of Colorado's 14ers. Our foursome group from the night previous had doubled. Joining Bad Foot, Bangs, Legs and me were German Mountain Goat, and a couple who went by Froggy Legs and Wild Woman and their dog, Winston.

The view from our campsite was filled with vistas of grey trees in a devastated forest. The dead evergreen trees seem to outnumber the living here.

"Isn't it crazy how devasting something the size of a grain of rice can be to a forest?" German Mountain Goat said as she untied her hiking boots to let her feet breath.

I felt the same way, amazed at how one drop of water the size of a pinhead could destroy my entire digestive system.

"Normally, the beetle population is held in check by long cold winters," she explained, "But as the winters are getting warmer and shorter, they aren't sufficient to kill off enough of the beetles to prevent an outbreak."

In addition to her biology knowledge, she had an amazing personal story. Living in California two years prior, she began suffering from some type of auto-immune disease which she believed would abate if she left the humidity of California. So, she moved to the dryer climate of Buena Vista, Colorado. Two years before she could barely hike a single mile. Now she was conquering the 486 miles of the Colorado Trail.

I sat there amazed how making one change can have such an impact on someone's overall life.

Maybe my change was this trail experience? That after this is all over, maybe my life will start to look different?

This 100-mile stretch is the least-traveled part of the CT. It doesn't have any nearby towns convenient for resupply nor does it have cell phone coverage. Which meant no access to the internet for a week — no emails, no social media, no news stories that enrage you and cause you to hold fictious debates in your head with the author. One of my favorite photos from my trip was of this crew laughing and cooking dinner together. No one was distracted by their phones. It felt great.

And I think it had a lot to do with no social media, which makes people more unempathetic, polarized, angry, agitated, frazzled and distracted. It also makes us think in a shallower way, damages our ability to focus, ruins our ability to be still and present.

But we were still and present at our campsite below San Luis Peak. I was far from that anxious and frayed way my brain feels after scrolling on a phone for an hour. During Covid, the strolling was filled with dreary news that they invented a term for it: doom scrolling. When our brains are constantly bombarded with negative images like you see on a Facebook feed, it also destroys our ability to distinguish what's relevant and irrelevant. In other words, it plays havoc with our attention. In her book "Peak Mind," Amishi Jha uses a "Back to the Future" reference to describe what social media does to our attention, writing, " . . . attention morphs into a glitchy DeLorean, hopping through time without intention or control, ruminating on regrets and predicting catastrophes that may never come to pass; it fixates on things that are not productive: it fills up working memory with irrelevant clutter."[41]

The Oxford Dictionary's 2024 word of the year was the trending term "brain rot," which it defined as the "supposed deterioration of a person's mental or intellectual state, especially viewed as a result of overconsumption of material (now particularly online content) considered to be trivial or unchallenging."

The trail is the opposite; it feels like the trail actively clears the clutter. I call it "Boom! Strolling."

Social media uses algorithms whose goal is to show you things that keep you engaged. And unfortunately, what best generates engagement is enragement.

For every word of moral outrage that you add to your tweet, your retweet rate will increase by 20 percent[42]. So adding "blame" or "attack" to your tweet will give you a boost. *That's disgusting.*

Not only does outrage spread easier on social media, the social feedback on emotionally charged posts increase the likelihood of future outrage. It's quite literally making us angrier and meaner. Reward outrage and you'll train people to give you more of it — not unlike Pavlov's dog.[43]

With 24-hour access to social media, we let our inner voice rant. No time to reflect, no compassion, it's just unabated emotional responses. What ever happened to the old saying, "when you are angry count to 10?" Social media has actively thrown that out the window and promoted an environment where anger and outrage rule the day.

So that algorithm, whose sole purpose is to keep you engaged, will inevitably prioritize the things that anger and outrage us. The algorithm favors sensationalist content[44].

To put it simply, I think social media makes us jerks.

It's basically the opposite of what the trail does to you.

Social media teaches us to condemn more. To forget compassion. To act and comment immediately. What's even more insidious is that 24-hour connectivity to social media negates the two tools that help regulate our negative emotions: time and empathy. Empathy is one of the keys to forming connections with others. Time lets us process upsetting experiences. Time allows reflection which helps temper our opinions.

The trail teaches us to understand more. To Listen. To empathize. And to give things time. After thinking about something while you hike six miles, your response is miles different from what your immediate one would be.

At the current moment, my immediate response was, "these noodles are hard to stomach."

I slowly forced down a packet of Ramen Noodles while I was enjoying the group's company. Before I started the trail, I took note of when the full moon would be during my trek, which was tonight. I woke up around midnight to what I thought was someone shining a spotlight on my tent. It was just the moon.

I thought about a few lines of the Robert Service poem, "The Spell of the Yukon," on this full moon night camped below San Luis Peak.

I've watched the big, husky sun wallow
In crimson and gold, and grow dim,
Till the moon set the pearly peaks gleaming,
And the stars tumbled out, neck and crop;
And I've thought that I surely was dreaming,
With the peace o' the world piled on top

I had a professor in graduate school who had a unique quirk when he lectured. While he thought and spoke, he'd raise his arm vertically over his head like he was a student trying to ask a question. Then he'd flap his hand to a 90-degree angle as the cadence of his voice matched his wrist movement.

After watching his quirky lecture posture for four hours a week, I caught myself subconsciously mimicking his arms and wrist doing a conductor impression. Two months into the semester, I was tutoring an Econ 101 student about supply and demand and caught myself leaning back in my chair at the white board in my office with my hand vertically up in the air, while my hand flapped in rhythm to the tempo of my explanation.

Mirror neurons are the reason. Mirror neurons sense then mimic the actions and feelings of someone else. They help explain why emotions and behavior are also contagious. That is, ambient attitudes and actions influence us. Our brains sense subtleties whether they be inflection of the voice, a roll of the eye, slouched posture and these clues quickly prime others to feel the same way. This can happen subconsciously.

This is why you laugh more at a comedy when there are more people in the theater laughing along with you. As you spend several days hiking with someone, you begin to feel in tune with them. The neurons in your brain are actually mirroring your hiking partner. You might be so in sync that your trekking poles swing in rhythm together.

But it works both ways. Negativity can be just as transmissible as positivity. Your tired, pessimistic, negative mindset can just as easily seep into the consciousness of fellow hikers.

Therefore, on my 25th day on the Colorado Trail, I was wondering if my sour attitude was influencing my tramily.

"Yeah, yeah," I muttered to Bad Foot as he was starting up the trail and wishing me a good morning while I was just stumbling out of my tent.

The day would be a shorter mileage day, but those miles were steep and at high elevation. Our goal was only 10 miles down the trail to camp by Middle Mineral Creek, but to get there was 3,000 feet of elevation gain over four different saddles — up and down four times. And most of it was above tree line.

I started the morning off strong — to my surprise — gaining the 860 feet of elevation over the first two miles of the day to the saddle (12,612 feet) of San Luis Peak. Many hikers detour the 1.25 miles and 1,400 feet of elevation to stand on top of the 14er, particularly if they have the energy and good weather. I had neither. I was chock-full of negativity because I was chock-full of giardia. Which also meant I was chock-full of diarrhea.

I had originally believed that San Luis Pass would be on this saddle right beside San Luis Peak. It wasn't. The trail doesn't get to San Luis Pass for four more miles at the very end of Segment 20 where an old sign marks the pass. That was still two up-and-overs away.

If the peak was closer to the Front Range with easier access, the gentle class 1 ascent up San Luis Peak would likely see the same conga-line crowds scurrying up it on weekends that Greys, Torreys and Bierstadt do. Since it's tucked in the San Juans and requires several hours on dirt roads to access the trailhead, it's one of the least-climbed 14ers.

It was on a 14er climbing trip with my buddies Jace and Shawn that I had first-hand experience with the power of one hiker's positive mindset. After a long day above tree line bagging two 14ers — Mt. Wilson and El Diente Peak, we made our way back to our tents. But we couldn't relax yet. We still had to pack up our gear and move camp six miles into neighboring Navajo Basin so we could position ourselves to get the third 14er the next day. Putting 30-pound packs on our back after a long day was challenge enough. That's when the rain came. And a near mutiny came soon afterward. We were in the rain and in a mental low, which made the steep trail up to Navajo Lake miserable.

Not that he necessarily knew about mirror neurons, but Shawn did know a lot about leadership and maintaining a positive affect for the good of the group. (Shawn: "It's just a bit further; the campsite will have a great view." Me: "A view of what, the sideways rain?")

If Shawn hadn't been optimistic and essentially deceptive with his positive comments (even though he later admitted being very negative but did his best to keep the negativity inside for the group's sake), we wouldn't have summited Wilson Peak the next day in fantastic sunny weather. His positivity kept us going.

Fortunately for me on this day of the CT, the role of the positive fellow hiker was being played by Bad Foot. He had me focus on a goal about 25 yards ahead and strive for it. Then take a break and restart the same cycle until we Little-Engine-that-Could-ed it up to the top of the saddle.

I was able to get my tent set up beside a huge beaver pond before the heavy rainstorm came through. Bangs and Legs, who opted to climb San Luis Peak, weren't so lucky. Froggy Legs and Wild Woman camped with us again this night. We enjoyed watching the beavers at work a few dozen yards from our camp site.

"I'd put your trekking poles inside your tent tonight, otherwise you'll wake up and find your walking sticks covered in mud and holding up the next layer of that beaver dam," I snarked.

I was trying to maintain my good humor, but my stomach was nauseous, and I was zapped of energy. All that stair climber training was completely useless against a parasite multiplying in my intestines. I felt powerless.

I sent a message through my Garmin Inreach to Ed about my bout with giardia and how low I felt. I was yearning for my mom's homemade chicken noodle soup, a staple growing up when we were sick. The best thing I had was a packet of chicken Ramen Noodles, which I barely choked down. It was not even close to the 4,000 calories I was burning each day.

Then I laid in my tent admiring the beaver ponds and worrying about my strength to make it the final 10 miles into Lake City tomorrow morning. Twenty minutes later, my In-Reach made a little jingle with an incoming message. It was from Ed. The message increased my appreciation for Ed's friendship and humor. The message harkened back to a comment I made to him in Leadville when he was feeling upset about mistakenly only booking one night at Airbnb and subsequently getting kicked out. It read:

"It'll eventually become a good story!"

CHAPTER EIGHTEEN:

Cannibal

The first thing I did when I woke on my 26th day on the Colorado Trail was to check and see that no one's trekking poles had become a permanent addition to the impressive beaver dam next to our tents.

They hadn't.

"Those carbon fiber trekking poles would be a great leg for our beaver coffee table," the beaver leader would be thinking.

I figured that the beavers had performed a reconnaissance mission that night and were currently laying plans to siege our poles the next evening under cover of darkness.

Then I had three additional thoughts:

1) We outsmarted you, beaver! We will be in Lake City tonight.

2) Why am I arguing, in my own head, with a talking dark-ops beaver?

3) Does giardia mess with your brain?

We had bolted out of our camp spot by 5:45 a.m. The morning clouds were eerily dark, which was especially worrisome since Snow Mesa stood between us and Lake City. And between me and some antibiotics.

Snow Mesa has a 3.3-mile very flat stretch with no bailout abilities. Which means it is not the place you want to be during a thunderstorm. Unlike a mountain ridge from which you can quickly drop elevation if needed, being on the mesa is like a flea being at the center of a kitchen table with no quick way to get to the edge and get lower. It was as though someone clicked, "delete all physical features," when designing this section of Colorado. No trees, no discernable rocks, no real distinguishable features except a single-track trail beelining across the level tundra.

There's a feeling of complete seclusion and desolation on Snow Mesa. The uncharacteristically flat section does, however, provide awesome views of the Uncompahgre Peak. It's as though the trail on the mesa is aiming right one of my favorite 14ers in the distance.

Despite the gray clouds when we broke camp, Bad Foot and I were lucky to cross the mesa in decent conditions. An hour into our morning, the clouds cleared for a nice weather window. But that wasn't the case for Spoons, a red-headed college gal whom we'd meet the next day in Lake City. She threw down her pack, pulled out her tent's footprint and ran for a small trench in which she'd wait out the electrical storm. The trench couldn't have gotten the Emory student more than 20 feet lower from the surrounding ground, but at least it got her from being the highest thing on the mesa. She lived to tell us her story.

Five miles into our morning, I had to ask Bad Foot an awkward question.

"Can I borrow some toilet paper?"

"*Borrow?*" asked Bad Foot. "Like you want to use it and *return* it to me?"

"OK, can I use some of your toilet paper, do you have enough to get to Lake City?" I said sparingly, "I do teach economics, and toilet paper is a *rival* good."

Fortunately, Bad Foot had plenty of squares to spare because I had to divert from the trail four times that morning to utilize that TP.

"What's a rival good?" says Bad Foot.

"A piece of pizza is a rival good, once you eat it, I can't also eat it. But a hiking trail is non-rival since we can both be on the trail at the same time. But this also means non-rival goods tend to get overcrowded or overused."

I pictured the frustrated faces of the bartenders at Two Mile Brewing in Leadville who complained about the repeated theft of their toilet paper. Many of the latrines along the trail have toilet paper that is on a locked axle so hikers can't readily swipe the whole roll. In economics, this is called the "Tragedy of the Commons." It's a problem where a few people can get away with certain behavior, but when everyone acts irresponsibly, then a common resource gets ruined or used up for everyone.

A few can get away with it, but once everybody does it, the commons get destroyed. It's also the reason why we've seen more and more permitting in popular overnight backpacking and camping spots in Colorado's mountains, where human waste is ruining the commons. A better solution than permitting is for backpackers to embrace an identity as stewards of our wilderness and act accordingly.

I was using a microeconomics 101 lecture as a distraction because any slight incline was exhausting with hardly any calories in a giardia-ridden stomach. Luckily, the trail crossing Snow Mesa was all but flat. After 3.3 miles of flat hiking, Snow Mesa abruptly ends, and the trail feels like it drops off a table. It descends through a very rocky section in the 1,200-foot drop to Spring Creek Pass and CO Highway 149. Here the trail heads back into the trees. And trees provided me much better cover than the non-existent cover on the mesa to use Bad Foot's rival toilet paper. This was important since the number of day-hikers we began to see walking toward us on the trail increased as we got closer to the highway.

After four trips off the trail that morning, we finally made it to the end of Segment 21.

We met a hiker named Brad sitting in what little shade was around the trailhead as we waited for Froggy Legs, Wild Woman and Winston, with whom we camped with the two previous nights, to arrive at the parking lot. They had left their truck parked at Spring Creek Pass and had plans to stay in Lake City that evening, which was perfect because that was our plan as well. This allowed us to avoid hitchhiking.

With 1,700 feet of elevation gain, we had hiked 10.5 miles which is about perfect for a town day.

Bad Foot and I shared the truck bed with Brad as we sped down Highway 149 over Slumgullion Pass, named for the Slumgullion Earthflow, a huge landslide whose soil the miners thought was reminiscent of the hodgepodge of beef, tomatoes and noodles called slumgullion stew. The term also describes the slurry-like mud left behind from washing gold through a sluice.

The earthflow is still moving, which explains why the trees growing on the newer slide are leaning at odd angles. That's a rather unappealing name considering the etymology of *slumgullion* basically means slime and cesspool. (That would not be a flattering trail name.)

The landslide damned the Lake Fork of the Gunnison River and created Colorado's second-largest natural lake: Lake San Cristobal. Unlike most natural dams that don't hold up over time, this one has. As the highway drops down into Lake City, you get great views of the lake.

I was telling this to Bad Foot over the windy noise in the back of the truck.

"Wait, how can Lake San Cristobal be the second largest natural lake in the state? Seemed like we've hiked past bigger lakes?" asked Bad Foot.

"What about Twin Lakes from earlier on the trail?"

"It falls into the man-made category," I explained.

It was a single natural lake once but was dammed and artificially enlarged in 1978. Likewise, Turquoise Lake by Leadville was also dammed. Those big lakes I was familiar with, they weren't natural. As its name suggests, Grand Lake ranks No. 1 on the list of Colorado's largest lakes at 507 acres[45]. Lake San Cristobal for comparison is about 333 acres.

"San Cristobal" Is Spanish for Saint Christopher, the patron saint of travelers who earned that title by carrying people across a dangerous river. Saint Christopher, when he refused to make a sacrifice to a pagan god, was beheaded, which was the similar fate of a victim of Colorado's famous cannibals near Lake San Cristobal.

In 1858, 10 years after miners would spill into California during the first gold rush, William Green Russell turned up a few deposits of gold in the Southern Rockies. Suddenly "Pikes Peak or Bust" was the cry, as thousands of miners descended upon Colorado territory in the second-greatest gold rush in American history.

As miners eventually spread across Colorado Territory, they would reach the San Juan Mountains. As Enos Hotchkiss's productive silver claim near Lake San Cristobal made news, a Denver Tribune article published in October 1873 headlined, "The San Juan Silver Mines," said there were "hundreds of rich discoveries still remained to be found." The article was reprinted throughout the southwest.

Living in Sandy Utah (just south of Salt Lake City) when that article came out, a 31-year-old drifter would hear about Colorado's mineral-rich land and hatch a plan to get from the Salt Lake area to Breckenridge, Colorado.

This drifter had wandered out west after a disability discharge from the army. He was just shy of his 19th birthday when bombs exploded at Fort Sumter and in April 1862, he would join the 16th Regiment of the U.S. Infantry. This is when he got a tattoo that misspelled his own name.

At one point, the drifter got a job leading burros laden with mining supplies up mountain trails — the job title: "jack whacker" (short for Jackass Whacker.)

Jack Whacker would make a great trail name.

During his odd mining jobs, he lost parts of two fingers on his left hand. This physical oddity along with his unique high-pitched and whiny voice would get him caught when he was on the run for nine years after being convicted of cannibalism. The newspapers would give him many epithets: The Ghoul, Human Hyena, Fiend. The name his parents gave him when he was born back in Pennsylvania was Alfred Packer. Because of the misspelled tattoo you sometimes will see Alferd or Alfred.

In November 1873, Packer and a large group left Utah. They would make it to Montrose, Colorado, in late January at the encampment of Chief Ouray. After ignoring the Ute Chief's warning not to cross the Rockies in Winter, Packer and five other men set out on Feb. 9, 1874. The lust for riches wouldn't be the only thing gnawing at them. Two months later, Alferd Packer emerged alone from the harsh San Juan winter with several wallets, another's man's knife and looking a bit too well-nourished.

Many of the stories of Alferd Packer were embellished over the years. Even witness accounts of Packer's arrival would differ significantly. One account claimed Packer was wild-eyed and haggard when he showed up in civilization. Another account insisted Packer looked well-fed and turned nauseated at the sight of food — the first thing on his shopping list was whiskey!

In honor of the latter account, Bad Foot and I strolled into Lake City after seven days without bathing and requested the first thing Packer requested — whiskey.

Well, I did at least.

I ordered a shot of Tin Cup Whiskey on the rocks as Brad, Bad Foot and I snagged an indoor table at the Cannibal Grill. The restaurant is called the Packer Saloon and Cannibal Grill. Packer also has a double meaning; in addition to referring to Alferd Packer, it also represents the NFL team from Green Bay. A cartoon sign of Alferd Packer hangs outside the entrance. It's complete with flowing black hair and a man in a characteristic black mustache, goatee and green and yellow football jersey.

Along with the whiskey order to pay homage to Packer, we also ordered Diet Cokes served in mason jars the size of fishbowls. We down three of them and still didn't have to pee. We were as dehydrated as we were hungry for hamburgers.

"Packer initially claimed that he was abandoned by his party," I continued to tell Bad Foot and Brad.

Then his story changed. His new version of the events admitted that the group had resorted to cannibalism. But something wasn't adding up.

With Packer awaiting trial, a reporter stumbled upon the bodies of five dead prospectors piled together not too far from what would become Lake City, Colorado — and not too far from the Cannibal Grill which we were currently stinking up with a week's worth of hiker B.O.

One body was missing a slice of thigh, one had no head, a third was missing flesh around the breast. The mutilated bodies all piled in one place directly contradicted Packer's claim that the deaths were spread out across the tough journey. But when they went to confront Packer in the Saguache Jail, he had escaped.

Nine years later, his high-pitched laugh gave him away in a saloon in Wyoming. He was carted back to Lake City for trial.

The Lake City Silver World wasn't reluctant to keep Packer in the news. In one story, a drunken miner arrested and tossed in the jailhouse for disorderly conduct started yelling in the middle of the night, "I ain't going to sleep in no jail with a man-eater! Packer the man-eater is in that cell, and I'm damned if I'm going to stay here!" Evidently, the commotion woke Packer, and the convicted cannibal purportedly snarled back, "Dry up there, goddamn you, or I'll chew you up!"

Packer was convicted of murder in Lake City. The Hinsdale County Museum in Lake City, which hosts ghost tours, is home to a collection of Packer memorabilia, including the skull fragment of one of the victims. In the past, you could visit the site where the Packer's victims were found, but no longer because it's on private property.

Of all the various lore and legends surrounding Alferd Packer, the most enduring was the fictitious and cartoonish speech that Judge Gerry delivered during Packer's sentencing. "Stand up, ye voracious man-eatin' son-of-a-bitch, stand up! There was seven Dimmycrats in Hindsdale County, and ye ate five of them, goddamn ye . . . "

Amazingly, Packer didn't face the newly built gallows in Lake City nor did the double-loop noose special-ordered from Denver ever touch Packer's neck. That was because of another murderer from Denver and a weird legal technicality.

I was telling Bad Foot and Brad about the Colorado legislature's error that kept Packer from being hanged in Lake City. Hungry, tired and sore from our longest stretch without a resupply, my audience was more interested in devouring fresh grilled burgers than hearing the story of Colorado's most notorious murderer. Fortunately, my bacon cheeseburger and Bad Foot's mushroom swiss burger arrived right at that moment.

In between bites of my hamburger, I said, "The legislature repealed an 1870 murder statute in a way that allowed Packer's loophole."

In 1881, the Colorado legislature repealed the 1870 murder statute in favor of a new law that would correct a loophole and allowed for the death penalty even in cases where the defendant pleaded guilty. But in doing so, the legislature made a huge blunder: it didn't include a "savings clause." Such a clause would have given the state the right to seek a conviction under the 1870 statute, even once it had been repealed[46]. With a savings clause, the repeal of one part of the law wouldn't invalidate the rest of the law. Without the savings clause, it was another story.

Since Packer had dined on his traveling buddies in 1874, he couldn't be tried for murder under the 1881 law, nor could he be tried under the 1870 law since it was invalidated without the savings clause. The Colorado Supreme Court agreed. Packer received another new nickname; the newspapers dubbed him the "unhung fiend."

He didn't avoid another prosecution, however. Packer was then retried and convicted, this time in Gunnison, of manslaughter and sentenced to 40 years. He was charged with the deaths of Israel Swan, Shannon Wilson Bell, James Humphrey, Frank "Reddy" Miller and George "California" Noon. (Apparently, the other three hadn't earned their trail names before they were consumed.) He served 15 years when he was released from prison on parole in 1901. Rumors say Packer lived his life after prison as a vegetarian. You can see his grave today in a Littleton cemetery.

After lunch and my cannibal history lesson, we checked into the Raven's Rest Hostel. The haven for thru-hikers is owned by a long-distance hiker from Wicklow, Ireland, who was passing through Lake City during his thru-hike of the CDT in 2007. He got to Lake City, looked around, and said, "Yeah I could live here." Then he met a gal named Amy Jo at the saloon and said, "Yeah I'm going to marry this gal and live in Lake City." And he did! His name is Cionnaith O'Dubhaigh but goes by the easier-to-pronounce trail name of "Lucky." The Raven's Rest opened in 2012[47].

Lucky knows about the sense of community found on long-distance trails, which is why we had no trouble making great conversations with him.

With Lucky's influence, Lake City has grown in a special way to cater to backpackers. On Sundays during July and August, the Presbyterian Church offers a free community hiker meal. We hadn't timed Lake City for a weekend, so we missed that chance. It's an extra thought to keep in the back of your mind as you plan your itinerary around Lake City. There's also a group of folks who coordinate a free shuttle that transports hikers the 17 miles back to the trail at Spring Creek Pass. The Lake City Trail Angel shuttle, which runs daily during July and August, leaves at noon from the Lake City library.

Once we found our bunks, I washed a week's worth of hiker grime off my body in the shower. About that time my pal Matt made it into Lake City from Denver with a trunk full of hiker food and fuel. But we didn't bother with resupplies at that moment, instead, we strolled two blocks over the Lake City Brewing Company. My plan was to enjoy at least one beer before my appointment at the Lake City Area Medical Center, where I'd no doubt receive industrial strength antibiotics.

The 27th day of my trip was my second zero day that would begin with donuts and other bakery goods.

For its guests, the Raven's Rest Hostel provides communal bikes, which we used to get to the Lake City Bakery 0.7 miles away. The bakery opens at 7 a.m. We showed up at 6:50 a.m. to find 10 other people already in line ahead of us. Once it was my turn, I ordered a breakfast burrito, donut, cinnamon bun and coffee. They were as delightful as they were caloric.

The zero day in Lake City felt so refreshing. I had no schedule, no emails, no responsibilities, no next project to continue. No papers to grade. Only ice cream to consume and rest to seek. I could just soak in the day. If I wanted to sit on a park bench and people watch, there wasn't anything nagging. It's hard to describe. I wasn't bored, I was just content. Much of the zero day was spent chatting with other hikers and strolling through Lake City with my phone strategically left behind on my bunk bed.

One of my big criticisms of social media platforms like Instagram is that people seem only to post good stuff. Their curated and manicured photos make it seem like their lives are all scuba diving trips and expensive restaurants. They don't show the bad stuff; it's only edited highlights of the good stuff. Well, here's my bad stuff, the stuff that doesn't get posted on social media: projectile vomit.

I had started taking the antibiotics, which I had picked up at the Lake City Area Medical Center, the night before. Somehow my hiker hunger trumped the queasy stomach in the morning, but it all went south in the afternoon. Luckily, I found Lucky's cleaning supplies under the sink which I used to thoroughly scrub down the shower of the remnants of my stomach lining.

I laid in my bunk bed that night not sure if my condition would require us to take a second zero day or not.

CHAPTER NINETEEN:

High Point

We started our second morning in Lake City the same way we did our first, by biking to the bakery before it opened at 7am. We had an extra in our breakfast crew this morning, *Spoons.*

After I was confident that my breakfast was going to stay down, we made the decision to head back to the trail instead of taking a second zero day. The decision was aided by the fact that the obvious camp spot on the next segment of the trail was only eight miles away. It would make for a good half day of hiking. After that the trail remained above tree line for two days of hiking. Also at that spot was the Colorado Trail yurt.

Instead of waiting around for the noon shuttle to Spring Creek Pass, Bad Foot and I rode in Matt's Subaru back over Slumgullion Pass. Matt would join us for the eight-mile hike and a night in the yurt. We were back on the trail at 10:30 a.m. starting the beginning of Segment 22.

After the trail leaves Highway 149, it heads west climbing again on a Jeep road before it crosses the Jarosa Mesa.

While hiking I asked, "Hey Matt, what's bigger: a butte, mesa or plateau? I mean, we are walking across the Jarosa Mesa, why isn't it the Jarosa Butte or Jarosa Plateau? Do you know the difference?"

After a few out-of-breath mumbles, Matt huffed, "All I know is that this heavy backpack and this hike is kicking my butte!" followed by his patented and infectious chuckle.

"I told you not to pack that grandfather clock," I taunted referring the extra items he brought in his pack including a very thick novel. Then I explained my rudimentary understanding of each: "I think plateaus are the biggest and don't have to have cliffs on all sides."

I learned later that each is an elevated area with a flat top. Plateaus are generally the largest. The one important distinction is that plateaus don't necessarily have to have cliffs that go all the way around. Buttes and mesas are generally smaller than plateaus and have cliffs on all sides, but what separates a butte from a mesa is the width-to-height ratio. A mesa is usually wider than it is tall. As opposed to the smaller butte that has eroded away now stands taller than it is wide.

Matt responded, "I hiked up to the edge of the Snow Mesa yesterday — that didn't look like it had cliffs on all sides. Shouldn't it be the 'Snow Plateau?'"

Hmm, good question.

"Maybe it should geologically be the 'Snow Plateau,' but the people who gave it the name didn't like the rhyme?" Matt concluded.

"There's a thought," I said. Then I spent the next mile reciting "snow plateau" with various rhythms as I made my way toward the Colorado Trail yurt

I got to wondering if all the features in Colorado already have destinated names? Like suppose during your CT hike, you wonder off the trail to heed the call of nature when you wander across a surprise tarn — a small mountain lake — that isn't named on your map. Nor can you find a designation on your GPS. Can you name that body of water? Maybe you want to give it a moniker after your CT trail name. Nugget Lake has a quaint ring to it, right?

Well, not so fast. The odds aren't good.

As the places in Colorado were being settled in the 1800s, the process was so chaotic that President Benjamin Harrison signed an executive order creating the United States Board on Geographic Names in 1890. If you really have your heart set on Nugget Lake, there is an application process. But it's not easy. You'd have a lot of hoops to jump through and numerous agencies to appease from the Department of the Interior and CIA to the Post Office and the Department of State and the Library of Congress and the Colorado Board on Geographic Names. Nugget Lake doesn't stand much chance of being in the updated CT Guidebook in future years.

I went to the website of the U.S. Board on Geographic Names and did a quick search of "nugget" in its geographic names information system. Turns out there are zero Nugget Lakes, but there are four geological names in the state that include "Nugget." A mining Site in Gilpin County is called "Nugget." There are two valleys in Colorado called "Nugget Gulch." One is just outside of Leadville, and the other is in Boulder County below Nugget Hill. A quick search of "Bad Foot" turned up no results. Nor are there any geological features in Colorado with the name "Wangler."

"Though Wangler Waterfall would make for a tourist destination...for skinny dipping," I told Bad Foot as we sat down on the deck of the yurt. We got there at 2:30 p.m. having hiked eight miles with 1,800 feet of elevation gain.

The dell that surrounded the yurt looked like it would make for good tent camping, but the slope and tufts of grass and sod prevented it. If you weren't camping in the yurt, the next viable campsites were where the CT ran back into the trees.

We could hear the voices of tent campers stationed for the night carrying across the valley as we sat on the deck of the Colorado Trail yurt and looked at the approaching thunderstorm over the San Juan Mountains — the mountains that awaited us over the next several days.

We sat on the yurt deck platform and gazed at the mountains, needing nothing else.

In the off-trail world, I discovered that I never followed a thought all the way to completion. Instead, one thought would ricochet through my brain to another thought, which would bounce me to another thought and on and on. If I could manage to stay on one concept long enough, I'd be inevitably distracted by a text message, another unfinished task, an email, a screen or an alluring YouTube video.

But on the trail, it was much different. I could much more easily explore one idea in depth or hold a deeper conversation; my brain felt still, and calm, yet energized — like it was full and had accomplished something but still had found peace. I kept using the term "mossy" to describe my settled and still brain, as if my brain resembled a serene receptive growth of moss on a rock as opposed to a turbulent pinball machine.

Gazing at the mountains, I realized the San Juans were in a separate league compared to the other mountain ranges in Colorado. Each new mountain range is a new phrase of the trail with unique character, topography and character.

As we were making our dinners, the familiar face of a hiker strolled through the yurt's door. It was the Pippy-Long-stocking-red-braided visage of Spoons, the college student from Emory.

After eating dinner together, we all four did the ninth RAT.

As the thunderstorm pounded down upon the yurt, we drifted off to sleep atop the springs of our cots quite cozy and dry.

When we went to bed, there were four of us in the yurt. When we awoke the next morning, there were five. We added "Chicken Fat."

At 11:05 p.m. the night before, we were all awakened up by a red light peering at us through the yurt's window from a hiker trying to get out of the rainstorm. Eleven at night doesn't seem that late, but let's remember that hiker midnight is 9 p.m. We'd been sleeping for two hours at that point. Bad Foot welcomed him into the yurt right away. The stranger took the empty cot next to me.

A high school teacher from North Carolina hiking the CDT northbound (we learned over breakfast), Chicken Fat had done a 37-mile day on the trail to get to the Colorado Trail yurt that night.

I was struck at how unapologetic Chicken Fat was in the morning. He had woken up four strangers and came into the yurt soaking, getting our gear wet.

Since Bad Foot had done the PCT, he had a deeper knowledge about long trail hiking's social mores. I was curious to ask him what he thought of the whole late night yurt arrival.

Bad Foot knew right away that someone shining their flashlights and waking up four strangers at night wouldn't be done by someone who hadn't learned long-trail principles. Hikers become family, and it is expected to help out a fellow thru-hiker.

"If it wasn't raining, the hiker etiquette would be to set up your tent and be as quiet as possible trying not to disturb sleeping hikers, but rain is a different scenario," Bad Foot explained. "Fellow thru-hikers have an obligation to help out. I figured he was a CDT right away, because a hiker unaccustomed to long trail ethics wouldn't dare wake up strangers. He's used to relying on fellow hikers. He expects it. That's why he didn't apologize. He saw us as fellow thru-hikers."

I thought back to my fifth day on the trail, before I had received my trail name, when I was selfish with my resupply food when Bad Foot's resupply package didn't get to Jefferson. I was understanding trail family mores better now.

Making our breakfast in the morning, it was cold enough to see our breath. We were at 11,700 feet in elevation.

I was out of the yurt by 7:25 a.m. on the start of my fifth week on the trail. Bad Foot and Spoons were out earlier. Chicken Fat had gone earlier headed the opposite direction all excited about a town day in Lake City. After filtering water, Matt turned and hiked back to his car at Spring Creek Pass while I turned and headed for the Colorado Trail high point.

Leaving the yurt and pushing up through the trees, the trail stays about 12,000 feet for the next 35 miles. The first big push of the day is gaining the 2,000 feet of elevation over the first seven miles of the day to where the Colorado Trail reaches it high point of 13,271 feet. Weirdly, this spot is not on a crest of a ridge but on a relatively flat and rolling point below Coney Summit.

I spent most of this section looking over my right shoulder toward stunning views of Lake San Christobal, Red Mountain, Red Cloud and Sunshine Peaks.

I caught up to my hiking partner shortly before the trail's highest point. Bad Foot and I posed together for a selfie in front of the brown sign with carved text: "High Point 13,271 FT. The Colorado Trail." From there, the trail drops 1,350 feet over the next three miles passing the Carson saddle and the start to Segment 23. Then the trail dips to 11,900 feet before charging up to the top of another ridge at 12,900 feet at the start of Segment 24. Our goal for the day was Cataract Lake, which required 14.5 miles and 3,100 feet of elevation gain.

At the top of ridge, we were greeted with wind and hail. Throwing on our rain jackets, we hustled down to Cataract

Lake to pitch our tents before the downpour came. This was the highest camp we'd make on the trip at 12,200 feet and above tree line. We were just off the trail by the second lake next to Cataract Lake.

After the first wave of thunderstorms came, the clouds gave us a break, which we used to cook dinner and filter water. As we sat filtering water by the lake, I spotted a familiar figure wearing a purple beanie and pink down jacket strolling along the single-track path bordering the lake.

"Sketcher!" I yelled as a hiker was meandering toward us.

"Nugget!" she yelled back.

We had last seen Sketcher at Tank Seven Creek eight days before. These surprise reconnections are a wonderful feeling on the trail. It feels like serendipitously bumping into a great friend you haven't seen for years — a friend you've known your whole life with whom you have spent countless hours together.

Only we hadn't.

At the very most I had hung out with Sketcher for three hours in my life. We had camped with Sketcher one evening by Marshall Pass and had run into her on the trail a few times during the day, but in all, I had spent very little time getting to know Sketcher. Yet she felt like a lifelong friend.

There's something amazing about friendships formed on the trail.

It's amazing how you can go from a low point being pelted with hail to suddenly being pepped up by reconnecting with (what feels like) old and lifelong friends. The sun comes back out, the wind dies down, you get a meal in your belly and your mind recovers. I realized I got my pep, energy and ability to socialize back since the mental valley I fell into with giardia.

After dinner, I recited some Robert Service poetry for the audience of Bad Foot, Froggy Legs, Wild Woman and Sketcher. As Bad Foot reclined in his tent listening, he snapped a photo that embodied the ethos of the trail. It's a side angle of myself, with Sketcher, Wild Woman and Froggy Legs in a line sitting on the tundra each with a slight smile staring at me as a rhythmically recited *The Cremation of Sam McGee*. Their facial expressions show them fully engaged, fully present and not even 1% distracted by anything else.

In the book *Stolen Focus*[48], Johann Hari describes the fragmented and frazzled way we live our lives as though "our civilization had been covered with itching powder, and we spent our time twitching and twerking our minds, unable to simply give attention to things that matter . . . " Our minds bounce around a lot more. There's no stillness. We struggle to stay on topic of conversation for long. This means we are losing our ability to be present which means we are missing our lives.

That photo makes me lament how many distracted conversations that I have in the off-trail world — ones where I am pecking on my phone as I half-heartedly listen to someone. No one was distracted by an electronic device at Cataract Lake.

After my audience retired to their tents, I reclined in my tent journaling at 8:15 p.m. when I heard the rumble of thunder. I got to thinking how the sound of thunder was so much more relaxing than the sound of the city.

Even if you are good at ignoring city noise, your body still subconsciously reacts to it. It doesn't matter if they are awake or whether they were asleep, participants who were monitored while sleeping through traffic noise had sympathetic nervous systems responses to the sounds with measurable reactions like elevated heart rates and blood pressure[49]. Being subconsciously vigilant during sleep makes sense from an evolutionary perspective — the animal that doesn't alert to a predator in the middle of the night doesn't live long enough to pass on their genes. Our strongest startle reactions are set off by sound. That's why I sleep with earplugs in my tent, so every twig snap doesn't cause me to engage my evolutionary response.

Sound pollution can also harm your ability to enjoy the scenery. In one study, visitors who hear loud vehicle noise rate parks as 38% less scenic than people who don't hear the noise[50]. So, the noises we sense with our ears can actually detract from what we see with our eyes.

Noise pollution is also linked to a bunch of health ailments, most notably an increase in hypertension. Noisy neighbors boost your stress hormones. Even kids' reading scores drop in loud localities[51]. Replace the urban noise with birdsongs, and you can get a benefit. Students listening to birdsongs were more attentive after lunch than students who didn't hear the chirps. I added "the absence of urban noise pollution" and the "presence of bird sounds" to the growing list of why I felt so good on the trail. No wonder the Wilderness Act mandates "outstanding opportunities for those who seek solitude."

Clues for RAT Quiz #9
Batter, sell, make
Church, light, lip
Fig, new, table
Flower, bug, rest
Circuit, fall, cut
Notch, tip, dog
Lift, lounge, wheel
High, house, bus
Toe, door, packed
Kitchen, salt, water

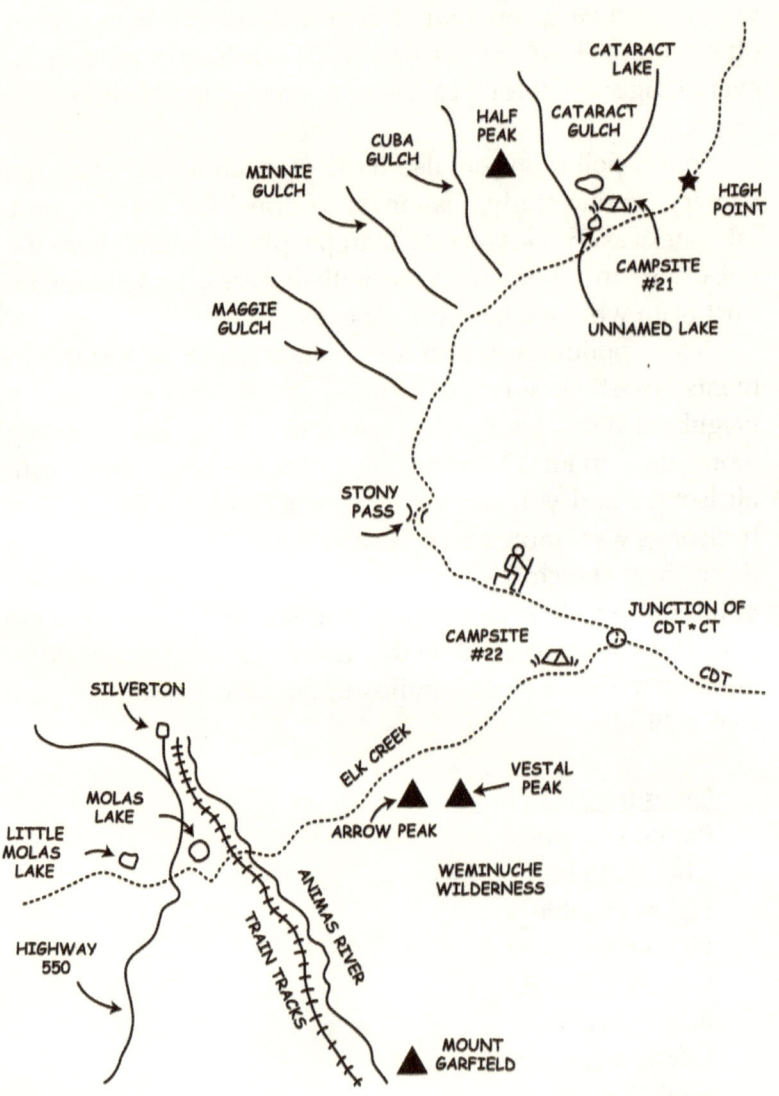

CATARACT
LAKE

HALF
PEAK

CUBA
GULCH

CATARACT
GULCH

MINNIE
GULCH

HIGH
POINT

CAMPSITE
#21

MAGGIE
GULCH

UNNAMED LAKE

STONY
PASS

JUNCTION OF
CDT * CT

CAMPSITE
#22

CDT

SILVERTON

ELK CREEK

VESTAL
PEAK

MOLAS
LAKE

ARROW PEAK

LITTLE
MOLAS
LAKE

WEMINUCHE
WILDERNESS

HIGHWAY
550

TRAIN TRACKS

ANIMAS RIVER

MOUNT
GARFIELD

CHAPTER TWENTY:

A Shot in the Arm

The 30th day on the Colorado Trail found me trying to distract Bad Foot as we climbed the day's first big uphill to reach the first of several saddles. We both woke up in our tents nervous about the day's ups and downs and elevation above 12,000 feet. In addition, I was still not 100% from the antibiotics upsetting my gut.

"Hey, Bad Foot, imagine this scenario: you're in a bank on Monday morning when a robber busts into the lobby scaring you and 50 other people in the bank lobby that day . . ."

"Wait, why is there 50 other people in the bank?"

"Don't worry about it, but yes 50 other people . . . let me continue: the robber fires a single shot off from his pistol and it hits you in the arm."

"The right or left arm?" Bad Foot asks.

"Doesn't matter . . . let's say the left arm if you promise to stop interrupting."

Then we pause to catch our breath as we make our way up out of Cataract Gulch toward the next valley over, Cuba Gulch.

"So, the robber shoots one bullet, and it hits you in the arm. But here's the important question: Do you feel lucky or unlucky?"

We are silent for a while as the elevation gain makes it hard to talk.

"I mean, there's 50 people in there each with two arms, so it seems fairly unlucky that my one out of a hundred arms gets maimed," Bad Foot reasons.

"But on the other hand, get it, the bullet could have hit me in the heart and killed me. So, from that perspective I'd feel pretty lucky," he concludes.

"Exactly, it all depends on how you frame the counterfactual event," I say.

"If you compare getting hit in the arm to getting hit in the heart, you're lucky. If you compare it to the scenario where someone else gets shot instead of you, well then you are unlucky," I explain. "But the counterfactual scenario is all up to you. If we can reframe things, we can find the positive in things. Basically, the story they compare things to decides whether the actual event is lucky or unlucky. The trick is to control which story we tell ourselves."

This was part of several topics I had been researching in my pre-trail preparation: happiness and neuroplasticity. My goal was simple. I wanted to figure out ways to train my brain to deal with the tough times on the trail.

For a long time, it was understood that our brains were fixed, immutable — that we are just stuck with the brains we have, with the emotions, with the depression issues, with the anxiety, with the negative. But experiments in the last 30 years have shown that the brain is malleable.

The brain can basically reorganize itself depending on the process it engages in regularly.

One notable example of that breakthrough work comes from the brains of London bus drivers and taxi drivers[52]. London is an old city with a spaghetti plate layout of roads — unlike newer cities whose roads systematically crisscross like a grid and are easier to navigate. Finding the best route from memory for a taxi driver requires them to hold those tricky London streets in their head and mentally solve for the best route. London taxi drivers call this "the knowledge," and it takes years to acquire it.

This is unlike the bus drivers who only had to memorize and use the same specific route over and over. The study showed that taxi drivers' brains grew differently than bus drivers. As did, I imagine, the variety of odors each vehicle collected. The hippocampus, the part of the brain that does spatial navigation and memory, was noticeably bigger in the brains of taxi drivers but not the bus drivers. Even though both spent their day driving the streets of London, the taxi drivers grew bigger brains.

But that's a double-edged sword, I realized, as I learned about the "Tetris Effect."

In "The Happiness Advantage," Shawn Achor describes how people, who for hours a day, played the addicting block-arranging puzzle game Tetris, reported seeing Tetris-like patterns in shelves and brick walls[53]. It was like their brains were suddenly primed to take a tall building, turn it sideways and see if it fit between another two. Achor then describes how our brains can be conditioned to view patterns, but it also showed that we can condition our brains to see what we want to see.

Because our brains can't take in every single bit of information, we must choose what we filter in. But it can go both ways. If you're in a rut and only seeing the negative, you'll continue to amplify and only selectively see the bad. Someone's emotions match their thoughts and actions. Psychologist call this "mood congruency." Simply put, if you're sad, you think of sad things and you are more likely to interpret ambiguous situations as negative. Happy people go the other way, they have more positive thoughts and are more likely to interpret that ambiguous situation as positive. Our moods can be a filter on how we see things. A big goal of psychotherapy for depression is to train people to get rid of the inaccurate filters through which everything looks dreary.

But train your brain to notice the good and you'll start noticing additional good things — like a happiness lens. I notice a similar feeling when I trudge around a national forest near Fraser, Colorado, each November looking for the perfect evergreen tree to place in my living room for Christmas. After an hour scouting trees, finally cutting one, and dragging it back to the truck, my mind is primed to evaluate every tree. On the way back to Denver, my mind is still stuck in a tree-evaluating mode. I size up and analyze every tree I pass.

"Nah," my brain says, "not enough limbs at the base" as I evaluate what, I then realize, is a telephone pole.

"Basically, you can rewire your brain to get better at noticing the positive," I told Bad Foot.

"I don't know if I have many wires to rewire left," he said.

The hike between Cataract Lake and Stony Pass Trailhead are a series of saddles/passes that unlock views to new, distinct valleys. It's as though each new drainage from Half Peak near where we camped said, "I can out-do the gulch you just came from." Like each new turn around a corner or step up to another pass turns the page into an even more picturesque gulch. The views, jagged ridges and colors got better and better as we moved through Cataract Gulch to Cuba Gulch to Minnie Gulch to Maggie Gulch.

My caloric intake was aided by two trail angels this day.

Seven miles into my day and just after the day's high point of 12,988 feet, I met Jeff and Val — a couple from the Durango area. They were filling the day by handing out peanut butter and boysenberry jam sandwiches to thru-hikers. After feeding me, as they hiked away, I could barely make out Jeff cheerfully saying, "Today might be a two-bag day!" referring to the auxiliary bag of sandwiches which they always packed but seldom got to open for lack of thru-hiker recipients. Twenty minutes after scarfing down that sandwich, I had a tortilla with two buffalo chicken packets. My appetite was finally fully back!

The section's proximity to Silverton and the four-wheel Jeep roads provided a fair bit of day hikers, that can be an abrupt transition from the seclusion of the previous day. One group of those day hikers was a four-person family who stopped their Jeep beside me on the road to offer me Rice Krispie treats and an apple. The husband and wife had thru-hiked the Colorado Trail 14 years prior and obviously knew how welcome free food is to thru-hikers.

Toward the end of Segment 23 that ends at Stony Pass, we met a CDT-completer named James. He had noted how much he enjoyed this section of the trail and vowed to return when he could better savor it. He was true to his vow. He was back armed with a large camera — one that, needless to say, didn't make the cut as an ultralight thru-hiker during the previous year's hike.

James joined Bad Foot, Sketcher and me for an early afternoon break at the start of Segment 24 next to the remnants of an old cabin. We took turns leafing through and admiring

Sketcher's daily journal pages filled with water-colored sketches and haikus.

"Hey, this sketch looks familiar," I said, pointing to an arrangement of pebbles on the trail spelling out "300."

"Yep, I figured that was you two who made that rock mile marker," Sketcher said, smiling.

She decided to camp here for the night. Bad Foot and I still had seven miles ahead of us to camp at a spot that had, what I later realized, was the most dramatic view on the entire Colorado Trail.

I'd been talking it up for weeks now.

"Wait 'til you see the Weminuche!" I kept telling Bad Foot.

Segment 24 enters the Weminuche Wilderness immediately south of Stony Pass, where the trail runs through a high, treeless shelf for the next several miles, ranging between 12,100 and 12,700 feet of elevation. The trail passes several lakes and follows a plateau as it heads toward Arrow (13,817 feet) and Vestal Peak (13,864 feet). Those two peaks pop up across the horizon like two dark, giant and intimidating shark's fins. They are part of the Grenadier Mountain Range, whose peaks are carved from quartzite.

Rocks like this are unlike any other on the entire Colorado Trail. Because that rock is particularly resistant to weathering, the peaks give off a shiny, black and polished gleam. That glint is more pronounced after a recent rainfall in the late afternoon, when the sun's light is at a perfect angle to make those mountains glare with darkened brightness. Bad Foot and I had just those conditions.

After crossing six miles of the plateau from Stony Pass, the trail came to a key intersection where we would depart from James, the CDT hiker we'd met earlier in our journey. This I the spot where the Continental Divide Trail separates from the Colorado Trail.

The Continental Divide Trail heads southeast at this point, while a mile later the Colorado Trail runs due west down to the headwaters of Elk Creek. There's a wooden trail sign here pointing CT hikers to the right and CDT hikers to the left.

At this spot, I imagined hearing the Colorado Trail taunting the Continental Divide Trail. "You've been co-located with me for the last 314 miles, and now you decide to diverge? Like a mile before the best view of my entire trail?"

Then I'd imagine the CDT responding, "It's not you, CT, it's me. I've got other places to be . . ."

The headwaters of Elk Creek greet hikers with a dizzying steepness. This view is on the cover of the ninth edition of the Colorado Trail Guidebook. To the right are two high alpine lakes perched above a shear drop-off. To the left is the black, glimmering rock of the canyon. In the middle is the Colorado Trail zigzagging through a valley of luscious green grass and the rivulet that is the start of Elk Creek meandering through that verdant field as well. The original 1989 Colorado Trail guidebook describes this section poetically as "on an extremely steep mountainside seemingly held in place by the intertwining roots of an exquisite alpine flower garden."

The view is awe-inspiring.

Bad Foot and I had the same response: we stopped hiking and just stared in silence with our mouths agape struggling to fully absorb the view. I'm not sure how long we stood this way, but it was like time was standing still.

Psychologists would call a moment like this part of the "extended-now theory," which purports that focusing on the present moment can help elongate time perception. Being in the present moment makes life more satisfying. It helps us focus on the here and now. When time feels expansive, it also makes people want to acquire new knowledge.

Maybe that's why in my research, I learned that awe has the power to put people into the present moment and can literally expand our perception of time. Awe is defined as an "emotion that arises when one encounters something so strikingly vast that it provokes a need to update one's mental schemas." The vastness of something awe-inspiring basically alters our ability to understand the world.

"But awe and happiness are not the same thing," I tell Bad Foot. "They do experiments on the two."

"How do you test such a thing?" he asks.

"You pay college students 20 bucks to watch LCD televisions," I tell him.

In this experiment, some students watch clips of waterfalls, whales and astronauts in space. The control group was shown a clip of people smiling during a parade filled with confetti. The one clip aimed at happiness the other aimed at awe. The people who saw the awe-inspiring whales were more likely to feel that they had more time compared to the group inspired with just happiness videos.

They also found the people inspired by awe were more likely to answer yes to questions like "how willing are you to donate your money to support a worthy cause?" Therefore, awe causes more people to support charities. This means experiencing awe makes us less selfish.

Do you choose the watch or Broadway show tickets, a jacket or a restaurant meal, a scientific calculator or a massage, or between a backpack or a $50 iTunes gift card? People experiencing awe are more likely to prefer experiences over material goods.

Simply put: a dose of awe gives a boost in life satisfaction and makes people feel like they have more time available, and that feeling leads them to value experiences and their community higher than simply happy-elicited people do. So, if you feel starved for time, it can help you to get out and experience the awe of nature.

When's the last time you've felt rich in time?

Survey data confirms that it is probably not very often. There's even a term for feeling like you don't have enough time: "time famine." Constantly feeling like you're running low on time is linked to a bunch of negative health effects like trouble sleeping, stress and difficulty delaying gratification. Running low on time also makes you a worse neighbor. It's been shown that people who feel hindered by time constraints are less likely to help someone in distress.[54] People with a dearth of time are also much less likely to volunteer or engage in their community[55].

At this point, the trail took a right turn and started a series of tight switchbacks that zigzagged like the icing on a toaster strudel.

Back and forth like a security line at Denver International Airport, we bobbed down nearly 30 hairpin switchbacks. I felt like I could almost high-five Bad Foot from one switchback, they were so tight. At the bottom of the switch backs, we ran into two northbound CT hikers headed up the hill who went by "Washer" and "Pocket Snacks."

The trail descended into the remnants of an old mining operation. What's left of the operation looks just like a small shed. There was already another tent set up by a flat spot next to the mining shed, so I stopped a bit before that spot and climbed 20 feet to a flat perch. From the spot we could see all the switchbacks we had just come down. We camped just one mile shy of the 400-mile mark after a day of 18.5 miles with 3,800 feet of elevation gain. We were still camped at around 12,000 feet, but it felt lower since we were surrounded by cliffs and ridges on all sides rising above us.

After we set up our tents, we sat staring at the view: the switchbacks we had just come down, the face of the canyon wall, the green grass, Washer and Pocket Snacks slowing working their way up the icing-swirl switchbacks.

This view, I thought, is the exact opposite of social media. In the off-trail world when I sit down on the couch, I just feel frazzled and antsy — like I need to look up something or watch a YouTube video or scroll through my social media feed. I never feel calm, rested or content. Instead, I'm wired from being wired. What's good to get your eyeballs absorbing more ads, is not good for my mental health, sleep or concentration.

But Elk Creek was.

The feed of Facebook or Instagram is fast and temporary, which makes us feel amped-up and on edge. Social media makes you feel anxious and envious. I think social media makes you believe the world is infatuated with you — like you're the biggest thing. But staring at that mountain makes you realize how small you are in the whole world. But the rock wall of the Elk Creek Canyon was steady, unchanging and constant. There are no fleeting moments. There was only static stone.

The silence was broken when Bad Foot finally said, "You know, I was apprehensive when I went to bed last night. I was worrying about the big miles and the numerous climbs we faced. But as it turns out, today was one of my favorite days backpacking ever!"

That's saying something from a guy that spent the previous summer hiking from Mexico to Canada.

"What was the secret?" I ask.

"The key was letting the day come to us," Bad Foot explained, "instead of pushing to cover the miles."

He added, "Being surrounded by the most beautiful scenery imaginable also helped."

The day had been Bad Foot's solidification of the newly found relax-don't-press mentality. The first pass with the eraser to Bad Foot's hurry mentality occurred 20 days before in the Holy Cross Wilderness when he, The Wangler and I ended the day at a time Bad Foot had deemed "premature," at 3:30 p.m. The overwhelming beauty of the canyon above the headwaters of Elk Creek fully whipped clean the hurry mentality.

The hike between Cataract Lake and the Elk Creek drainage was very difficult but one of the most rewarding days of my adventure. Each day I'd make my dinner and reflect about the day's hike, mileage, effort, the people I met and switchbacks or lack thereof. There was a profound sense of fatigue and accomplishment. Like your body was tired, ready for sleep and very proud of what you did that day to get it to that condition.

We stayed as long as we could, soaking in the view until darkness began to fall upon us and it was time for the tent.

In the gratitude section of my journal, I wrote, among other things, "start to finish breath taking 360 degree views today." And, "I almost had a completely solid poo tonight!"

What a thing to be grateful for: half solid stool.

The optimist sees the glass half-full instead of half-empty. I decided the optimistic hiker-suffering-from-giardia sees the stool as half firm instead of half runny.

As if given the same gift twice, but in different colors, we woke up early and got to experience that same amazing view at Elk Creek as the sun rose into the sky.

We got the evening setting sun on the sheer cliff face, but also got to wake up to what John Muir called "one of the most impressive of all the terrestrial manifestations of God,"[56] the morning alpenglow of pink lighting up the rock at 5:30 a.m.

Looking at the rock face glowing in the morning beauty reminded me of the Bible verse Philippians 4:4 that says, "Rejoice in the Lord always. I will say it again: Rejoice!" In Paul's letter, he repeats himself. I got to rejoice in the best spot on the Colorado Trail twice.

From our campsite, the trail squeezes you into a narrow gorge with a steep drop-off to your left and sheer cliff face to your right. It's just past this section and less than 10 minutes into our hiking day that we stopped, shed our backpacks and began looking for small rocks to construct a mile-stone figure on the trail to mark where it crossed the 400th mile.

This one was extra delightful to create since we knew it would be drawn by Sketcher the next day in her journal.

The trail follows Elk Creek, eventually reaching tree line. After spending the last two days above the trees, being among them again was comforting.

The winter of 2018 was a big one for avalanches and their destruction and power was evident on this section of the trail. "Every chute in the Weminuche ran that year," a ranger from Bayfield, Colorado told me. Avalanches along Elk Creek that year created four football field-sized debris fields of dirt and downed timber that were 20-feet high atop the trail. Clearing something like that is tiresome. But it's more difficult here given its remoteness — it required a 10-mile hike to reach the area. Plus, it is hand tools only in wilderness areas. No chainsaws, but weirdly though, dynamite is OK. We had been fortunate with our timing through this section. The next day they were clearing debris with dynamite.

The trail exits the Weminuche Wilderness Area before crossing the train tracks.

We spent the last two days among the giant peaks above 12,000 feet, as if we hikers and the peaks sat together as equals on high thrones. But after dropping from 12,690 feet down the steep descent into the gorge toward Elk Creek all the way to 8,918 feet beside the Animas River, suddenly Mt. Garfield towered above us again. It was like we were again peasants looking up toward those parked on the high thrones above.

The trail doesn't stay below 9,000 feet for very long at all. It's a quick skip across the train tracks and over the Animas River, and then the trail starts its switchbacks up the side of the valley toward Molas Pass.

The last time I hiked across the Animas was a year prior after a four-night backpacking trip into the Chicago Basin. Back then I was elated from my longest backpacking trip of 40 miles. Today, I hit 400. That 40-mile trip gave me the final jolt of confidence I needed to do the Colorado Trail. Before that trip, I had done dozens of two- or three-night backpacking trips. And at the end of each of them, I had an urge to get back to town and back "home." I've learned that there's something magical about that fourth night. After the fourth night, you begin to see the trail as your home.

The anthropologists who study pilgrimages would call this "entering liminality." From the Latin word *limen* meaning "border" or "threshold," the liminal realm is the space between states.[57] It's a phase different than normal life. When pilgrims enter liminality, status distinctions are gone, pilgrims carry few possessions, wear simple clothing, embrace humility and do the same things as their fellows. The liminal realm is usually simple, calling for self-sacrifice and perseverance through pain and fatigue[58].

Sounds a lot like thru-hiking, doesn't it?

Pilgrims share a belief that there's a transformative power in being away from ordinary life. I believe thru-hikers are very similar in that aspect. Three nights in a tent isn't enough to cross the threshold out of normal life. The fourth night does it.

Scott Stillman articulates it very similarly when describing the peace he finds after a few days in the wild writing, "I believe that the answer lies here, in wilderness . . . Once you get past the jitteriness of day one, the cravings of day two, and the loneliness of day three, meditation comes easily and naturally."[59] For the hiker unsold on the idea of thru-hiking for fear of missing home, I tell them to try a four-nighter and see how they feel.

The four-night trip to the Chicago Basin really opened my mind to the idea of sleeping in nature for a month straight. The area is one of my favorites in the state, and if the Colorado Trail followed the originally proposed path, it would have gotten a lot closer to the Chicago Basin and those four remote 14ers.

When the route of the Colorado Trail was being proposed in 1973, the biggest discussion was the path it would take through the Weminuche Wilderness Area, the largest Wilderness area in Colorado — three quarters the size of Rhode Island. That was before four of the Wilderness Areas the CT now meanders through existed. Meanwhile, the Continental Divide National Scenic Trail didn't get its designation until 1978.

The originally proposed route crossed Hunchback Pass and dropped into Vallecito Creek, then up Johnson Creek and up to Columbine Pass, which dropped into the Chicago

Basin (a popular backpacking destination for 14er climbers which provides the standard routes up Sunlight, Windom, Eolus and N. Eolus). But the route didn't drop into the Chicago Basin, it made a southern turn on Columbine Pass toward Trimble Pass before heading south to City Reservoir, then due west toward West Virginia Gulch, where it left the Weminuche. It then dropped down toward Lemon Reservoir and up Missionary Ridge to Spring Creek and on to Durango.

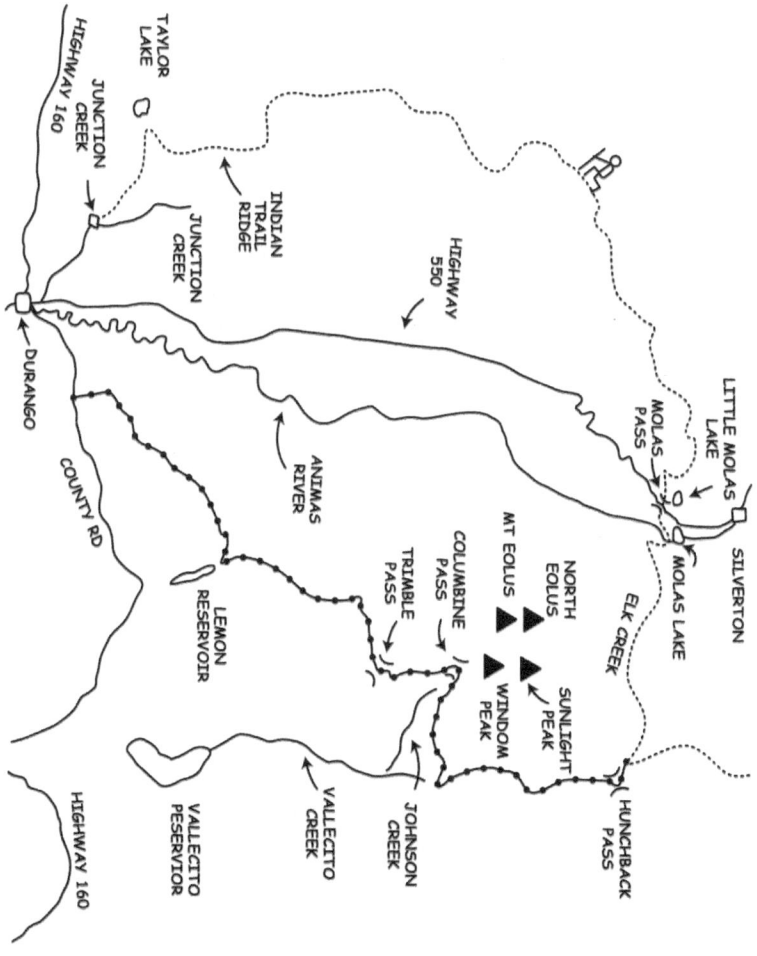

The Forest Service's Environmental Assessment Report from the 1970s warned that the Vallecito drainage was already the most heavily used portion of the wilderness area. If the CT had followed the original proposal, it would have never dropped down into the picturesque Elk Creek Drainage headed toward Silverton nor would it have passed the beaver ponds with views of Vestal and Arrow Peaks. It never would have traversed the features that lay ahead of us in the next several days: Molas Pass or Blackhawk Pass or Taylor Lake. It would have stayed on the east side of CO 550 and the Animus River.

I was now on the west side of the Animus River making my way up to Molas Pass. The views of the valley and Mt. Garfield get better and better as you gain elevation. After re-gaining a thousand feet, I heard a train whistle echoing through the valley of the Durango and Silverton Narrow Gauge carrying tourists into Silverton. I took a photograph of Aspen leaves framing the valley with the train running alongside the Animas River with Mt. Garfield towering above. The tourists that would spill out of those train cars into the streets of Silverton would still be there when we got to town.

After four miles and 2,000 feet of elevation gain since crossing the Animas River, I should have been relieved when the trail topped out at Molas Pass, but I had one more challenge standing between us and burgers.

This hike had already been a trip of firsts (first time with giardia and the first time beer tasting without underwear). It was time for my first attempt at hitch-hiking. The Colorado Trail crosses Highway 550 at Molas Pass, seven miles south of Silverton.

"It's going to take a bit longer without our 'ride bride,'" said Bad Foot. I learned that Tall Tale had much better luck flagging down rides than Bad Foot did last year on the PCT.

It was up to me now.

My friend Rob, who hiked the Appalachian Trail after college, gave me similar advice that lower income drivers were much more likely to pick him up hitch-hiking. I wondered if that was true.

I thought about this while I thumbed it alongside Highway 550 at Molas Pass. At least 25 expensive pickup trucks, all with room in their truck beds, flew by. I was surprised how rejected I felt as each vehicle failed to stop.

I wish I had sign that said "Thru-hiker to town." I figured people would be more likely to transport me four miles and assist my thru-hike than take the risk that I wanted to hitch to Albuquerque.

After about 15 minutes, we were in luck. A retired gentlemen from the Montrose area in a Subaru who spent the morning mountain biking in the San Juan mountains, decided to offer us a ride into town. He was delighted to drive us into the center of Silverton, and we were delighted to be transported.

In speaking about hitch hiking with other thru-hikers I gathered some further tips:

- Look like a hiker and not like an axe murderer.
- Your smile does more than your thumb.
- Make you trekking poles conspicuous to signal you are a thru-hiker.
- It's best to be thumbing 50 yards up the road from the parking lot, since a vehicle driving by 60 miles per hour only has a several seconds to see you, access whether you're not crazy and then decide to pick you up.

As soon as we hopped out of the Subaru and thanked our driver, we beelined it to High Noon Hamburgers. We decided

to walk over to the post office to pick up our last resupply before Durango after we had lunch.

I scarfed down a bacon cheeseburger, fries and a Cherry
Coke while Bad Foot enjoyed his signature town day meal of
a swiss mushroom burger, fries and Diet Coke.

"What if a robber busted in here and shot you in the arm
right now?"

"Can I still finish my burger?" Bad Foot asked.

"Yes."

"Then I choose Lucky!"

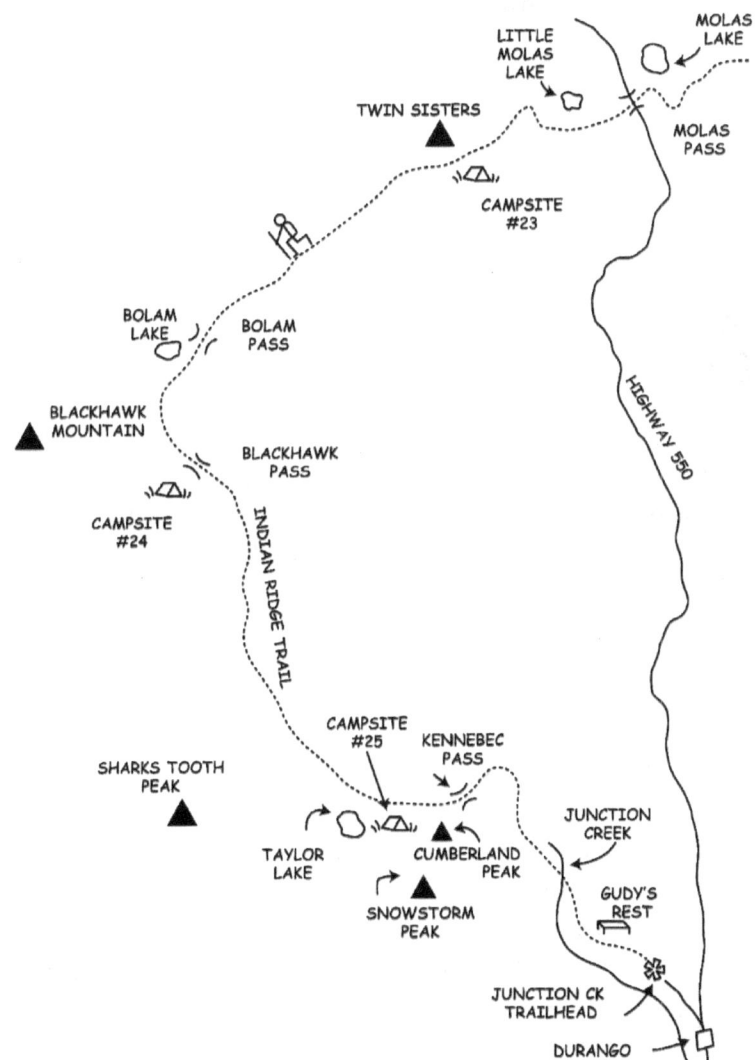

MOLAS LAKE

LITTLE MOLAS LAKE

MOLAS PASS

TWIN SISTERS

CAMPSITE #23

HIGHWAY 550

BOLAM LAKE

BOLAM PASS

BLACKHAWK MOUNTAIN

BLACKHAWK PASS

CAMPSITE #24

INDIAN RIDGE TRAIL

CAMPSITE #25

KENNEBEC PASS

JUNCTION CREEK

SHARKS TOOTH PEAK

TAYLOR LAKE

CUMBERLAND PEAK

GUDY'S REST

SNOWSTORM PEAK

JUNCTION CK TRAILHEAD

DURANGO

CHAPTER TWENTY-ONE:

Molas to Blackhawk

After a big breakfast, Bad Foot and I organized our packs in our triple-level bunk bedroom at the Avon Hotel and Hostel. We learned our third roommate for the night was the same guy who camped by the mining shed in the Elk Creek valley the previous night. We'd slept near him before. Except that the trail, a valley and 150 yards separated us the previous night. Last night, we were literally stacked on top of each other.

Shouldering our packs, we meandered south out Silverton with our thumbs out. We needed to catch a ride back to Molas Pass. It took about 15 minutes thumbing at the gas station just outside of town for someone to pick us up, but we wished it took a few minutes longer.

The downside of hitch-hiking is that you don't know how weird someone is until you commit to get into their vehicle.

It wasn't until our packs were in his trunk and we were headed south on Highway 550 that the driver, a 28-year-old kid with messy brown hair, said, "Don't try anything, I'm packing."

Then he asked, "So how long have you been hiking?"

"For about 30 days." I told him.

Satisfied with that answer, he lights a cigarette, then says, "So, you've been hiking for how long?"

He kept repeating himself and asking the same questions. It was obvious that he was a little more than just high on the Rocky Mountains. It felt like the same unsettling pressure you'd get when a depressed drunk at a bar starts talking to you, and you know if you said the wrong thing he might erupt. Or in this case, drive off Highway 550.

The driver, who suddenly seemed confused as to why we had been in his vehicle for the past five minutes in the first place, said looking at Bad Foot, "Tell me an interesting story from your hike, old timer."

I caught Bad Foot's eye. His expression said something like, "How about you concentrate on safely navigating this mountain road, eh?"

I'd like to believe my expression said, "Well, it'll eventually become a good story." But I know I was telepathically willing this guy to drive us safely up the pass. The seven miles back to Molas Pass felt like it took an hour, but we did make it there safely.

Once we got our packs out of the trunk, Bad Foot and I hustled away from the parking lot and away from the driver, deciding this was the best way to avoid fact checking if the driver really did have a gun.

To think, I had worries of run-ins with mountain lions, bears and moose. I didn't expect my closest call to come from a weirdo in a Honda Civic.

We walked away faster than we ever had thus far on this journey. Each step I took that created more distance between us and that crazy guy garnered a sense of relief. We lived. I had never been so happy to be back on the trail, walking.

Once we felt comfortable back on the trail, Bad Foot and I, like we had most days on the trail, resumed our own pace of hiking.

Segment 25 of the Colorado Trail starts on the west side of the highway and winds its way past a campground. This is an important spot in the trail's history. Along with two other spots — Camp Hale and Mt. Princeton, Molas Pass was the site where a "Golden Spike" ceremony was held on Sept. 4, 1987, that celebrated the linking of the trail from Denver to Durango.

Bad Foot and I had my own reason to hold a ceremony at this spot. We were top dogs again.

For the past 24 days we'd been sharing the trail with Continental Divide Thru-Hikers. The CDTers were the most badass thru-hikers to people in the towns shared by the CT and the CDT of Breckenridge, Leadville and Lake City. Now that we separated from the CDT, we were no longer overshadowed by the CDT hikers.

Since we were near accessible trailheads, the trail was filled with day hikers. They were generally impressed when they learned we'd hiked from Denver and extremely interested in the Colorado Trail.

"Wow, you look like an experienced hiker, how far are you hiking?" one group asked.

"Another 10 miles today," I'd say, "but we've come 400 miles since Denver . . ."

The impressed look in their eyes gave me such a sense of satisfaction that I wanted more of these moments.

Another group of tourists was impressed with the idea of hiking 20 miles a day. "How do you do that?"

"Well, it's actually pretty easy when you do the math," I said, standing a bit taller. "Say you hike 2 mph, if you hike for 10 hours, that's 20 miles. If you're on the trail at 7 a.m., you'll be 20 miles down the trail by 5 p.m."

It wasn't long before I even had a bit of a prance.

Or another couple I told, "Yep, that's right, I've been hiking for 32 days . . . 400 miles since Denver."

To which they said, "OK, but all we asked was, 'Do you know if the trailhead has a latrine?'"

My prance stopped in its tracks, I pointed them in the direction of the bathroom and kept hiking.

But my confidence was rekindled by the views. As if nature came out to celebrate our rise to the top of the food chain, the rocks were decorated with grays, browns, reds and greens. A mile into hiking, we were back above 11,000 feet, I realized the San Juan Peaks were very different than the rock of the mountains on the middle of the CT. It's as though the artist painting the San Juans had extra colors on their palette — extra browns and reds. The Sawatch Mountains from earlier seemed to be made of green and gray alone. The San Juans were like a layered cake of shale, sandstone and limestone.

I couldn't help but slow down and stare as I walked. The view was breathtaking and almost surreal — like a graffiti artist made some random red stripes on these mountains.

The basin above Molas Pass meanders through Upper Lime Creek, a drainage area that used to be a forest until a fire ran through it in 1879. Although it hasn't been reclaimed by the forest, it has become home to abundant wildflowers. Yellow and purple heads of flowers splatter the green grass that frames the trail.

Several miles into my 32nd day on the CT, I realized my mind wasn't as clear as the previous days. I had the unrested mind of a town day. Like some of the benefit of my brain being in nature was zapped by civilization. There was just a slight uncluttered and unrelaxed sense to me today.

Maybe it was the distractions of phones and modern life pulling me from the trail brain. Town days are fun, but I craved to get back into trail mode. The anxiousness could also be the product of a few beers and the ensuing disturbed sleep that comes from alcohol in your system at night. I didn't drink any alcohol when camped on the trail, but in town I did.

Alcohol diminishes the quality of your sleep. Specifically, it impacts the amount of mind-rejuvenating REM (rapid eye movement) sleep. In the habit of drinking alcohol several days a week, I realized how much better I can feel when I take a few weeks off.

I noticed the stark benefits of not drinking alcohol when I did a 31-day alcohol-free month to kick off the year. The first thing I notice is the improvement in my sleep. Then I notice more energy and motivation. It caused me to drink less throughout the year. Giving up alcohol for a month has benefits months later — that's what I found out and what academic literature confirms.[60]

Starting the day in Silverton meant hitting the trail three hours later than usual. We wouldn't get 10 miles by noon. Our goal was 10 miles for the entire day. This required 2,400 feet of elevation gain and got Bad Foot and me into camp around 3 p.m.

I napped, completed a crossword puzzle, and ate Fritos around a fire while I waited for some fellow backpackers to show up at this magnificent campsite. I figured we'd start a new chapter of new hikers. With a view of the valley and downed trees for seating around a great rock-made fire ring. The site below Twin Sisters rocks was designed for a party of backpackers.

Yet none showed up. That surprised me.

I was hoping to introduce the RAT clues to more hikers. Alas, it was just Bad Foot and I setting the eight-minute timer as we quizzed ourselves.

I supplemented the food in my re-supply package with a block of cheddar, tortillas and a bag of Fritos from the grocery in Silverton. I would spork my dehydrated meals into a tortilla with cheese and chip crunch. This was a method I adopted to get extra calories.

The day's gratitude portion of my journal included the topics: "cheese Frito tortilla goodness," "crossword puzzles," "easy miles" and "surviving a weird hitch-hiking experience."

Segment 25 of the Colorado trails runs for 21 miles between Molas Pass and Bolam Pass. We had hiked the first half of Segment 25 the previous day, which meant our goal of 10 miles by 12 o'clock required finishing up Segment 25 of the trail by noon, which we did.

Since leaving Denver, I had lost 15 pounds. Supplementing tortillas and cheese to my meals was a new way to maintain my weight. I had a sizable chicken and tortilla meal at 10 a.m. and another dehydrated meal wrapped in a cheesy Fritos-laden tortilla at 12:30 p.m. The extra meals really allowed me to keep up my energy during a monster hiking day. You burn a lot of calories hiking 21 miles and 4,200 feet of elevation. It also helped that the previous day was a rejuvenating relatively-low-mile day.

It's funny how my perspective had changed; hiking 10 miles used to be a huge day. Now 10-mile days were basically a rejuvenation day. Twenty-mile days were the new 10-mile day. Even saying the words, "We hiked 21 miles today," made me puff up my chest and put my shoulders back in confidence.

The start of Segment 26 begins by the edge of Celebration Lake. Despite the dirt roads and parking lot, the area feels very remote. Along the way to gain the saddle beside Hermosa Peak, the trail passes several signs with yellow lettering carved into the brown wood saying, "Colorado Trail."

They are great picture spots, particularly since you can also get Hermosa Peak in the background. The mountains in this area have red blotches that seem to stream down their sides like the red splotches that form under the nostrils on the nose of someone with a cold who has blown their nose too much — only these were pretty.

Next was the climb up Blackhawk Pass, which, I discovered, revealed one of the best views on the entire trail. That was saying something. The rugged San Juan Mountains don't disappoint.

We had the added benefit of getting the view from the pass with the sky being partially filled with recent thunderstorm clouds. We got the whole spectrum from dark storm clouds to bright blue sky above and the entire spectrum of colors down below between the dark greens of the grass and pine trees and the stark gray rock contrasted with stripes of red. From the pass, you can see the Wilson Group 14ers and what appears like a giant finger sticking up from the gray peaks in the distance known as Lizard Head Peak, whose spire-like shape makes it one of the most distinctive 13,000-foot peaks in Colorado.

We would've sat at the saddle taking in the views much longer if the rain hadn't been moving right at us. The top of Blackhawk Pass sat at 11,988 feet in elevation. The next two miles descended 1,100 feet to the last reliable water source before a day's hiking worth of dry stretch. We were able to drop 500 feet before the rain dumped on us.

"It's raining," Bad Foot said over the clatter of droplets slapping against our rain jacket hoods.

"Thanks for the update," I said with a puzzled expression in my eyes.

"'It's raining' is different than saying 'It's raining on me,'" he elaborated. "There's a subtle distinction. The minute you add 'on me' you make it personal."

Bad Foot was imparting some wisdom he'd learned from months of backpacking.

"Language matters. That subtle distinction keeps your mind from taking weather personally. It's not. We are all getting rained on."

"You trying to change your trail name to 'Stoic?'" I joked, even though I knew his advice was important.

We can't control the rain. And the rain doesn't just happen to me. We can only control ourselves, our own actions and how we respond and the judgments we ourselves make.

We crossed Straight Creek that was running fast with brown muddy water from the rain fall, and we started to do some trivia because it reminded me of the Mississippi's nickname — "The Big Muddy." So, at the tail end of our day, I tried to distract from our fatigue and quiz Bad Foot.

"OK, I'll give you a clue, and the answer has the word 'big' in it," I said.

"Lanky Lefty Pitcher from MLB . . ."

"The Big Unit," said Bad Foot, a little quicker than I had hoped.

"OK, how about the tunnel project in Boston?"

"The Big Dig," said Bad Foot.

"Jeff Bridges movie character?"

"The Big Lebowski."

He's good

The guidebook noted that Straight Creek was the last reliable water source for 22 miles until reaching Taylor Lake. Given the recent downpour, we figured the "unreliable" water sources up ahead on the trail would have enough water for us. So, we decided to hike on past Straight Creek in search of a better campsite in the trees. This had the added benefit of shortening the dry stretch that we'd cover first thing the next day. We found a good camp spot another half mile down the trail beside a flowing seasonal stream. This made it a perfect spot to camp for the night, allowing us to fill up our water bottles fully in the morning before tackling that arid section.

Once our tents were up and dinner was consumed, into our camp rolled a mountain biker from Flagstaff, Arizona. He put up his tent next to his bike, next to Bad Foot and me.

"I'll admit I was a bit confused as I rolled my bike into your campsite I heard you saying, 'Yeah, I agree it's 'stand' — Band Stand, Kick Stand, Stand Off,'" he told us.

Admittedly, he had reason to be a bit bewildered. We were comparing the answers to the 11th RAT I brought with me.

We both got seven out of 10 correct. Our best score yet. There really might be something about stunning days in nature.

Only 75 trail miles run from Silverton to Durango. The math works out to five 15-mile days. After 10 miles the first day, our 20-mile day caught us back up to a 15-mile day average. We finished the day only 44 trail miles from Durango. We were back on pace. Three 15s would get us to the end of the trail.

Or back-to-back 20 plus days . . .

Clues for RAT Quiz #10
bench, book, check
top, car, soap
mare, fort, time
trade, ground, play
garage, man, bell
stop, house, night
home, mine, line
band, kick, off
fast, art, paper
burn, flower, shine

Clues for RAT Quiz #11
cheap, board, figure
tree, smoke, out
love, story, line
field, shopping, lane
bull, pig, pal
first, wrist, tower
red, lid, ball
immediate, tree, doctor
ruled, wall, clip
mail, letter, key

CHAPTER TWENTY-TWO:

Last Camp

I emerged from my tent just as Bad Foot was leaving camp. Our initial plan, discussed the night before, was to get to a seasonal stream 15 miles down the trail called Deer Creek and assess if that was where we'd put up our tents for the night.

I took my time making oatmeal and enjoying my morning coffee before fully filling up all my water bottles. The mountain biker from Flagstaff was still asleep when I left.

The first four miles of my 34th day on the Colorado Trail were either flat or had a gentle downhill slope. On an easy path like this section, your brain doesn't need to devote a ton of conscious effort to walk, and this means my brain was free to wander. I got into a great thinking space. As you allow your mind to wander, your subconscious guides you to places you didn't know you'd visit. This, I realized, is why insights seem to pop into my head on a stroll.

Why does walking help you think?

The first and most obvious reason is that walking makes our hearts work faster, which helps circulate more blood and oxygen to muscles and organs including the brain. But that's not where the benefits stop. Just as upbeat music helps us run fast, walking at our own pace allows our thoughts, mood and inner speech to match the cadence of our feet.[61] That's right, the crunch, crunch, crunch of the trail beneath my trail runners was helping shape my thoughts.

Some of the world's greatest thinkers were avid walkers: Darwin, Nietzsche, Einstein, Wordsworth, Thoreau, Woolf and Aristotle. Nietzsche said, "All truly great thoughts are conceived while walking." Thoreau said, "Me thinks that the moment my legs begin to move, my thoughts begin to flow."

Researchers at Stanford decided to test if walking really does measurably boost creativity.[62] In a series of experiments, college students completed creative thinking tests (like coming up with unique uses for, say, a brick, tire or paperclip) while either walking or sitting. The walkers came up with about four to six more unique uses for a tire than students who were seated.

So, walking through campus boosted creativity.

But was it the walking? Or was it the movement in nature that was boosting creativity? To answer that question, they grabbed some wheelchairs and some treadmills and ran some more experiments. Some students tested their creativity while walking on a treadmill staring at a blank wall, while others were walking through Stanford's campus, while still others were thinking about unique brick uses while being pushed in a wheelchair around campus.

In this way, they were able to isolate the difference between movement outdoors from physical walking. The walkers scored higher in creativity than those pushed in a wheelchair along the same path. Walking on a treadmill staring at a blank wall also beat those who sat. Other studies show that walking can help delay the negative effects of an aging brain.[63] I figured this CT hike added back the few years of my brain's life that I lost during late nights in college.

The trail zigzags south staying close to the ridge line between 10,600 and 11,000 feet for nine miles of Segment 27 of the CT. That elevation is still among the trees, but high enough and on top of the ridge enough to have expansive views of the greens, reds and grays of the San Juans. The bonus of the ridge run means wide views to your left for a few minutes, then suddenly the trail zigs on the other side of the ridge and delivers the great views to your right.

I didn't catch up to Bad Foot until 12 miles into the day. We split a dehydrated beef stew meal wrapped in tortillas.

When we got to the seasonal water spot, Deer Creek, I said to Bad Foot, "It's only 1:30, and there's not great camp sites around here. What do you think?"

Bad Foot checked the FarOut App and said, "It looks like the trail continues up from here. We either camp here or it's another eight miles and 2,000 feet of gain to Taylor Lake, the next water source."

We were currently at 11,100 feet in elevation. The trail continued to climb to 12,300 feet. It was still early in the day, yet we knew we'd start to feel sluggish in the late afternoon after coming off a big 20-miler the day before.

"It'll be our last time above 12,000 feet of the entire trail," I offered. "If we get over Indian Ridge today, it's downhill sailing to Durango tomorrow."

"That's true . . . but I don't know . . ." Bad Foot said.

"Is that fatigue talking?"

"You know, there are studies that ask long-distance runners how steep they think a hill is, and cross-country runners are typically much better than the average person at guessing gradients . . . except when they are tired . . . after a long run, the cross-country runners overestimated a hill's steepness like the rest of us."

When we are exhausted, we shift toward the negative and underestimate our abilities. Knowing that helps you get better at doing something about it.[64]

"Maybe it's not as bad as it looks then, because I am definitely exhausted" Bad Foot concluded.

"Clever reasoning," I told him. "Let's think of another 20-mile day as a challenge."[65]

After yesterday's Stoic philosophy lesson on "raining on me," I decided to teach Bad Foot a lesson on underestimating our abilities when we're in a tired mood.

We decided to push it to Taylor Lake, which meant crossing, in the late afternoon, Indian Trail Ridge, a rocky spine above tree line. The trail makes a linear path across the ridge. The elevation plot of Indian Trail Ridge looks like five ascending teeth of a saw blade, the tallest point at 12,300. It's 3.5 miles long with no great spots to ditch, in the case of a stacking thunderstorm or lightning strike.

On the first of five saddles on the ridge, we ran into two guys lingering in the sparse trees that were able to grow that high up. The hikers were called Tin Goat and Daddy Long Legs.

"I've been waiting here for the past 45 minutes," Tin Goat explained. "I saw lightning strike the ridge further on up."

They confirmed what I had feared since we left Deer Creek: the afternoon thunderstorms that were common in July were forming overhead.

"Do we turn around and drop elevation and get below the trees while the thunderstorm passes?" I suggested, but no one really responded.

There were patches of blue sky above us, but also threateningly dark thunder clouds forming blotches in all directions — the kind of sky that could just as easily clear up into perfect blue evening or build into a massive thunderstorm.

We sat, chatted and waited at the saddle knowing we could quickly descend back down the trail below the trees if the weather turned worse. But it didn't get worse, and it didn't get better either. The blue sunny patches were in a stalemate with the heavy gray rain clouds. So, we decided to hike ahead.

As a foursome, we pushed across the three-mile stretch under the menacing clouds. The ridge offers tremendous views of the amphitheater-like valley formed by Diorite Peak, Lavender Peak, Sharkstooth Peak and Hesperus Mountain. With nicer weather, we would have taken a few rests on the ridge to savor the views. Instead, we never stopped. We were a nervous conga line covering the ridge miles as quickly as possible while intermittently scouting the clouds overhead.

We reached the last lower summit of the ridge at 5 p.m. and got our first view of Taylor Lake. The descent is steep and rocky. We were still exposed and still in a hurry.

The heavy, gray storm clouds began dissipating about the exact moment we reached Taylor Lake. We took our time filtering water and basking in the sun.

During this whole hike, I was intrigued by how quickly friendships can form on the trail. The bonds we made with Tin Goat and Daddy Long Legs formed especially quickly.

It's like suffering through that lightning storm on an exposed alpine ridge sped up our relationship. Could that be possible? Could cohesion, trust and solidarity be strengthened by experiencing a miserable lightning storm together?

There's research data to back that up. A trio of psychologists from Australia fed college students either a raw Bird's Eye chili pepper — which is super spicy — or candy, then tested their cooperation.[66] They found that people in the pain condition group who ate the pepper tested higher on social bonding and cooperation than the students who ate candy. Sharing pain becomes a very salient shared experience. As the authors note, "Pain, it seems, has the capacity to act as social glue, building cooperation . . ."

As we lounged next to Taylor Lake, the adrenaline began to wear off and the fatigue of a monster hiking day started to set in. We got to learn the etymology of Tin Goat's trail name.

"Well, I was blown up when I was in Afghanistan. Between the shrapnel and the rebuilt body parts the Army put into me, I figured I'm a walking Tin Man. Then some hikers a few weeks back thought I hiked like a Mountain Goat. So, we combined Tin Man and Mountain Goat."

I wondered if the hiker bond was somewhat akin to a soldier's bond. I was surprised that Tin Goat would open up to us non-soldiers so readily.

Maybe it's the bond of being a true thru-hiker?

From the lake, we could see a patch of trees a half mile down the trail. The comments on the FarOut app confirmed our hope for a good camp spot.

The four of us slowly meandered down the trail toward the spot. I was so tired that rocks were beginning to look like pillows.

Tin Goat didn't stay, however. He wanted to log several more miles on the day. Daddy Long Legs camped with us. We made it to our camping spot around 6:30 p.m.

The day's totals were 23 miles and 4,100 feet of vertical gain. Bad Foot was completely wiped out. Once he got his tent up, he fell asleep.

I used the term "surreal" in my journal that night. Waking up this morning, we thought we had two more nights on the trail. But after such a big day today, we were only a day away from Durango. This was my last night camping on the Colorado Trail.

I made my dinner and chatted with Daddy Long Legs, whose moniker came from his height and the hiking he does with his children. I learned about the unique tradition Daddy Long Legs has for each of his children once they turn 13. He takes them on a thru-hike of the 211-mile John Muir Trail in California.

Intrigued, I asked, "How hard was it for your kids to adjust to trail life?"

"They are uncomfortable, they miss their friends, they miss their screens and social media. Then a transformation happens, usually about day four or five," Daddy Long Legs tells me, "They start to embrace the challenge. They start to break their phone addiction. They embrace the 'badassness' of accomplishing something difficult."

Wow, so day four is really a thing. I felt it too.

"What a great way to strengthen your relationships with your kids," I added. "Sounds like a rite of passage?"

"It instills in those teens a sense that you can accomplish big things if you keep your nose to the grind and have a little grit," he said. "Though it takes a few days for them to get to that head space."

I learned that the initial days on the trail through the Sierra Nevada for a teen whose eyeballs are too often marinating in the blue light of a cell phone scrolling through social media are what you'd expect from an addict.

I didn't know much about the John Muir Trail at this point. But Daddy Long Legs filled me in.

Then I learned about the "mini triple crown." The full triple crown of thru-hiking in America is hiking the AT, PCT and CDT. But there's a standalone subsection of each of the triple crown hikes. The John Muir Trail (211 miles) is part of the Pacific Crest Trail, the Long Trail (272 miles up and down the length of Vermont) is part of the Appalachian Trail, and the Colorado Trail is 486 miles sharing 314 of the Continental Divide Trail.

As we were talking about the JMT, a 37-year-old blonde female hiker stopped by our campsite to chat. She was also a day away from finishing a thru-hike of the Colorado Trail. She introduced herself as Tooth, a trail name given to her because of the luxury item she carried with her from Denver: an electric toothbrush.

I had already been impressed with some of the unique stories I heard about why fellow hikers were on the CT. There was German Mountain Goat who left the humidity of California to help cure some sort of autoimmune disease. Only a few years earlier, she could barely hike two miles, but in 2022 she was hiking all 486 miles of the Colorado Trail.

There was Tin Goat, who had been blown up in Afghanistan and had been confined to a wheelchair and told he'd never walk again. He was a day away from thru-hiking the entire trail.

Tooth had a similar inspirational reason for hiking. Tooth had very little backpacking experience before starting the Colorado Trail, but she was driven to hike to find catharsis. She had recently gotten out of a 12-year relationship in the same month that her brother passed away. Tooth told us that she spent the first three weeks of the trail crying every single day.

"Until I found a trail family," she told us triumphantly.

The trail eventually brought her relief.

I saw it the same way Tooth did. I was becoming more extroverted. My brain didn't feel like a pinball machine mixed with six shots of espresso and itching powder. I wasn't struggling with mental chatter when I was trying to fall asleep. The trail transformed me, too.

"I'm going to try to hike another mile or two tonight. I hope I see you in Durango tomorrow," Tooth told us.

I felt a pang of regret that Bad Foot didn't have the energy to chat at the campsite on our last night on the trail. Plus, I had one last RAT to do. Maybe I could recruit someone else.

"Hey, Daddy Long Legs, do you know what a remote association test is?"

"I don't think so."

I pulled out my papers and began explaining the three clues when I when Daddy Long Legs interjected with a chuckle.

"I think I've heard about these quizzes, yeah there were two women camped in the yurt outside of Lake City talking about these."

"That had to be Bangs and Legs," I said. "Small world on the trail, right?"

These serendipitous moments are recurring events on a long trail.

We had introduced Bangs and Legs to remote association tests around the campfire 12 days before. Daddy Long Legs also knew Spoons. They had run into the college gal outside Lake City.

As I was digging in my pack for my pens, I heard a voice call out from behind me, "Better give me one of those tests too."

Bad Foot was unzipping his tent and sliding out to join us.

I tried to hide my emotions as he crawled out of his tent to join us, "I'm glad you're up, so we can enjoy our last campsite evening together, man."

I felt a tad queasy expressing my feelings, but I knew Nugget was getting better at it; 35 days ago, I'd have avoided saying anything about my feelings.

We set the eight-minute timer and the three of us tried to solve the 10 clue-triplets.

This was the 12th of 12 Remote Association Tests that I brought along. I can't say that I had a control group. And I don't know if one quiz was harder than the others, but what

I can say is that I was better at them on days when I let the day come to me. On days I was worried about the weather or when I was occupied with making a set time to meet part of my trail crew, I wasn't as creative. I didn't have the energy to see broader connections. But on a few days, where we didn't have to rush, we didn't have to worry about getting down from a mountain pass before lightning came, we could just be. Hike, camp, be. On those days, the Remote Association answers came easier.

Before I crawled into my tent, I received a ping on my Garmin. It was as message from my friend Heidi, "I've been following your GPS. It looks like you're getting close to Durango. Congratulations." My mom also sent me a message advising me to "soak up the last night on the trail." My pal Shawn said, "Past Taylor Lake, looks like you'll finish the trail tomorrow."

It was more than a month ago that I had been sitting in the sandy dirt next to the South Platte River at the end of Segment 1 of the Colorado Trail, as Chris, alone. Those Garmin messages meant so much to me.

Now I was Nugget, with my tent feet away from Bad Foot, with whom I'd been hiking for the last 31 days and Daddy Long Legs, whom I'd been hiking with for the past three hours.

I felt invincible. I felt different. I felt a change.

Yet the messages from friends still stirred a tingling in my stomach (different from giardia) and some tiny tears in my eyes.

How lucky am I?

I sat with my back against a tree staring out as the setting sun cast a pink glow on the neighboring peaks from the island of a campsite we had found in a patch of trees amongst a sea of willows. I felt like the trail gave me a farewell present — the most amazing sunset.

I began remembering all the amazing campsites I had the past 34 nights. Then I made a list of the most spectacular campsites that I experienced along the Colorado Trail. The current spot, I assigned it the second-best awe-inspiring-view-campsite of my journey. We were still at 11,600 feet of elevation.

Here's the list I jotted in my journal:

#5 the campsite in the Holy Cross Wilderness (about 7 miles into Segment 9) in an open grassy meadow which looks out at the snow in the couloirs of the granite ridge that forms the eastern flank of the Sawatch Range and the Continental Divide.

#4 the campsite in the long valley by Cochetopa Creek (mile 8 in Segment 19) the creek snakes through the grassy open valley and it's framed by evergreens and ridges on both sides.

#3 Marshall Pass (Segment 15): The view of the setting sun casting its light on Mount Ouray.

#2 Tonight's spot (around mile 20 in Segment 27) in a small postage stamp of a patch of trees down into Cumberland Basin below Taylor Lake.

#1 The site by Elk Creek (mile 7 into Segment 24) just before mile 400.

In my gratitude section of my journal that night, I listed "not getting struck by lightning" and "Bangs and Legs talking about RAT."

Then I thought, with a sharp tinge of sadness in my gut, that my email's automatic away message wouldn't be truthful after tomorrow.

If you need me in person, I can be found on the Colorado Trail.

<u>Clues for RAT Quiz #12</u>
dry, funny, wish
cheap, board, figure
about, off, card
green, board, place
sun, side, out
leader, wall, school
extra, card, rating
hold, print, note
cold, water, page
waiting, bird, curtain

CHAPTER TWENTY-THREE:

Durango

As usual, Bad Foot was up with his tent packed on his back leaving camp about the time I was emerging from mine. Like I had been doing the 24 other times I slept in my tent on the trail, I packed my quilt, pad and pillow up before I popped out of the tent. It was my routine, my habit of making my bed every morning first thing. Then I'd start heating water for my coffee. In the time it got hot, I would pack my gear into my backpack. With everything all neatly packed, I sat sipping my coffee, staring at the clouds casting the sun's early pink light above Snowstorm Peak and Cumberland Mountain.

It was awesome, like watching Mother Nature's Imax.

We continued the same morning trail routine as we had for the past weeks. Bad Foot got up earlier than me and I tried to catch him. Bad Foot was on the trail at 6 a.m. I was hiking at 6:30 a.m.

From our campsite, the trail gently drops elevation as it heads to the Kennebec Trailhead, the official start of the last segment of the CT. If my body was sore from back-to-back, 20-mile, big elevation days, the adrenaline of the last day masked it. The anticipation and its accompanying dopamine of seeing that trailhead sign at the end of a 486-mile hike was fueling my legs.

The 28th and last segment of the Colorado Trail has more vertical travel than any other — 6,500 feet of elevation in one direction, and that direction graciously is down! The Kennebec Trailhead sits at 11,642 feet, and the Colorado Trail southern terminus is below 7,000 feet. It's not all downhill, however. There's still 1,900 feet of gain. Most of that gain is between mile 7 and 11, which meant once we got halfway through this segment, it was a clear 10 miles sailing downhill to Durango.

From Kennebec Trailhead, the trail crosses a talus slope named Sliderock. Across the valley from Sliderock, is a miner's cabin seemingly built on the red rock cliffs. It's a quick transition as the trail drops elevation from the rocky talus slopes of Sliderock, to the thick green vegetation of the valley. The trail drops 3,250 feet in 6.5 miles as it heads down to cross Junction Creek. It felt like a lush, wet, jungle compared to the arid, high elevation trail we'd been on the past few days.

It was at Junction Creek that I caught up with Bad Foot sitting next to Tin Goat enjoying a snack and filtering water.

"Hey, how many days of the past year do you remember?" I asked them as I chowed down a Pop-Tart. "Like 'wow' moments that you can re-live and savor? Because I can remember every single day of my 35 days on the trail. Why do you think that is?"

"Because you are on high alert to make memories and look for adventures," Bad Foot suggested.

After our snack break, Tin Goat, Bad Foot and I began the last notable climb of the Colorado Trail. We'd already climbed 88,000 feet of elevation since the start at Waterton. This was the last 1,000 feet of gain.

The trail climbs up from Junction Creek then parallels it 1,000 feet above it in the narrow, verdant gulch. Achieving the last 1,000 feet of elevation, the trail turns right and reveals views of the rolling ridges of evergreen trees.

I had seen Bad Foot smile and laugh before — when I body slammed the Wangler in the Holy Cross Wilderness he let out a big hoot. And he chuckled at what I said when we were chatting with fellow hikers in the hostel in Lake City — as we were discussing how our cell phones listen to us and target ads to what we say, I told the group, "because I've been hiking with Bad Foot for the past three weeks, all my ads have been suggested medicine for erectile dysfunction."

But I realized at that moment at the top of the last climb of the Colorado Trail that those were only Bad Foot's 80% grin. At the top of that ridge, with 10 miles left on the Colorado Trail — all downhill — that's when I saw Bad Foot's 100% smile.

I felt honored that he showed that smile because I knew he reserved it for special friends and special moments. I returned his smile with one of my own.

We were 10 miles away from the finish — 98% of the way done. Those last 10 miles maintained a gentle 300-foot drop per mile. That's easy strolling.

The gentle downhill slope was the perfect time for reflection. Most of the miles on the trail together, we'd hike alone at our own pace — separated by several hundred yards. But for these remaining miles, it just felt right that we stayed together.

I thought back to the Angel of Shavano Trailhead when I had a fear of sharing my feelings with my mom. I missed that opportunity to apologize and express my feelings in person.

Don't waste that chance with Bad Foot.

"You really made my first thru-hike special, Bad Foot, I'm really glad that I met you," I was surprised to find myself saying. It wasn't effusive, but it was a major improvement for me.

And as we ambled along, Bad Foot let me in on the philosophical debate he'd been pondering in his mind over the last several days.

"Back when I first started backpacking as a teenager, I got into a debate with my father about the backcountry," Bad Foot said.

"In what way?" I asked.

"Well, my dad felt that the views and mountain trails that we've been hiking should be accessible to all people regardless of their age. But I argued that there should be areas only for those who were willing to pay the physical price to get there."

"Has your opinion changed?"

Bad Foot then said, "Well . . . back then it was easy for me to argue when I was a teenager and squarely in the group that could pay the price to enjoy the mountains. But I've been thinking about that debate a lot today, and my father's view is starting to make more sense."

"So, more switchbacks and more spots that are accessible by car? Should more people be able to see the views from Blackhawk Pass like we saw?"

"Well . . . I don't think. I think I'm going to stick with the same side of the argument I took as a teen," Bad Foot explained.

"My experience last year on the PCT was very much about the people I met along the way. This year, it was more about the mountains and their raw power," Bad Foot continued. "I realized that some places are magical because they aren't crowded, and you can lose yourself completely."

"Yeah, I remember you saying something similar when we had that valley camped next to the Cochetopa to ourselves."

"Yeah, if that was easy to access, it would have been packed with people," Bad Foot said. "There needs to be obstacles and steep sections. Those steep sections mean there are indeed 'No Country for Old Men' and they need to stay that way."

"Make people earn the views? They are more meaningful then?" I suggested.

"The Colorado Trail has made me acutely aware that my days of no limits are numbered."

"But not yet, huh?" I said.

"We are completing a 486 mile thru-hiker today aren't we?" Bad Foot smiled, "So, I guess not yet."

On my 35th day on the Colorado Trail, Bad Foot and I encountered four separate groups who were starting their first day. They were all headed northbound from Durango to Denver. They all looked so refreshed, yet unbeaten by the elevation gain and the strong Colorado sun.

I was the veteran thru-hiker now dispensing advice to the newbies. And I was proud and nostalgic about it.

"Did you download the FarOut app?" was my first question. "I'd recommend avoiding giardia," was my second piece of advice. "Don't pass up the Lake City Bakery," was the third. And the fourth was "Don't feel bad about pulling a Shade Patch."

'What's 'pulling a Shade Patch' mean?" asked the first thru-hiker we met that day, whose trail name was "Sol."

"It means taking more breaks, slowing down and noticing your surroundings," Bad Foot added.

We later met a husband and wife from Wisconsin. Another group was a guy from Italy and a gal from France. All were bound for Denver. And all faced a big uphill day in front of them, but the same trail was a nice downhill for us.

Four miles from the Junction Creek Trailhead and the southern terminus, the trail passed another memorial to the Godmother of the Colorado Trail — Gudy's Rest. The bench at that spot decorated the scenic overlook above the evergreen trees and Durango lounging below. I shared the bench with Tin Goat, Bad Foot, a female hiker only four miles into her trek to Denver and her boyfriend, who had hiked those first miles to Gudy's Rest with some champagne to send her off.

We convinced her to download the FarOut app right there.

From the bench overlook, I was intentional about walking the last four miles of the trail in solitude to allow my mind to process the entire 35-day journey. Besides the first 300 yards when Ed accompanied me, I walked the first four miles of the trail alone as well. Back when I was unsure of myself. When a 10-mile hike was a monster day. When I was intimidated to be in the wilderness alone. When I let troublesome, yet tiny, interactions rankle me all day. Since then, I had shed 15 pounds of body weight and quite a bit of self-doubt. My mind was clear. I'd found a tribe. I was a better listener, and my legs were boulders.

Exactly 34 years to the day earlier (On Saturday, July 24, 1988), the Colorado Trail was officially dedicated at Junction Creek Trailhead. The ceremony coincided with the end of a five-week Trail-A-Bration hike.[67]

Over 200 people watched as a ribbon was cut to officially open the Colorado Trail.

There weren't 200 people watching Bad Foot and me as we took our photos in front of the Colorado Trail sign, but it felt like there were. At that moment, a flooding realization came over me. I understood how thru-hiking the Colorado Trail and the transformation I experienced was one of the most rewarding experiences of my life. In my bones, I felt happier, kinder, calmer and more confident than I had ever felt before.

Shortly after we took our pictures in front of the Colorado Trail sign, Bad Foot blurted out, "Is that Tin Goat?"

He was pointing to a guy, loaded with a monstrous backpack, barreling down the trail in a fast jog. In keeping with his military tradition of running the last mile of a big hike, Tin Goat was running the 486th mile of the CT. It made my eyes tear up to witness someone, who in the mid-2000s was contemplating suicide after being blown up at war and didn't think he'd ever walk again, finish the Colorado Trail.

I didn't run any steps that day, but the highest step count I had on the trail was my last day. My daily step average in my off-trail life is around 7,700 steps. This is better than the average American step count of 5,400. To put the trail into perspective, my daily average in July on the Trail was 25,000 steps. My iPhone recorded 48,454 steps on my last day on the CT. That was hiking 23 miles of the trail and strolling around Durango between breweries, ice cream shops, restaurants and the hotel.

But it didn't include having to walk from the trailhead into Durango. Because fortunately for us, the champagne-wielding boyfriend from Gudy's Rest showed up at the trail head shortly after Daddy Long Legs did. Four of us were looking to hitch a ride into Durango, and the boyfriend had just enough room in his Jeep once we Tetris-blocked our backpacks, poles and bodies.

Over the past 35 days, time and time again, I had been amazed at the quick bonds formed by people on the trail. The last leg of the trail was no different. The boyfriend with champagne was set to make the long drive back to Denver when Daddy Long Legs, who knew the boyfriend for all of 10 minutes, decided to ride along. The bonds of the trail trump six hours in a car with a stranger and their hiker stench. There's no way the boyfriend had "embraced the stench" yet.

With five men, and five backpacks crammed into a Jeep, we headed for town. The ride gave me time to think about myself 35 days before, out of water slogging to the end of

Segment 1 of the trail to get water from the South Platte and daydreaming about my top list of best beer experiences.

That was back when I asked myself, "Am I craving a cold beer? Or am I craving my good friends? What makes a top beer experience?"

I found my answer.

It's the company — it's celebrating something difficult that you accomplished with your tribe — something you're immensely proud of, like the Colorado Trail.

The beers with Silent Nomad in Leadville made the list. So would the free Colorado Trail Nut Brown Ale from Carver Brewery Co. in Durango. Luckily for the other patrons, who were spared our hiker stench and our enthusiastic storytelling, Carver Brewery has outdoor seating.

Epilogue

I t's a Monday in July 2024, a full two years after Bad Foot and I took Colorado Trail finisher photos in front of the Junction Creek Trailhead in Durango.

I'm back in Pennsylvania visiting my parents. We are loading up my mom's Jeep with soda, snacks and fresh fruit, and my parents and I drive 67 miles east of my hometown of Bedford to Caledonia State Park in search of the painted white strip blazes of the Appalachian Trail.

Once we find them, we set up our trail magic on two picnic tables right beside the 2,200-mile trail from Georgia to Maine and wait for hikers to hear out our trade proposal, written neatly on a small sign: homemade chocolate-chip cookies for trail stories.

Because the hikers we meet will cross the halfway point of the AT the following day, they are already talking about a rite of passage they will encounter at the Pine Grove Furnace General Store: a challenge to devour an entire half gallon of ice cream in one sitting to mark that halfway point.

At 5:30 p.m., the shadows of the trees are getting longer, and the sun is at a perfect angle. It's throwing around a perfectly soft, golden light, the kind that photographers love. There's a half dozen backpacks strewn on the ground.

Scattered around a picnic table sit Cash, Freight Train, 9 to 5, Bliss, Riley and Milk Man.

I met them only 20 minutes and three chocolate chip cookies ago, but I juke into their conversation like we are lifelong friends. My parents fit right in as well; they found common ground despite never having done a major thru-hike. It could have been the fact that handing out milk and cookies puts you into thru-hikers' good graces fairly swiftly.

"It's time to pay up!" my dad declares. "It's time for hiker stories. But first, I must know, why do they call you Freight Train?"

I am delighted to see my dad embrace my passion for the thru-hiker culture since he couldn't get to Colorado when I was on the CT.

"Because I have a joint condition and it takes me awhile to get moving, but once I do, I can move and I'm hard to stop," Freight Train tells us.

Cash, the Canadian hiker whose gray horseshoe mustache makes him look like a Civil War reenactor, is next. He tells us the origin of his trail name. "Do you know what a pain it is to book hotels without a credit card? You have to put down a cash deposit, which they only give you back after they inspect the room for damages. Which sometimes might take a few hours before they get around to it." Cash lost his credit card early in his journey, and his new one could only be mailed to his permanent address north of the U.S. border. I stare at his socks as he talks. They look brittle from two months of sun, dirt, dust and sweat.

The laughter, the instant friendships, the proud feeling of a big day, the hiker stench. I miss it.

A fluttery feeling of excitement springs into my stomach. I can only describe it as overwhelming joy.

Three days after hanging out with Cash and Milk Man on the AT, I'm back in Colorado parking my truck at the

Eddiesville Trailhead, where Segment 20 of the Colorado Trail overlaps the CDT.

On my 10th day on the CT two years ago, I ran into the Colorado Trail Foundation's field operations manager, Darin, near Tennessee Pass. He had mentioned there was a remote section of the CT up for adoption.

Well, not anymore.

The eight-mile stretch of trail past the Eddiesville Trailhead is my adopted section now. Alongside the coolers and grill in the bed of my blue F-150 truck is a 48-inch-long refurbished crosscut saw. The kind that looks like mini arches between the lance-like teeth and rakers of the blade. It will help me clear the trees that have fallen across the trail over the winter.

As an official trail adopter for the Colorado Trail Foundation, I'm responsible for walking my section twice a year, keeping it clear of treefall, making sure water isn't eroding the trail and filling out reports on the condition of the trail and the work I do.

To get permission to use that four-foot saw, I had to acquire my sawyer certification, which required a 16-hour course on how to safely cut felled trees into logs (called bucking). The class had a connection to the Colorado Trail. The classroom portion took place in the North Fork Fire Station — the one whose spigot is used by hikers finishing the waterless Segment 2 of the CT. While we were looking at PowerPoint slides about compression and tension, two CT hikers walked past the window of the meeting hall. It was a nostalgic moment for me.

They're probably still new to thru-hiking and on only their second day. They'll develop confidence.

At the saw training, I met John, who, along with his dog Banjo, had come along to help me maintain my adopted section of the Colorado Trail. John is two years older than me and talks with an Alabama accent. Banjo talks with a beagle accent. If you want to make friends who love the Colorado outdoors and love giving back, go get your sawyer certification. It gave me a similar feeling to the camaraderie on the trail itself.

I didn't even have to sell trail work very hard to John.

"You want to drive five hours, hike five miles into a wilderness area so we can cut and remove downed trees on your day off?" I flippantly suggest.

"Will my car make it to the trailhead, and can Banjo come along?" says John.

"Yes."

"I'm in."

This is my second year as a trail adopter, and I'm hooked.

I found it so funny that the minute I learned how to build trails correctly, I turned into a total trail snob, pointing out poor draining paths as I would take my own leisurely hikes. Wangler didn't find it amusing and would always remind me how far I've come since he first met me. That would always spark a reminiscing session.

"When I met Nugget in 2022," Wangler teased, "he wasn't a trail adopter yet, and we were blissfully ignorant of trail design, but then hiking with him the summer after he became a trail adopter, every half mile he'd be like, 'Hey, Wangler, look right here, this drainage isn't good right here, this could be built up better.' It was like a running trail conditions commentary for the week we hiked."

Wangler and I remained good friends over the past two years. I've learned people look at you funny at Christmas parties when you call someone whom every single other partygoer knows as Scott, "The Wangler." (Even weirder when, after saying his name, you whistle spaghetti western music).

Bad Foot and I stay in touch. Our text messages usually involve brainstorming reasons for us to reunite on some new adventure. (Hike across Michigan next or the West Highland Way in Scotland?) In the summer of 2023, he came back to Colorado to join me in helping Wangler hike a portion of the CT for a week. It didn't take much convincing to get us back on the trail, particularly since the Collegiate West Route would all be new to us. I feel giddy inside when I get to reconnect with my trail family.

In addition to Bad Foot and Wangler, I've stayed connected with Sketcher. She drew the maps in this book. I've also managed to yogi my way into staying at her cabin in Steamboat Springs Colorado on ski trips. Ed and Julie often tag along to Steamboat. The two don't miss a burro race I run.

I've also spent the past two years on another journey to unwind a seeming paradox. On the trail I was sleeping on the ground but waking up fully rested. I was walking 20 miles but felt energetic. Most of my food had to be rehydrated, but I felt great. My social battery seemed to always be fully charged. My mind was still. I was present in conversations with people. I had more energy for people. I was establishing deep relationships. I was less anxious. And I was better at soaking up and savoring every detail of my environment. It's like thru-hiking fast tracks your health and well-being.

I found my best self on the trail. And I wanted to figure out why.

I spent the next two years on a research expedition that took me through the various fields and academic literature of psychology, neuroscience, philosophy, sleep science and biology to help figure out how what I was doing during a 35-day thru-hike made me feel so much joy.

It had me digging through scrap books at the Colorado Trail Foundation's Office in Golden. It had me dusting off typewriter-written speeches in the archives of History Colorado and had me pestering a historian who helped me dig up the original 1974 Forest Service Assessment of the first proposed route of the CT.

And in my research and writing, I was able to activate a lot of what I learned on the trail.

The past two years, I've used walking to help prime my brain for writing. The two-block path around my house is 0.6 miles. I usually walk three laps in the evening before I sit down and write. I've noticed that my mind is scattered for the first lap, then midway through the second lap, my brain calms down, then by the third lap, I don't remember my surroundings because I'm lost in thought; a good lost in thought, not frazzled and pinballing from one anxious thought to another or rumination, but good continuous mind wandering. Ideas seem to flow more readily to me while walking. I walk with a pocket-sized notebook in which I jot thoughts. I try to avoid having my phone with me.

Writing this book, I've also discovered I can do my best writing after a weekend backpacking trip into Colorado's forests.

Since the trail, I'm intentional about sleep hygiene. The phone goes away after 10 p.m., and I read by red-light headlamp — the same one that made it from Denver to Durango with me.

I've discovered that grit isn't fixed. It can be learned, strengthened, improved and grown.

On the trail, I found my tramily, and I found ways to help my tribe out. I've continued chasing that dragon with trail maintenance. In addition to my adopted section of the Colorado Trail that I maintain, I've made overnight backpacking trips to the Lost Creek wilderness to clear trails of fallen trees. I help a retired Forest Service Ranger named Ralph whom

I met at my sawyer class. I've discovered that tree clearing makes a backpacking trip into the Colorado wilderness twice as rewarding because it gives you a purpose in addition to the awesome benefits of being in nature.

Investigating those benefits of nature, I came across survey data that shows people underestimate how good they feel when they are outside.[68] So bad predictions — people not being fully aware of how happy outdoor walks can make them feel — means people aren't experiencing natural environments enough.

Get your brain on nature. Even if you don't think it will make you feel better — it will!

Also, in my research trying to answer why I found my best self on the trail, I read "Blue Zones." In Dan Buettner's book, the author travels across the globe interviewing people who have made it to 100 years old and live in pockets with statistically higher concentrations of centenarians. The author documents the characteristics, habits, reasons and lifestyles that possibly explain their longevity. It's striking how similar the blue zones secrets of longevity match up with the lifestyle that I adopted on the trail.

- Find sanctuary in time
- Maintain healthy body mass index
- Get regular exercise
- Spend time with like-minded friends
- Snack on nuts
- Give something back
- Drink plenty of water

But these wellness-enhancing activities get easily crowded out by the off-trail ways we live our lives. Lasting change is hard to install. You need to instill habits to break the addiction to screens and scrolling and getting riled up by the news. Modern life will quickly creep back in. To keep reminding myself to be more like Nugget, I have a written summary, which I keep on my refrigerator as a reminder, of why I was the happiest on the trail. It also reminds me how hiking has lived on inside of me.

Think of these as my Happiness Nuggets:

- An ingredient to finding happiness is finding "relatedness." Find your tribe. Find your community.
- Find ways to contribute to your tribe.
- Create situations to smile, create memories, find luck and put yourself in situations to make lasting stories that you'll be proud to tell on your death bed.
- Get on a natural light caveman sleep schedule. Which means avoiding the blue light before bedtime, and get more sunlight in your eyeballs once you wake up.
- Social media and online news are engineered to get clicks, and since anger gets more clicks, it's designed to make us angry. Get away from it! Put your phone away.
- Happiness is in the mind. Our culture forces us to make comparisons to others. Forget them. The only person you need to compare to is the person or hiker you were yesterday.
- Have big goals and break them down into noticeable small goals to accomplish along the way. Take note of progress.
- Find Flow. Note what you are doing when you lose track of time being fully immersed in something.
- See difficult tasks as challenges not threats.
- Get into nature. There's something about awe and nature that makes us better.
- Rewire your brain to see the positive (gratitude practice, mindfulness mediation and celebrating small achievements are three good starts).

- Do hard things, seek novelty, pursue challenges to expand your comfort zone and be intentional about putting yourself in situations that force growth.
- Invest more in experiences.
- Walk more.
- Be present with people.

Just barely missing making the list was "Embrace the stink."

I hope this book has convinced you to give thru-hiking a shot. Or, at the least, see for yourself if the Four-Day Effect is real and go spend four nights in a tent.

Maybe you too will realize that you are happiest when surrounded by people with names like Freight Train and Pipe Dream and Roaster Chicken and Bad Foot, 9 to 5, Feeling Good, Tall Tale, Caddy Shack, Sketcher, Spoons and Milk Man.

Maybe you too will learn life lessons from the people you meet on the trail. Look at me, I met Connie, who taught me to take time to reflect, and Shade Patch, who taught me to slow down and enjoy the moment. There was Bad Foot who taught me to let the day come, and Kyle, who made sure others didn't miss out on noticing the beauty of nature. There was Silent Nomad, who taught me to laugh at my mistakes, and Rosy Maple and Santiago, who really listened and made people feel heard and special. There was Lilly, who taught me to laugh a little extra at cow jokes, and Andrew, who taught me, if I'm ever in a bacon-eating competition, to roll it into a burrito-like wad.

The trail has a magical way of pulling the best out of you, or rather, creating the best in you.

Let me know if it does that for you, via the email Christopher.Stiffler.author@gmail.com.

Or maybe thru-hiking isn't your thing and you have another quest in mind? Happiness is often a byproduct of pursuing a quest. A good rule of thumb to determine if you have a quest is to ask yourself, does it have clear goals? Measurable progress? A sense of calling? And does it require sacrifice and effort? Golfing is a hobby. Golfing every course in Scotland is a quest.[69]

But be warned. A lot of folks have the big idea for a quest, but they never act on it — just like the guy who owned my home in Denver and never took the leap to leave his front door and walk to Durango.

Go do it.

And no matter what happens on your journey to push your comfort zone, whether it's difficulty, discovery or diarrhea, remember:

It'll eventually become a good story.

Author's Note

owe special thanks to my friends, family, and colleagues who graciously helped edit the manuscript and give feedback: Tim Hoover, Mike Lukas, Shawn Adrian, Katie Mitchell, Stephanie Wilson and Jan Rastall. Without your guidance and encouragement, the book would have fewer laughs, more redundant sentences, and been a lot less readable. You've translated my academic writing into story telling. Thanks to all the trail angels, crew members, and volunteers that make the Colorado Trail such an amazing hike. Thanks to all the friends and family that supported me during my hike: Doris Stiffler, Nancy Kriek, Ed McConnell, Julie Terrill, Matt Valeta and Rich and Heather Kunckel. Thank you also to the folks at History Colorado and the Colorado Trail Foundation for letting me raid your archives and old scrapbooks. Finally, thanks to you, the reader. If you enjoyed the book, consider leaving an online review.

Happy Trails
Christopher "Nugget" Stiffler

About the Author

Christopher Stiffler is an economics professor and senior economist at the Colorado Fiscal Institute in Denver, Colorado. But he's also worked as a high school Latin teacher, trained as a professional wrestler and climbed all of Colorado's 14,000-foot peaks. He is a burro racer, public speaker, thru-hiker of the Colorado Trail and dabbles in things like ice climbing, stand-up comedy and cowboy poetry. He hosts the Non-Standard 14er Podcast and cohosts the Funny Muscle Podcast. He does his best writing after weekend trips backpacking into Colorado's wilderness away from cell service. Christopher got his start explaining economics in 2009, writing an explanatory economics column for his small hometown newspaper in Bedford, Pennsylvania. The column was geared at explaining complicated economic concepts in simple metaphorical terms that everyone can understand. His other published works include two children's books titled, "An Igloo Half-Made" and "A Burro Named Bedford" and an economics book titled "Economics In-Other-Words; What Your Boring Economics Professor Tried to Teach You."

Contact him at Christopher.Stiffler.author@gmail.com
Follow him @econ_comic

APPENDIX:

Remote Association Test Answers

Clues to RAT Quiz #1:

law, birthday, case	suit
stop, ground, ache	back
off, beer, way	run
wash, food, off	power
good, salad, head	egg
hat, poll, last	straw
work, back, line	yard
wreck, town, shape	ship
silver, hard, house	ware
back, camp, enemy	fire

Clues to RAT Quiz #2:

without, Indian, dinner	reservation
new, through, loose	leaf
school, ball, chair	high
paper, castle, bag	sand
coffee, dance, down	break
bottom, hard, music	rock
rest, chair, side	arm
sheet, bed, out	spread

see, horse, dust	saw
moon, shoe, sun	shine

Clues to RAT Quiz #3:

wild, man, fly	fire
down, dance, out	break
foot, pad, high	note
eight, bearing, park	ball
game, dead, front	end
book, law, study	case
rise, five, mile	high
broken, time, book	record
under, zone, paper	construction
apple, tomato, hot	sauce

The clues to RAT Quiz #4:

kin, flag, shape	ship
fall, chill, law	out
play, under, water	ground
air, knife, watch	pocket
chip, sweet, salad	potato
moral, rose, reading	compass
stool, first, dance	step
open, work, trip	road
phone, sick, work	home
shoe, elbow, game	tennis

Clues to RAT Quiz #5

camp, seat, fire	work
grass, blood, moon	blue
drain, window, thunder	storm
gray, ground, wheel	water
bill, book, ground	play

will, back, last	call
black, carpet, hat	magic
hand, smoke, turn	signal
box, hung, duty	jury
light, natural, station	gas

Clues for RAT Quiz #6

think, drunk, dunk	tank
one, phone, line	number
through, side, board	walk
mixed, road, car	race
sound, book, hat	check
man, arm, lift	chair
line, piece, event	center
TV, light, airplane	pilot
play, fold, board	bill
over, mark, end	book

Clues for RAT Quiz #7

Eye, tickled, slip	pink
Wind, puppet, monkey	sock
Pillow, town, fall	down
Coffee, bag, magic	bean
Note, food, river	bank
Fishing, flat, line	line
Fall, second, trade	wind
Line, floor, hall	dance
Night, mother, house	hen
Boat, knot, up	slip

Clues for RAT Quiz #8

False, slide, ladder	step
Boxing, diamond, leader	ring

Super, cereal, over	bowl
Glass, country, fine	wine
Blood, cast, writer	type
Prime, dance, line	number
Rope, start, high	jump
Office, hitching, card	post
Greeting, flash, punch	card
Plug, elephant, worm	ear

Clues for RAT Quiz #9

Batter, sell, make	up
Church, light, lip	service
Fig, new, table	leaf
Flower, bug, rest	bed
Circuit, fall, cut	short
Notch, tip, dog	top
Lift, lounge, wheel	chair
High, house, bus	school
Toe, door, packed	jam
Kitchen, salt, water	table

Clues for RAT Quiz #10

bench, book, check	mark
top, car, soap	box
mare, fort, time	night
trade, ground, play	fair
garage, man, bell	door
stop, house, night	light
home, mine, line	land
band, kick, off	stand
fast, art, paper	clip
burn, flower, shine	sun

Clues for RAT Quiz #11

cheap, board, figure	skate
tree, smoke, out	house
love, story, line	life
field, shopping, lane	center
bull, pig, pal	pen
first, wrist, tower	watch
red, lid, ball	eye
immediate, tree, doctor	family
ruled, wall, clip	paper
mail, letter, key	chain

Clues for RAT Quiz #12

dry, funny, wish	bone
cheap, board, figure	skate
about, off, card	face
green, board, place	card
sun, side, out	burn
leader, wall, school	board
extra, card, rating	credit
hold, print, note	foot
cold, water, page	front
waiting, bird, curtain	call

Endnotes

1   [1]Atchley RA, Strayer DL, Atchley P (2012) Creativity in the Wild: Improving Creative Reasoning through Immersion in Natural Settings. PLoS ONE 7(12): e51474. https://doi.org/10.1371/journal.pone.0051474

2   The theory separated attention into two components: involuntary attention (where you're intrigued) and voluntary/direction attention (where attention is directed by cognitive control.)

Sitting in traffic, doing complicated math problems, picking the right letters on your Wordle all require voluntary attention. They give us mental fatigue. In contrast, using our involuntary attention occurs when something effortlessly draws us in and intrigues us. The ripples on the river beside the trail and the aspen leaves shimmering in the summer breeze gently captivates our attention by a process that the Kaplans called "soft fascination." They help our brains replenish. So, after time in nature, a person is able to perform better on tasks that require direction attention.

3   Kaplan, S. (1995). The restorative benefits of nature: toward an integrative framework. Journal of Environmental Psychology, 15(3), 169–182.

4   Jiang, B., Schmillen, R., & Sullivan, W. C. (2019). How to Waste a Break: Using Portable Electronic Devices Substantially Counteracts Attention Enhancement Effects of Green Spaces. *Environment and Behavior, 51*(9-10), 1133-1160.

5   Matsuoka, R. H. (2010). Student performance and high school landscapes: Examining the links. Landscape and Urban Planning, 97, 273-282. doi:10.1016/j.landurb-plan.2010.06.011

6   "Why plants in the office make us more productive." ScienceDaily. ScienceDaily, 1 September 2014. <www.sciencedaily.com/releases/2014/09/140901090735.htm>

7   Bratman GN, Hamilton JP, Hahn KS, Daily GC, Gross JJ. Nature experience reduces rumination and subgenual prefrontal cortex activation. Proc Natl Acad Sci U S A. 2015 Jul 14;112(28):8567-72.

8   Robert S. Ulrich, "View Through a Window May Influence Recovery from Surgery," Science 224 (1984): 420-421.

9   MaryCarol R. Hunter, Brenda W. Gillespie, Sophie Yu-Pu Chen. Urban Nature Experiences Reduce Stress in the Context of Daily Life Based on Salivary Biomarkers. Frontiers in Psychology, 2019; 10 DOI: 10.3389/fpsyg.2019.00722

10   Van Hedger SC, Nusbaum HC, Clohisy L, Jaeggi SM, Buschkuehl M, Berman MG. Of cricket chirps and car horns: The effect of nature sounds on cognitive performance. Psychon Bull Rev. 2019 Apr;26(2):522-530. doi: 10.3758/s13423-018-1539-1. PMID: 30367351.

11   Felsten, G. (2009). Where to take a study break on the college campus: an attention restoration theory perspective. *Journal of Environmental Psychology, 29*(1), 160–167.

12   Kardan O, Gozdyra P, Misic B, Moola F, Palmer LJ, Paus T, Berman MG. Neighborhood greenspace and health in a large urban center. Sci Rep. 2015 Jul 9;5:11610.

13   https://www.nytimes.com/2018/10/25/style/journaling-benefits.html

14   McRaven, William H. Admiral "Make Your Bed" commencement address to the graduates of The University of Texas at Austin on May 17, 2014.

15   Kratz, A. and Delmatier, C. (2014) Old-Man-of-the-Mountain

(Tetraneuris grandiflora). U.S. Forest Service available at https://www.fs.usda.gov/wildflowers/plant-of-the-week/tetraneuris_grandiflora.shtml

16   Williams, F. (2017). The nature fix: why nature makes us happier, healthier, and more creative. First edition. New York, W.W. Norton & Company, independent publishers since 1923.

17   See the discussion of ignition and primal cues in Coyle, Daniel. The Talent Code. Arrow Books, 2010.

18   Clear, J. (2018). Atomic habits: tiny changes, remarkable results : an easy & proven way to build good habits & break bad ones. New York, New York, Avery, an imprint of Penguin Random House.

19   https://www.gse.harvard.edu/news/20/04/harvard-edcast-benefit-family-mealtime

20   L. Wong. "Why They Fight: Combat Motivation in the Iraq War," Strategic Studies Institute, 2003.

21   *Camp Hale Ski-Zette* 1, no. 12 (March 23, 1943).

22   Grant, Adam (2023) Hidden Potential: The Science of Achieving Greater Things. Page 74

23   The Complete Guide to Colorado's Wilderness Areas. Mark Pearson and John Fielder. Westcliffe Publishers, Inc. Englewood, Colorado

24   Stewart I. Donaldson, Barbara L. Fredrickson, and Laura E. Kurtz, "Cultivating Positive Emotions to Enhance Human Flourishing," in *Applied Positive Psychology: Improving Everyday Life, Schools, Work, Health, and Society* (New York: Routledge Academic, 2011). Research shows that we need three positive thoughts to counter only one negative thought.

25   Glenn R. Fox, Jonas Kaplan, Hanna Damasio, and Antonio Damasio, "Neural Correlates of Gratitude," Frontiers in Psychology 6 (2015): 1491

26   People who have a journaling gratitude practice tend to exercise more, report fewer illnesses, and report feeling more

optimistic about the future than people who don't make the time for daily gratitude. It also increased resiliency and ability to cope with stress. It also underscores that our ability to react is under our control and not determined by bad weather.

27   Wiseman, Richard. (2003). The luck factor: four simple principles that will change your luck and your luck and your life . London: Arrow Books

28   Peak Performance chapter 4 The Paradox of Rest by Stulberg, Brad and Magness, Steve

29   T.D. Wilson, D.A. Reinhard, E.C. Westgate, D.T. Gilbert, et al. "Just Think: The Challenges of the Disengaged Mind," *Science* 345, no. 6192 (2014): 75-77

30   Tamir, D.I. et al. Media Usage Diminishes Memory for Experiences. *Journal of Experimental Social Psychology* 76, 161-8 (2018).

31   Blue light (emitted by phone) can be beneficial during the daylight hours because it helps boost attention, working memory, and mood. That's good when you're trying to finish a 10-page term paper in college. But when restful sleep is your goal at 1am and not 1,000 written words, all that blue light is counterproductive.

32   Winter, W. Chris. *The Sleep Solution: Why Your Sleep Is Broken and How to Fix It* First edition., New American Library, 2017.

33   Artificial light is the reason so many of us in modern society don't get enough sleep. And it's bad for our health. There's a short line from poor sleep to increased risks of depression, diabetes and heart problems. Still, 65 percent of Americans get less than the recommended 7 to 9 hours of sleep per night.

34   I didn't have to go far to find professor Kenneth Wright of the University of Colorado at Boulder who researches questions about melatonin and campers. He and his colleagues tested melatonin production on test subjects who headed into the Rocky Mountains for a 6-day summer camping trip. The

campers' bodies started to release the hormone melatonin around sunset and stopped making it around sunrise. This was a shift on average of 2 hours difference than the melatonin release schedule of non-campers.

Wright KP Jr, McHill AW, Birks BR, Griffin BR, Rusterholz T, Chinoy ED. Entrainment of the human circadian clock to the natural light-dark cycle. Curr Biol. 2013 Aug 19;23(16):1554-8.

35 In another study, Professor Wright saw a shift in melatonin levels after just 2 days of camping compared to the control group that stayed home

Stothard ER, McHill AW, Depner CM, Birks BR, Moehlman TM, Ritchie HK, Guzzetti JR, Chinoy ED, LeBourgeois MK, Axelsson J, Wright KP Jr. Circadian Entrainment to the Natural Light-Dark Cycle across Seasons and the Weekend. Curr Biol. 2017 Feb 20;27(4):508-513.

36 Using Science to Optimize Sleep, Learning & Metabolism | Huberman Lab Podcast #3

37 Alcohol also decreases the later stages of sleep. It makes us fall asleep quicker, but the real cost comes at the lost REM sleep we get. Sleep is one of few things where there are increasing marginal returns to sleep because REM time lengthens with each sleep cycle. Said another way, that 7th, 8th, or 9th hour of sleep that many people aren't getting, are the most potent.

38 Anne-Marie Chang et al., "Evening use of Light-Emitting eReaders Negatively Affects Sleep, Circadian Timing, and Next-Morning Alertness," *Proceeds of the National Academy of Science of the United States of America* 112, no. 4 (January 27, 2015): 1232-1237.

To investigate the effects of blue light on sleep, Harvard researchers looked at the difference between e-book readers and traditional book readers. Participants read a traditional book or a blue-light emitting e-book 4 hours before bed. After just 5 days of this routine, there was a big difference: the e-book readers were much less sleepy when bedtime rolled around.

Biochemistry wise, the e-book readers melatonin release was 90 minutes behind the traditional book readers.

39 Palmer, Albert, W. The Mountain Trail and Its Message (Boston: The Pilgrim Press, 1911)

40 Flynn, Jim. (2016) A Compendium of Curious Colorado Place Names. Arcadia Publishing

41 Jha, Amishi P. (2021) Peak Mind Find Your Focus Own Your Attention Invest 12 Minute a Day, HarperOne. New York, NY.

42 William J. Brady et al., "Emotion Shapes the Diffusion of Moralization Content in Social Networks," *Proceedings of the National Academy of Sciences* 114, no. 28 (2017): 7313-18

43 Brady WJ, McLoughlin K, Doan TN, Crockett MJ. How social learning amplifies moral outrage expression in online social networks. Sci Adv. 2021 Aug 13;7(33): eabe5641.

The study combed through 12.7 million tweets to assess how behavior on social media changes over time. They isolated Twitter posts that both expressed moral outrage and got a lot of engagement from other users. Then they tracked the future posts of those Twitter users who recently received a bunch of engagement from a post filled with outage. They found that that those users were then more likely to incorporate additional outrage in the subsequent posts.

44 To make matters worse, there are no vocal intonations, physical gestures, and expressions online; it's just immediate text. This leads to trolling and bullying which are associated with host of bad outcomes like: anxiety, depression, headaches, sleep disturbances, and stomach problems.

45 https://www.uncovercolorado.com/largest-natural-lakes-in-colorado/

46 Schechter, Harold (2015) Man-Eater, The Life and Legend of an American Cannibal. Amazon Publishing.

47 https://www.backpacker.com/stories/people/profiles/the-hiker-who-never-left-continental-divide-trail/?scope=anon

48   Hari, Johann. "Stolen focus." New York : Crown, 2021

49   Barbara Griefahn et al., "Autonomic Arousals Related to Traffic Noise During Sleep," *Sleep*, vol. 31, no.4 (2008): p. 569

50   David Weinzimmer et al., "Human Reponses to Simulated Noise in National Parks," *Leisure Sciences: An Interdisciplinary Journal*, vol. 36, issue 3 (2014): pp.251-67

51   Williams, Florence, 1967-. 2017. The Nature Fix: Why Nature Makes Us Happier, Healthier, and More Creative. New York, W.W. Norton & Company, independent publishers since 1923.

52   Maguire, E., Gadian, D., Johnsrude, I., Good, C., Ashburner, J., Frackowiak, S., & Frith, C. (2000). Navigation-related structural change in the hippocampi of tax drivers. *Proceedings of the National Academy of Sciences, USA, 97(8)*, 4398-4403.

53   Achor, S. (2010). The happiness advantage: the seven principles of positive psychology that fuel success and performance at work. New York, Crown Business.

54   Darley, J.M. & Batson, C.D. (1973). From Jerusalem to Jericho: A study of situational and dispositional variables in helping behavior. *Journal of Personality and Social Psychology*. 27, 100-108.

55   Strober, M.H. & Weinberg, C.B. (1980). Strategies used by working and nonworking wives to reduce time pressures. *Journal of Consumer Research*, 6, 338-348.

56   Muir, John, "The Mountains of California." (1894). A Near View of the High Sierras.

57   Ives, Christopher. Zen on the trail : hiking as pilgrimage. (2018). Wisdom Publications. March 18 2024. Page 10.

58   Victor Turner, *The Ritual Process: Structure and Anti-Structure* (New York: Routledge, 1995), 106-107.

59   Stillman, Scott. Wilderness : the gateway to the soul. (2018). Wild Soul Press.

60   University of Sussex. "How 'Dry January' is the secret to

better sleep, saving money and losing weight." ScienceDaily. ScienceDaily, 28 December 2018.

Participants who completed a dry January were interviewed in February and again in August 2018. They found that participants completing a dry January decreased the number of days they drank later in the year---from an average of 4.3 days a week before a sober January to an average of 3.3 days per week afterward. Rates of excess drinking later in the year also fell. During the sober month participants reported sleeping better, saving money, having more concentration, higher energy levels and losing weight.

61   Why Walking Helps Us Think. Ferris Jabr (September 2014) The New Yorker.

62   Oppezzo, M., & Schwartz, D. L. (2014). Give your ideas some legs: The positive effect of walking on creative thinking. Journal of Experimental Psychology: Learning, Memory, and Cognition, 40(4), 1142–1152

63   Voss MW, Prakash RS, Erickson KI, Basak C, Chaddock L, Kim JS, Alves H, Heo S, Szabo AN, White SM, Wójcicki TR, Mailey EL, Gothe N, Olson EA, McAuley E, Kramer AF. Plasticity of brain networks in a randomized intervention trial of exercise training in older adults. Front Aging Neurosci. 2010 Aug 26; 2:32

The study took adults aged 59 to 80, who previously had a rather "couch potato" lifestyle and decided to make a change by joining a walking group They walked for 40 minutes, three times a week. Then they stuck them in a fMRI scanner. They found that walking improved brain connectivity and improved cognitive performance even compared to the control group that didn't walk but did toning and stretching.

64   M. Bhalla and D.R. Proffitt, "Visual-Motor Recalibration in Geographical Slant Perception," *Journal of Experimental Psychology: Human Perception and Performance* 25, no. 4 (1999): 1076-96.

65   Magness, S. (2022). Do Hard Things: Why We Get Resilience Wrong and the Surprising Science of Real Toughness (Unabridged.). HarperCollins. Page 47. A challenge is manageable, but a threat is something dangerous. People who can see a challenge are better able to assess the situation and their ability to address it. Whether we code things as a challenge or a threat also dictates our brain's biological response. The bodies of people new to skydiving are typically filled with the stress hormone cortisol that harms performance, while skydiver veterans have more adrenaline, which improves it. Both are jumping out of a plane, but the sky divers' expectations are different. Those expectations can prime a biological response. If we can see a stressful situation as an opportunity to grow---that is something hard but something we can ultimately handle---we'll get a challenge-response, and our bodies will release more testosterone and adrenaline instead of cortisol.

66   B. Bastian, J. Jetten, L. J. Ferris. Pain as Social Glue: Shared Pain Increases Cooperation. *Psychological Science*, 2014.

67   https://coloradotrail.org/wp-content/uploads/2019/09/TreadLines-1988-Fall.pdf

68   Elizabeth K. Nisbet and John M. Zelenski, "Underestimating nearby nature: affective forecasting errors obscure the happy path to sustainability." *Psychological Science*, vol. 22, no.9 (2011): pp.1101-6.   In a set of studies, students were asked to predict how happy they thought they'd feel on their walks of either a path by a canal or the underground tunnels connecting campus buildings The outside walk made them feel much happier than the students initially predicted. The students overestimated how much they'd enjoy the tunnels and underestimated how good the outside walks made them feel.

69   The Happiness of Pursuit: Finding the Quest That Will Bring Purpose to Your Life. (2016) Chris Guillebeau